PRENTICE-HALL SERIES IN WORLD RELIGIONS

Robert S. Ellwood, Editor

BEYOND "THE PRIMITIVE":
THE RELIGIONS OF NONLITERATE PEOPLES

SAM D. GILL

HINDUISM: A CULTURAL PERSPECTIVE

DAVID R. KINSLEY

ISLAM: A CULTURAL PERSPECTIVE

RICHARD C. MARTIN

AMERICAN RELIGION:
A CULTURAL PERSPECTIVE

MARY FARRELL BEDNAROWSKI

JAPANESE RELIGION:
A CULTURAL PERSPECTIVE

ROBERT S. ELLWOOD
RICHARD PILGRIM

CHINESE RELIGIONS:
A CULTURAL PERSPECTIVE

CHRISTIAN JOCHIM

CHRISTIANITY:
A CULTURAL PERSPECTIVE

JAMES B. WIGGINS
ROBERT S. ELLWOOD

Crucifixion plaque. Photo courtesy of the National Museum of Ireland.

James B. Wiggins

Syracuse University

Robert S. Ellwood

University of Southern California

CHRISTIANITY
a cultural perspective

Prentice Hall
Englewood Cliffs, New Jersey 07632

Library of Congress Cataloging-in-Publication Data

Wiggins, James B.,
   Christianity: a cultural perspective/James B. Wiggins and
Robert S. Ellwood
     p. cm.
   Bibliography: p.
   Includes index.
   ISBN 0-13-133570-7
   1. Christianity. I. Ellwood, Robert S.,   . II. Title.
BR121.2.W47 1988
270--dc19 87-22861
        CIP

Cover Art: Crucifixion Plaque. Photo courtesy of the National Museum of Ireland.
Manufacturing Buyer: Margaret Rizzi

 © 1988 by Prentice Hall
A Division of Simon & Schuster
Englewood Cliffs, New Jersey 07632

Printed in the United States of America

10 9 8 7 6 5 4 3 2 1

ISBN 0-13-133570-7   01

Prentice-Hall International (UK) Limited, *London*
Prentice-Hall of Australia Pty. Limited, *Sydney*
Prentice-Hall Canada Inc., *Toronto*
Prentice-Hall Hispanoamericana, S.A., *Mexico*
Prentice-Hall of India Private Limited, *New Delhi*
Prentice-Hall of Japan, Inc., *Tokyo*
Simon & Schuster Asia Pte. Ltd., *Singapore*
Editora Prentice-Hall do Brasil, Ltda., *Rio de Janeiro*

Contents

Foreword

The Prentice-Hall Series in World Religions is a set of introductions to the major religious traditions of the world, which intends to be distinctive in two ways: (1) Each book follows the same outline, allowing a high level of consistency in content and approach. (2) Each book is oriented toward viewing religious traditions as "religious cultures" in which history, ideologies, practices, and sociologies all contribute toward constructing "deep structures" that govern peoples' world view and life-style. In order to achieve this level of communication about religion, these books are not chiefly devoted to dry recitations of chronological history or systematic exposition of ideology, though they present overviews of these topics. Instead the books give considerable space to "cameo" insights into particular personalities, movements, and historical moments that encourage an understanding of the world view, life-style, and deep dynamics of religious cultures in practice as they affect real people.

Religion is an important element within nearly all cultures, and itself has all the hallmarks of a full cultural system. "Religious culture" as an integrated complex includes features ranging from ideas and organization to dress and diet. Each of these details offers some insight into the meaning of the whole as a total experience and construction of a total "reality." To look at the religious life of a particular country or tradition in this way, then, is to give proportionate attention to all aspects of its manifestation: to thought, worship, and social organization; to philosophy and folk beliefs; to liturgy and pilgrimage; to family life, dress, diet, and the role of religious specialists like monks and shamans. This series hopes to instill in the minds of readers the ability to view religion in this way.

I hope you enjoy the journeys offered by these books to the great heartlands of the human spirit.

ROBERT S. ELLWOOD, editor
University of Southern California

Preface

Books on Christianity are numerous, and many of them are excellent works. This volume is added to their number, though, in the hope that it will offer collegiate and other students of the religion a resource which in some ways is special. Like all religions, Christianity is multi-dimensional. We have tried to move beyond those presentations which look at its historical and denominational diversity chiefly in doctrinal and institutional terms to focus as fully on worship, sociology, and art; we have tried to capture the flavor of Christian life past and present, near and far as it has affected ordinary as well as elite persons.

How well we have succeeded the user of this book must judge. But readers must also realize that no book is complete in itself. Fully to comprehend what it wants to communicate one must bring an empathetic imagination able to reach the human experience behind the words, and one must supplement one book with others which explore more profoundly the meaning behind those words. We hope, then, that this little book will be only a gateway to your adventure in understanding the many dimensions of the Christian faith.

J.B.W.
R.S.E.

Acknowledgments

A great contribution was made to this book by Syracuse University's having awarded me research and editorial support in two summers, 1984 and 1985. Ms. Sarah Halford was extremely helpful in performing some of those tasks. The book appreciably benefited from her assistance and careful attention to detail.

The patience of my coauthor Robert Ellwood and the care and sensibility he has demonstrated are acknowledged and deeply appreciated; he and I share responsibility for the interpretations and judgments presented here.

James B. Wiggins

Ardagh Chalice. Photo courtesy of the National Museum of Ireland.

an ancient heritage

Dawn came quickly over the ancient Mediterranean city. As sentinel of the Roman world, it stood watch over the sea that had carried many other conquerors and their different creeds between the Orient and the western shores of the Atlantic. At the eastern end of that sea lay another city: Jerusalem, sacred to the Jews. Outside its walls a young Jew named Jesus had been crucified. One hundred and fifty years had passed since that time. Many had been crucified before and many after as the Jews sought heroes who would lead them out from under Roman domination. Yet that particular death had remained in the memories of a few who, like the event itself, stood apart from the rest. This execution had not only remained a vital memory but had fired their souls and transformed their world.

THE WINE OF REMEMBRANCE

But what lay at the heart of that transformative memory? Those who were claimed by it believed that Jesus, like the rising sun itself, had mounted out of the darkness of death and into the heavens above, lighting the world and carrying with him the hopes and visions of those who ''saw and believed.'' This death was different; it offered new and unending life. As morning followed morning, the heat of the passion on the cross was felt farther and farther afield, dispelling the haunted shadows of those who lived under the heavy burden of oppression.

On this first day of the week in A.D. 180,[1] the morning of the resurrection was remembered and celebrated in a symbolic reenactment of those miraculous events. The ascending sun caught and changed shadows to patches of light in the courtyard of a widow. She was a member of a faith as fresh and controversial as human culture was old and established around the Great Sea. The woman was a Christian. She and others of like faith were moved to name Jesus, the Galilean teacher, the prophet from Nazareth, as the Christ, the Anointed One, through whose death and resurrection all creation was redeemed. She and others like her named Jesus Christ as the Son of God who "became flesh and dwelt among us." That morning Christian worship was to be held at her home.

At one end of a rectangular room in the mansion rested a table. Behind it stood a dignified person dressed in white linen and, to fend off the morning chill, a colored pancho-like jacket. This was the *episcopos* or "overseer" of the church in that community—the office and title would find their way from the Greek into English as "bishop." This presiding officiant was flanked by two younger persons in white, the *deacons* (from a Greek word) or "servers." Their chief responsibility was the care of the poor, but they also had certain ritualistic functions in the Christian service. Behind the bishop was a semi-circle of *presbyters* (also from the Greek) or "elders." Much later, the name and calling of these ministers would evolve into that of the priest, but now they were more an administrative board that assisted the bishop, who in turn was more the pastor of a church than of a territory.

Facing the clergy behind the table was the congregation. Its body was also divided into various subsections. Widows, matrons, virgins, husbands, young men, and children all were in their respective places, making clear that the church though one unity was composed of people in many diverse life-situations, each meriting respect.

Behind the main assembly of the church stood persons in two other categories: *catechumens* (of Greek origin) or "neophytes," who were under instruction for baptism and admission to full membership in the church; and penitents, once full members whose privileges had been temporarily suspended because they had committed a serious sin; that is, an act, intended or otherwise, that was construed as being contrary to the individual's relationship with God and with the community of believers.

The service began with formal greetings by the bishop. Then presbyters and deacons read from the Scriptures. First they read aloud from scrolls of the Hebrew Bible—that group of writings that Christians call the Old Testament—probably

---

[1] A.D. From the Latin, *Anno Domini,* the "year of Our Lord." The Christian calendar begins from the date that signifies the time of Jesus's birth. Prior to that, time is referred to as being before Christ, B.C. Modern historiographical scholarship now tends to refer to B.C. as being before the Common Era, B.C.E. and A.D. as being in the Common Era, C.E. This acknowledges that the time referred to is common both to Jews and Christians, that their time is shared. It acknowledges that, in a pluralistic world, other religious traditions have other calendars, and that time is measured differently.

in the Greek version called the *Septuagint,* so called because it was compiled and translated by a group of seventy Jewish scholars.

Perhaps the selection was from a passage believed to foretell and ascribe meaning to the life and death of Jesus, the Messiah (in Greek, *Christos*—the "Anointed One" or "Christ"), the Sublime King for whom many Jews in recent centuries had ardently waited. Widespread were the stories that in his day he would deliver his people from all oppressors and establish a paradisiacal kingdom that would be the glory of the earth. Even nature, it was rumored, would unite with his triumph to produce harvests of fruit and grain a hundredfold those of the present hungry, tear-stained age.

The Christians believed all this, and much more as well. For they and they alone believed that in Jesus the Sublime King had already walked the world. It was necessary, they said, that he first appear in obscurity and that he suffer and die before manifesting his splendor in a new heaven and earth. For as he walked, he had talked of the Kingdom of Heaven, or the Kingdom of God, as a mysterious and fascinating reality that was both in the world, centered about his own presence and healing power, and yet somehow also coming. He had spoken of a "Day" which would dawn when least expected. Then he was tried, tortured, and executed by the powers of religion and state. His followers said the risen Lord had appeared again afterwards, and was made known to two of them in the breaking of bread.

The lines from the old Jewish Scriptures read in church, then, might be those from Isaiah, in which the prophet sings poignantly of an abused hero:

> He was despised, he shrank from the sight of men,
>   tormented and humbled by suffering;
>   we despised him, we held him of no account,
>   a thing from which men turn away their eyes.
> Yet on himself he bore our sufferings,
>   our torments he endured,
>   while we counted him smitten by God,
>   struck down by disease and misery;
>   but he was pierced for our transgressions,
>   tortured for our iniquities;
>   the chastisement he bore is health for us
>   and by his scourgings we are healed. (Isaiah 53)[2]

Or the reading might be the lines about the dry bones in Ezekiel, in which this prophet seems to envision the very resurrection of the dead: "This is the word of the Lord God to these bones: I will put breath (or wind, or spirit, from the Hebrew) into you, and you shall live" (Ezekiel 37:5).

Next in this Christian service of around A.D. 180 came a reading from the

---

[2] All scriptural passages are from *The Revised Standard Version of the Bible.* Copyright 1946, 1952, 1971 by The National Council of Churches of Christ in the U.S.A.

Letters of the Apostles. The Apostles were the personal followers of Jesus who (along with Paul, who had seen Jesus not in the flesh but in a vision) had spread word of his work throughout the world. Those missionaries of the first Christian generation had kept in touch with the growing *ecclesiae* (from the Greek, *ekklesiai,* "churches") or assemblies of believers by correspondence, and now their letters were much treasured.

In such a reading, the Beloved Disciple, John, might again be heard to say, "But should anyone commit a sin, we have one to plead our cause with the Father, Jesus Christ, and he is just. He is himself the remedy for the defilement of our sins, not our sins only but the sins of all the world" (1 John 2:1–2).

Or Paul might be heard thundering down the years;

We died to sin: how can we live in it any longer? Have you forgotten that when we were baptized into union with Jesus Christ we were baptized into his death? By baptism we were buried with him, and lay dead, in order that, as Christ was raised from the dead into the splendour of the Father, so also we might set our feet upon the new path of life. (Romans 6:2–4)

A passage from a Gospel, or account of the life of the Lord Jesus, followed. The assembly in the widow's house might have heard of a healing miracle, or a parable, or a discourse like the Sermon on the Mount, or even a somber account of Christ's last days. All these stories would be weighted with the mystery of the Kingdom and the strange mission of the young man who was to die to live anew. For instance, after he had cast a devil out of a dumb man and the dumb man began to speak, Jesus said in response to those who accused him of doing such wonders through alliance with the prince of devils, "If it is by the finger of God that I drive out the devils, then be sure the kingdom of God has already come upon you" (Luke 11:20).

The exact set of books called the New Testament had not yet been fixed, that is, made *canon* (from the Greek for "rule") and would not be until early in the fifth century. But letters and writings on the life of Jesus attributed to the Apostles had great authority, and the most important of these writings in today's Christian Bible were known and read in most churches in the first century A.D. Other writings, however, were also circulated in the early days, such as the Gospels of James, Thomas, and Mary (which present scholarship suggests were not actually authored by those eminent persons). They were favored in circles given to esoteric interpretations of Christianity, for example the Gnostic circles (from the Greek, *gnosis,* "extraordinary knowledge").

After the Scriptural readings, the bishop delivered a sermon, probably based on those Scriptures. Writings from the early church give us some idea of what such a sermon might be like.

Some scholars have suggested that the First Letter of Peter in the New Testament might actually be an Easter sermon by a second-century bishop. In this treatise, we find admonitions to honor Jesus Christ ("You have not seen him, yet you love him") and moral instructions for persons in the church's diverse categories—servants, wives, husbands, young men, presbyters. Finally, the text speaks of the ark of Noah, in which a few people were saved through water, as prefiguring the baptism, which then was usually administered at Easter.

Or we may turn to the Second Letter of Clement, *not* found in the New Testament but included in most collections of the works of the "Apostolic Fathers" or orthodox writers in the early church. This essay is widely regarded by scholars as the earliest extant Christian sermon outside the New Testament. It was probably addressed to the church at Corinth about A.D. 170.

The Second Letter of Clement emphasizes the importance of Christians separating themselves from the values of this world while at the same time fearlessly going into it. A day when grim persecution of Christians was far from uncommon is brought back to us by such passages as:

> Therefore, brothers, leaving behind life as strangers in this world, let us do the will of him who called us, and let us not be afraid to go forth from this world. For the Lord said, "You shall be as lambs in the midst of wolves." And Peter answered and said to him, "What if the wolves should tear the lambs?" Jesus said to Peter, "The lambs should not fear the wolves after they are dead. And so with you—fear not those who kill you and can do nothing more to you; but fear him who after your death has power over soul and body, to cast them into hell fire." And understand, brothers, that the lingering of our flesh in this world is short and passing, but the promise of Christ is great and wonderful and is a repose in the kingdom to come and in eternal life.[3]

We may note two things about this passage. First, the Kingdom already seems in the minds of some to be entirely associated with the afterlife. It is interesting to note that the dialogue between Jesus and Peter, while echoing Matthew 10:5 and 10:28 and Luke 10:3 and 12:4–5, is not found in just these words in any known Gospel or other source. The preacher must have drawn upon a gospel or tradition now otherwise lost.

Let us now return to the celebration at the widow's house. By the end of the bishop's sermon, the sun had risen, and yet the climax of the service was still to come. The deacons turned to say, "Depart, you catechumens" and "Attend the doors!" Those under instruction, and also the penitents, would leave, for what followed was only for the fully initiated and those in good standing.

When they were alone, the inner circle of the church offered prayers for the needs of those present and for the world. Then they embraced each other in the kiss of peace, confirming their sacred fellowship.

Next the deacons placed a plate and a chalice on the table, mixing wine and

---

[3] Francis X. Glimm, et al., *The Apostolic Fathers*. New York: Christian Heritage, 1947, pp. 67–68. Translation by Glimm.

water in the chalice. Each of the congregants solemnly came forward to place, on the plate, a small piece of bread he or she had brought from home. Then the bishop and presbyters laid their hands on those offerings. The former prayed the great *eucharistic* (from the Greek, *eucharistia*) or "thanksgiving" prayer over the bread and wine. The prayer gave thanks to God above for the gift of the Lord Jesus Christ, for the fruits of the earth symbolized by these offerings, and for the life empowered by the indwelling of the Holy Spirit in the faithful of the congregation; it asked God to make the partaking of this sacred food and drink an *anamnesis* (from the Greek for "remembrance"), a solemn remembrance of the dead and risen Lord.

Each communicant then came forward to receive a piece of bread and a sip of wine. Each did not necessarily receive the same piece of bread brought from home; their lives were now commingled like the offerings upon the dish.

The *Didache* (from the Greek, "to teach"), called in full "the Teaching of the Twelve Apostles," is a short text of Christian instruction from around A.D. 180 or perhaps even earlier. It contains the oldest extant eucharistic prayers, and their lines have an unforgettable beauty. Over the cup of wine, officiants were instructed to say:

> We give thee thanks, Father, for the holy vine of David thy son, which Thou hast made known to us through Jesus thy Son; to Thee be glory forever.

And over the bread:

> We give thee thanks, Our Father, for the life and knowledge which Thou has revealed to us through Jesus thy Son; to thee be glory forever. As this broken bread was scattered upon the mountain tops and after being harvested was made one, so let thy church be gathered together from the ends of the earth into thy kingdom, for thine is the glory and the power through Jesus Christ forever.

After the blessing of the bread and wine, a longer prayer might follow. The version of it in the *Didache* ends with the words:

> Let grace come, and let this world pass away. Hosanna to the God of David. If anyone is holy, let him come; if anyone is not, let him repent. Maranatha.[4]

Maranatha is a word in Aramaic, the language of Jesus, meaning "Come, Lord."

When those who were part of the holy fellowship had received the sacred food and drink, the bishop blessed and dismissed them, and the Christians departed into the streets of the old city on the shores of the turquoise sea.[5]

---

[4] Glimm, pp. 178–180.

[5] A standard study of early Christian worship, upon which this summary is based, is Dom Gregory Dix, *The Shape of the Liturgy.* London: Dacre Press, 1945.

probably the highest structure in the village proper, and most villagers had rarely been out of sight of it. Inside, the church represented another world, more ominous and more wondrous than the one outside. Paintings and windows told of the life of Christ, from humble nativity to the awesome Last Judgment. They told of the babe in the Holy Mother's arms, who was also judge of the dead, the one who would guide the destiny of souls to eternal bliss or torment.

These images of a transcendent and mysterious reality revealed far wider realms of mood and meaning than the cramped estate. In the church, the bedecked altar, the cross, the flickering candles, and the hint of incense in the air evoked the numinous into the midst of everyday lives. Virtually everyone in the village except the priest and clerk was illiterate (including probably the lord also); the church was not only the villagers' place of worship but also their place of learning and festival.

The parish priest would have had some schooling, though perhaps not nough fully to understand the archaic Latin of the Mass he celebrated regularly the church or perhaps even to know of the Mass's antecedence in the ancient use-service during the days of the Caesars, which we have already seen. The sic order of the Mass, though—Scripture, offering of bread and wine, prayers, great eucharist or thanksgiving, communion, blessing—remained the same. n the priest's ornamented ritual vestment, the chasuble, was a descendent of Roman pancho-like jacket. But that was not the main point.

The meaning of the ceremony lay in what was understood to be happening service, which was read by a clergyman who faced the altar and whose ations in the sonorous language of another age were punctuated with ornate gestures. Yet, the Christian rite still lived, for what counted to priest and was the sense of rich sacred presence that the Mass evoked, the occasion the priest to deliver simple instructions on faith and virtue in the Sunday , and the chance it afforded the village to gather together. Villagers under- at in the service something holy was going on. They could apprehend that of Jesus upon the cross portrayed over the altar, as well as his position al judge of souls pictured at the rear of the church, was about their lives deaths. That they were somehow lifted into a holy presence was the main

nt-day Roman Catholic worship is for the most part in the lineage of medieval church in western Europe, as is the worship of the Anglican in America) faith and some Lutheran churches. But the sweeping affected the Roman Catholic church after the Second Vatican Coun- y 1960s have made the Mass now strikingly much more like that of urch than that of the medieval village. As we shall see in more detail on Christian worship, the full participation of the community al offering is perhaps emphasized more than the mysteriou dicating once more the ability of Christianity to express in different contexts.

A DIFFICULT LIFE

The Christian experience was not over when the community left the widow's house. It was not always easy to be of this gathering. After the eucharistic service, women and men deacons took consecrated bread to sick members. In times of persecution, this was a dangerous assignment. More than one young envoy of grace suffered death rather than betray his or her holy burden and the home for which it was intended.

However, active persecution of Christianity in the Roman Empire was only occasional and often localized. But even when times were relatively safe, Christians had difficulties enough. Lucrative occupations such as idol-making, or anything to do with what they considered the generally licentious and barbarous arena, were closed to them. Some Christian leaders advised nonparticipation in the imperial armed forces as well. Further, Christians joined not only in the eucharistic Sunday worship, but prayed and fasted on the "station days" of Wednesday and Friday. In what they saw as a hedonistic society, they strove to dress and act chastely. All these practices brought them countless conflicts with the outside world.

Just as often, they produced internal division within families; for it frequently happened that one spouse was Christian and the other not, or children of pagan parents accepted the risen Lord. As the stern Christian writer Tertullian tells us, the pagan might wish to feast while the Christian must fast. In another case, the non-Christian may insist on attending to family business while the converted spouse is equally set on going to worship, or visiting the cottages of the poor brethren, or even (this was a common practice) going to a jail to kiss the chains of martyrs imprisoned for upholding their faith.[6]

If it was not easy to be a Christian, neither was it easy to become one. Baptism, the great rite of entry into the Christian experience, was the most important event of a believer's life. It was received by adults only after two or three years of study and preparation. (By A.D. 180, however, it seems to have been common to baptize the children of a Christian family with their parents or as infants.)

Prebaptismal instruction covered two areas: doctrine and the strict Christian moral life. Doctrine was apparently taught along the lines summarized in the Apostles' Creed, which comes down to us from perhaps the second century A.D., and is used today in innumerable churches. In the later chapter on the beliefs of Christianity, we will look more closely at its significance as a recounting of the founding story of Christianity.

The miraculous is strongly present in the Creed, from the virgin birth of Jesus to his marvelous resurrection and ascension. For the story of the Creed is

---

[6] Tertullian, *To His Wife*, IV. Cited in A.E. Welsford, *Life in the Early Church A.D. 33 to 313*. Greenwich, Conn.: Seabury Press, 1953, p. 332.

a narrative of the power of God, whom Christians believe had in Jesus set aside all the old rules to work a new wonder for human salvation.

Baptism, the gateway to participation in this wonder, was generally administered at Easter, a great central festival in the church calendar year when the events leading up to the crucifixion and resurrection are reenacted, as they are also each Sunday in the weekly cycle of the year. Before Easter, catechumens sufficiently advanced underwent a strenuous preparation during the forty days of Lent which led up to the great festival. They fasted, they were exorcized of evil spirits daily, and they received advanced training. Finally, on the Wednesday before Easter, the bishop gave each a final examination and a solemn blessing, layed hands on every candidate, breathed on her or him and signed each with the cross.

On Easter eve, the candidates maintained an all-night vigil, keeping watch through the night during which Jesus had lain in the tomb. At dawn they ritually undressed. Stripping themselves of all that had gone before and turning themselves toward the east and the rising sun, they went to the place of baptism, usually a tank or pool deep enough for immersion. There they would once again be exorcized. Next each took vows renouncing the devil and all his works, and affirmed her or his faith by reciting a brief creed such as the Apostles' Creed or answering questions based on its main articles.

Then the bishop baptized the candidates by immersing or pouring water over the head of each. The *Didache* insists that cold running water should be used if possible, and tells us that the water ought to be poured over the initiate's head three times as the officiate says, "In the name of the Father, and of the Son, and of the Holy Ghost." Afterwards the candidates emerged from the place of baptism to be clothed in radiant white linen and to partake of their first eucharistic meal in the fellowship of those with whom they now fully belonged. They were now ready to re-enter this hard world, in which the powers of evil held such sway, with the purity and faith of new beings, born again as Christians.

OVERVIEW OF THE EARLY CHURCH

The preceding pages have given a brief glimpse into the life of the Christian church in its first centuries. Much has had to be left out, especially in respect to its development, its diversity, its many changes from what was presented here. Such an examination will be the subject of later chapters. It can be said now, however, that the sort of second-century Christianity just described represents a formative version of the faith, and perhaps also a "classic" style of early Christianity, which if appreciated can help to give perspective to that which followed.

In passing, we may note that so often the early church seems to have maintained a "both–and" position toward issues that later were to divide Christianity.

Emphasis was given more or less equally to Scripture, sermon, and sacrament. The authority of the nascent New Testament joined, without conflict, the authority of the church as represented by the bishops of the major churches believed to have been founded by Apostles. The Gospels and Apostolic letters were thought to have been written by Apostles or to have the authority of an Apostle in them. The same authority lay behind both bishop and book. Adult and infant baptism and baptism by both immersion and pouring were observed, yet these practices were later to become the source of bitter conflict. We shall look more closely these conflicts in subsequent chapters.

Now we will briefly introduce the story of this church as it triumphed spread, finally, to embrace a quarter of the earth's population.

CHURCH AND VILLAGE

Let us leap forward in time a thousand years to the year A.D. 1180. The a year as any to use as a vantage point for surveying another "class Christianity, the medieval. The year A.D. 1180 falls in the very middle Ages, those seven centuries (counting from Charlemagne, wh man Emperor unified the western Christian world, to Martin splintering of the church). The Middle Ages were times of cast of cathedrals and cloisters, of romantic ideals, of splendor ar a faith grounded in a world-view nearly universal among Ch This medieval experience has indelibly colored all subseque

On another Sunday morning, this time anywhere in rope, the bells of a village church rang out around 9 A.M. the community to Mass. The village itself probably was li of mud-and-wattle cottages set near the grim walls of surrounded by the fields that its peasants worked for

The relation of lord and serf was complex. On fe banquet with the nobles in the great hall, and at har lords had to labor alongside their peasants. Mediev the importance of visiting the poor and sick of the v kitchen to prepare extra food for the beggars at the admonitions did not always fall on deaf ears an high and low were sometimes caring ones. Nev centered on fighting and collecting revenues th style. Caught between the threats of war and viewpoint a very difficult life.

One aspect of the peasants' life, how more than the daily struggle for survival. than the serfs' hovels, and more graceful

HEAVEN ON EARTH

Nowhere is the sense of transcendent reality in formal worship preserved more fully than in the Eastern Orthodox churches, and in those Roman Catholic churches that use Eastern rites.

The Eastern Orthodox church is predominant in Russia, Greece, and the Balkans. The worship in other Eastern churches, such as the Armenian and the Coptic church found in Egypt and Ethiopia, is similar. The basic pattern of Orthodox worship developed from the ancient rite in Constantinople (modern Istanbul) when that city was the hub of the Byzantine or Eastern Roman Empire. Its special theme has ever been a Christian celebration of resurrection and divine glory. When Russian envoys came to Constantinople in the Middle Ages and saw this worship for the first time, they said it was like entering heaven on earth, and they determined to bring it to their people.

Music, incense, lights, and slow ritual drama bring the attender at an Eastern Orthodox service into an expansive world that seems to point in a direction beyond the mundane. Standing between congregation and altar yet drawing them together stands the glittering *iconostasis* ("image screen" in Greek), a partition or screen that is bright with icons or sacred pictures of Christ and the saints. Its doors open at crucial moments of the service to reveal richly garbed ministers whose ceremonial processing punctuates the very ancient and conservative Divine Liturgy. Paradoxically, the Eastern church also presents a warm, homey, and somewhat uninhibited ambience. People come and go freely during the long service, as though in the mansion of a great and ancient friend; they stand and kneel and move about to light candles or kiss icons with a freedom seldom seen in Western congregations.

There is the sense in Orthodox services of the deep interaction of the Eastern churches with the varied ethnic identities of their adherents. The Eastern churches have had a very different history from those of the West. Most of the Eastern Christian peoples have suffered long centuries of rule by non-Christian regimes like the Ottoman or by autocracies like the Russian czardom. Even today the great majority of Orthodox people live under officially antireligious Communist rulers. In these situations the Orthodox church has been, and often still is, virtually the only vehicle for the expression of an independent national identity and culture. This historical role has made the Eastern church conservative, yet also deeply interwoven with the ethnic cultures where it ministers.

FAITH WITHIN

Protestantism expresses another important manifestation of Christianity. Even as medieval and Eastern services have tend to emphasize the second part of the ancient rite, the blessing, giving, and receiving of bread and wine, so the typical Protestant service is an expansion of the first part, with its reading of scripture, prayers, and sermon. This is because Protestantism has a somewhat different understanding of the meaning of Christianity, and of the church, than those other traditions.

Protestantism came into being espousing the fundamental principle of the reformation in sixteenth-century Europe, first articulated by Martin Luther, and briefly stated as "justification by faith." It is more fully and correctly put as, "justification by God's freely-given grace received through inward faith." "Justification" here refers to an individual's being put in right relationship with God despite his or her sins and limitations. "Faith" here means a deep interior openness to God and trust in him. It was this kind of faith, not outward deeds or beliefs or rites or even pious feelings, for which, Protestants believed, God looked. It was this kind of faith by which Protestants believed one was accounted righteous.

With its roots firmly planted in the writings of the Apostle Paul, Protestantism characteristically holds that the initial imparter of saving faith is not the sacraments. Rather, faith comes into being in the individual's internal response to the Word of God, communicated through the Scriptures and expounded in preaching. If the sacraments should impart faith to anyone, it is through their being, as it were, enacted sermons. Though words can, of course, be read silently as well as heard aloud—and the Protestant emphasis on Scripture was a great impetus to the expansion of literacy and book-publishing—the word is originally and fundamentally heard, and this basic meaning of word is reactivated in Protestant worship.

Today, Sunday service in a Protestant church centers upon the imparting of the word. The minister, garbed either in a simple gown or a plain suit, takes his or her place at the front of the church, which is probably marked only by a simple altar or a pulpit. Words of greeting and inspiration are followed by a reading from Scripture and a "pastoral prayer" offered by all for the concerns of the community and world. The preaching of the sermon follows, often explicating and interpreting the Scriptural passages that have just been read. An offering of money is taken up and its presentation, symbolizing the sacrifice of the congregation's time and talents for the Christian cause, has become something of a ritual climax in many Protestant churches. Afterwards, unless Holy Communion is celebrated, the service quickly comes to a close with final prayers and a hymn.

This outline of the pattern of worship can be said to be characteristic of most "mainstream" Protestant churches—Methodist, Baptist, Presbyterian, Congregational (United Church of Christ)—and it will be further amplified later. Unbound by any common rule, Protestant worship flourishes in a diversity of form and mood. The rather intellectual tone of traditional Presbyterian and Congregational churches offers contrast to the warm and more intense atmosphere of many Baptist and similar churches that often involve impassioned sermons denouncing evil or pleading for a return to Christ.

Some denominations, like the Lutheran and Episcopal which stand midway between Catholic and Protestant, have a much more formal, ritualized service, with vestments, set prayers, and responses. The Holy Communion or Holy Eucharist in them, particularly, are comparable to the Roman Catholic rite.

Other diversifications obtain too: the Quaker (Society of Friends) meeting, silent with no sacraments; the Pentecostal service—now found among "mainstream" Protestants and Roman Catholics as well as in traditionally Pentecostal churches—in which the Spirit moves freely to give spontaneous movement, preaching, interpreting and "speaking in tongues," as described by the Apostle Paul (1 Corinthians 14).

Finally, we note that today in many Protestant, as well as Roman Catholic, churches, traditional molds are again being broken open to introduce dance, drama, discussion, and modern styles of music into new types of worship. Within the last century, numerous new and vigorous movements of Protestant and Catholic background have arisen in Third World areas such as Africa and Latin America. They have frequently rejected the customary alliance of Christianity with Euro–American cultural styles, setting out to create new forms of expression incorporating indigenous features. Protestantism, potentially perhaps a very dynamic branch of Christianity, with its stress on inward faith rather than outward form, has continually found avenues in which to respond anew to the changing times, although there is a danger that too much diversity without a deeper unity can lead to disordered fragmentation.

THE HEART OF CHRISTIANITY

We have been looking at the religious tradition known as Christianity, or rather some samples of its outward forms. Numerically the largest of the world's religions, it is also, as these examples must have suggested, immensely varied and diverse.

Historically, nearly all its many forms can be traced back to the churches of the ancient Roman world like the one we described in the opening of this chapter. Although Christianity has undergone many changes, and experienced innumerable reforms and counterreforms in many distant cultures, traces of the language and logic of that Greco-Roman world are present throughout the changes.

Yet, fundamental to the church of the ancient world stands another religion and culture—Judaism. Christianity owes much to the ancient tradition and rich heritage of Judaism. At the heart of both Judaism and Christianity stands the solitary figure of the Messiah. For Christians the Messiah came in the human form of the Jew named Jesus—the Christ. For the Jews, the Messiah or Messianic Age has not yet come.

As the stories of the New Testament tell us, Jesus came as Messiah but not of the sort expected by his followers or his enemies. He did not try to liberate Israel by political coup from Roman oppression. Rather, he began his public life associated with the ascetic prophet John the Baptist, who preached the coming of the Apocalypse, the end of time, and the beginning of God's judgment in the world. John preached repentance in preparation for that event, repentance that would lead to a transformed state which was symbolized by baptism.

Jesus asked for baptism by John. After his immersion in the river Jordan, he moved out into the world to begin his own ministry. His message shared the same roots as that of John, but, like their two characters, each message had a distinctive quality.

The themes of their preaching spoke of the divine overthrow of the old and the beginning of a new order, the coming of the Kingdom of God, a new creation available to all who return to the intimate relationship with God established so long ago in the desert at Mt. Sinai. As recounted by the Gospels, John's proclamation stands out as clearly and as strikingly as the harsh and shadowless desert in which he spent most of his life. Clad in the skins of animals and eating only locusts and wild honey, he was sustained by his great faith. Empowered like the prophets of old, he drew people out to him in the wilderness to hear and to respond to the message of repentance and salvation.

The preaching of Jesus who, it is written, moved through the world eating and drinking, weeping and dancing, often appears enigmatic, elusive, hard to understand, yet universal in its significance. Jesus spoke of the Kingdom of God as the divine reality which is both present in the world and yet coming, is expressed in both God's judgment and his forgiveness. It is as treasure hidden in a field or a pearl of great price for which the finder sells all possessions, or again as a tiny mustard seed that can grow into the great tree it holds within. As the Gospels tell us, Jesus was the center of the divine activity that would transform the world. His preaching offered a way to live in harmony with it and his miracles were its signs.

The stories tell us that at about the age of thirty-three, in the context of a holy day of his people, Jesus was arrested and condemned. The holy day was the Passover, the festival commemorating the escape of the Hebrews from slavery in Egypt. The Book of Exodus tells us how Moses led God's people out of captivity. He did so after a plague, which killed the first-born of every living thing, had passed over the houses of the Hebrews, which in accordance with God's command were marked and set apart by the blood of a slain lamb. Jesus, and his followers, interpreted his death as like that of the lamb, necessary for the coming of the Kingdom and the liberation of those in captivity. On the night before his death on the cross, Jesus gathered his disciples for a Passover meal with bread and wine, that became a celebration of the Kingdom and a showing-forth of its inaugural sacrifice, which was to be the pouring out of Jesus' blood and the lifting up of his flesh. The feast of this night and the remembrances it evokes were to be the basis of the Christian Eucharistic ritual.

Yet, the meal showed forth not only a sacrificial death, but also ongoing life. For beginning three days after his crucifixion, various of the disciples of Jesus began reporting seeing him alive; he was made known to them in the breaking

Leonardo da Vinci's *Last Supper*.

of bread, in a gathering in an upper room, and while fishing by the shores of the lake. These encounters were brief; Jesus mysteriously came and went; and only believers were involved. Yet to the followers of Jesus, they were unmistakable and they vindicated their belief that the life of God, undefeatable by mankind, flowed in and through Jesus. The resurrection appearances, Christian tradition tells us, occurred over forty days and culminated in a final appearance (excluding Paul's later vision) in which Jesus was lifted up to heaven—the Ascension, as it is called.

CONCLUSION

The stories have led us into the heart of Christianity. It lies in the experience and faith that the life of God flows through Jesus to create the heavenly Kingdom of which he spoke while on earth. That faith and experience have been expressed in many ways. The divine life has been communicated in diverse media. But virtually all Christians would agree that something very special concerning the understanding of ultimate meaning and the effecting of the ultimate transformation of human life took place in a particular time and place, and in a particular person. For Christians, this bedrock fact affirms the irreducible uniqueness of Christianity, and yet simultaneously unveils its universal significance. We can now survey how this particular faith founded on these experiences has come to not one but myriad expressions through changing times and places and each recognizing itself as Christianity.

christianity in history

A HISTORICAL OVERVIEW

Variety and diversity are surely words that occur when anyone samples the contemporary world of Christianity, as has been the case throughout its history. The obvious gross distinctions between the Catholic, Orthodox, and Protestant expressions of Christianity include enormously different forms within each. Concurrently, one would find in many quarters of Christianity expressions of a deep concern regarding its fragmentation, with a corollary desire to work for the unification of Christians. If diversity is regarded by some as an unfortunate reality, unity is their hope. At a time when the Polish-born Pope John Paul II was visiting more countries of the world than any of his predecessors and prohibiting holding political office by priests, in the United States a self-avowed fundamentalist preacher, Reverend Jerry Falwell, was trying to forge an effective political force in the Moral Majority movement.

Engagement with the world or renunciation of the world? Diversity or unity? Doctrinal conformity or freedom of religious thought? Hierarchical forms of church organization or complete equality and responsibility for the religious community's well being on the part of every participant in the community? Such are but a few of the tensions inherent in present and previous expressions of Christianity, which is a name inclusive of remarkably different expressions and experience. No single form or conception has ever fulfilled the ancient Christian test: "that which is believed by all in all times and in all places."[1] St. Vincent 431 A.D. Historically viewed, there has never been such a time for Christianity.

"God was in Christ reconciling the world unto himself" (2 Corinthians 5:19). A concrete, specific life—a set of events in time and place—is affirmed by Christians to have been a decisive act by God to overcome the alienation by which humans, through sin and with no possibility of being otherwise, are separated from God (see Chapter 5). God has done what humans can in no wise do for themselves—this is the heart of the incarnational and historical proclamation of Christians through the centuries. But, as historians have necessarily come to recognize, any event in time and space is susceptible to radically diverse interpretations and meanings. And, further, any interpretation, once made, carries a power and force within it that modifies interpretation of every other event.

Christian recounting of history takes as its backdrop the Jews who were the first "people of the book" in Western religion. It was they who over a thousand and more years had recorded, preserved and revered the stories of the mighty acts of God in delivering the Jewish people out of Egypt and in giving the promised land to them. They also recorded the recurrent pattern of now forgetting the Covenant and then prophetic re-calling to trust in the Lord. Theirs was the gift of the Bible, first to and for themselves and then, by extension, to the rest of humanity.

Jesus was a Jew whose teachings, as scholars have decisively demonstrated, were not at all new or unique in content. He spoke as a Jew to Jews. He lived out his short life primarily among Jews. His disciples (followers) during his lifetime were Jews—numerically few at that.

After his crucifixion, however, his followers were emboldened to interpret his life and death as the turning point of history. In the religious language they employed, the Holy Spirit empowered and energized them to tell their radically revised story of God's mighty acts as having come down to a concentrated and incarnated presence in the life, work, and teachings of Jesus of Nazareth. So powerfully transforming was this conviction that over the course of the first four centuries of the existence of Christianity, the Bible of the Jews came to be revered and retained out of deference to and regard for its importance to Jesus, to the Apostles—especially Paul—and to the earliest Jewish Christians. But by calling that Bible the "Old Testament," the Christians were also declaring that the event of the life, death, and resurrection of Jesus had provided them with the basis for a radically revised interpretation of that earlier testament. They declared that selected writings by a few Christians, taken together, should also be regarded as Scriptural. Thus, the amplification of the Bible to incorporate a "New Testa-

---

[1] Around 434, Vincent of Lerins wrote *Commonitorium* as a critique of what he regarded as the errors of St. Augustine. He proposed that sound doctrinal teachings would be required to meet the tests of "universality, antiquity and consent." The one cited here, of course, is that of universality.

ment,'' though requiring centuries to accomplish, was at once a way of inex-
tricably retaining a connection between Jews and Christians and, paradoxically,
declaring an all-important distinction between them.

One of the widely recognized conclusions of Biblical scholars is that Jesus
taught in parables, several of which are preserved in the Gospels in the New Testament. From the outset, these powerful utterances provoked divergent in-
terpretive responses from those who experienced the words as a transformative
power in their lives and understanding. Those strands of the Christian tradition
that have tended to respond primarily to these enigmatic teachings of Jesus and
that have emphasized their regard for him as a teacher have tended to view their
religious community as a school of followers of the Way.

Other Christians from the outset, however, have tended to respond to the
Jesus story not by emphasizing his teachings but rather by regarding him as the
founder of a different kind of religious institution—the Christian Church. From
that perspective, the work of the church is to be a witness to the work of Christ
and to make the benefits of that work available to all who would partake of it. If
those who emphasize the teachings of Jesus hold that the Christian community
is like a school, those holding the other view of the proper work of the church see
it as sacramental in nature. In explanation of this nature, its champions emphasize
the conviction that Jesus instituted those rituals which it is the work of the church
to provide. Baptism and the Eucharist (in some traditions within Christianity this
is called Holy Communion or the Lord's Supper) are offered in virtually every
Christian community or church. But the beliefs regarding how the sacramental
rituals are to be understood and what happens in them are widely divergent. Some
Christians believe Christ to be physically present in the bread and wine of the
sacraments; others believe that the communion is a memorial feast (see Chapters
5 and 6).

Such differences as these are clear signs of the diversity within Christianity.
They also harbor the seeds of the terrible conflicts which have from time to time
erupted between defenders of one view of what Christianity is and what it requires
of its adherents and defenders of other views. The specter of Christians murdering
Christians in the inquisition or in the religious wars of the sixteenth and seventeenth centuries in Europe manifests the terrible side of the passion that gives
rise to and is expressed in these manifold expressions of Christianity. Christianity
was born in conflict, first between Christian Jews and other Jews, then between
Jewish Christians and Gentile (non-Jewish) Christians, then between Christians
and devotees of many other religions in the Roman Empire, then between Gentile
Christians holding to one system of Christianity against groups of Christians with
other interpretations of it, then between Greek-speaking Christians against Latin-
speaking ones, then between Latin-speaking ones and those emphasizing the importance of the vernacular languages, then between the Catholics and the Protestants—ad infinitum.

No form, no creed, no rituals, no institutions, no set of doctrines or dogmas

Charlemagne's Palatine Chapel. Photo courtesy of Ann Münchow.

has ever successfully gathered into itself the allegiance of all the people at any given time in history who were determined to regard themselves as Christian. This recognition gives rise to the possibility that the power of Christianity lies in its generation of diversity. The story told by Christians is such that some people of all races, cultures, political persuasions, and social differences feel themselves moved by the Christian experience. At the same time, critics and foes of Christianity over the centuries have unhesitatingly declared that Christianity's inability to achieve uniformity among its adherents may be an indication of a fundamental weakness or flaw. However, the fact of diversity among Christians from the religion's inception is undeniable. This history of change and diversity is one of Christianity's distinctive characteristics and suggests that future centuries may witness further and as yet unknown forms of expression of religious vitality that their devotees will insist on calling Christian.

An awareness of the history of Christianity suggests the possibility of characterizing at least the major shifts in it over almost two thousand years. In summary, and briefly characterized, these include the following. First, the emergence of Christianity as a distinct religion out of its Jewish origin, which occurred in the first and second centuries and which left a legacy of unresolved problems for both religions. Second, the shift from Jewish primacy to Gentile predominance required in the earliest centuries not only certain appropriations from Judaism but also attempts to express the Christian story and ideas in words, concepts, and symbols that were meaningful to Gentile participants. This has been called by some historians the Hellenization of Christianity. In spite of, or perhaps paradoxically because of, the restless, dynamic struggles to become accessible to every possible culture, while at the same time remaining constantly faithful to the stories of its foundations, Christianity not only survived but flourished in the mode of conflict, disputation, and occasional persecution.

An Emperor of the Roman Empire, Constantine, in 312 determined that Christianity was no longer an unlicensed, illegal religion. By the end of the fourth century, under the Emperor Theodosius, Christianity was adopted as the official religion of the Roman Empire and paganism was no longer tolerated. Within the geographical Roman Empire, the next challenge confronting Christians was the conversion of the barbarian Germanic peoples, who in wave after wave battled and subsequently conquered the western provinces of the Roman Empire. Their adherence to their native cults required ingenuity by Christianity yet again to find ways of expressing the faith that would be persuasive and acceptable to these powerful new forces. This process continued into the sixth century with impressive successes.

Concurrently, Christianity was spreading out from the Roman Empire. The British Isles, Armenia, Mesopotamia, portions of the Persian Empire, Arabia, north-central Europe, India, and China—all of these sites and various cultural and ethnic groupings of peoples were enfolded in diverse ways into Christianity. Even in cataloguing them by geography and culture, we can see that the forms and institutional expressions of Christianity would necessarily have to be significantly diverse.

The spread of Christianity, so impressive in many respects, was bought at the price of adaptation and accommodation—even compromise. Some Christian purists were appalled by what they regarded as indefensible corrupting of the faith. They became the schismatics in some instances, the monastics in others. On the other hand, defenders of the adaptation of Christianity to the new demands posed by the challenges of proclaiming the faith to new and diverse peoples were equally adamant in insisting that theirs was the way to be faithful. The internal seeds of discord were manifesting themselves in these crucial decisions. Christianity may be understood not only by comparing and contrasting it with other religious positions, practices, and traditions but also by examining the seemingly incompatible differing views and practices within the religion itself.

CHRISTIANITY IN THE LATE IMPERIAL AND MEDIEVAL WEST

One aspect of the eventual triumph of Christianity over its competitor religions in the Roman Empire was its adoption of a form for the institutional church directly modeled on the structures of Roman government. Early on, Paul had proposed the image of the human body as that which best characterized what the church could be like—all organs and parts meshing mysteriously to form a functioning whole. He also offered other images that suggested an ideal of unity and mutuality. But like all the others who served as leaders of early Christian communities, Paul experienced their frequent disunity and fragmentation. Varieties of forms were tried, but for decades none was accepted universally as *the* appropriate form.

However, one pattern of organization did emerge by the end of the first century that has persisted ever since, although there has never been a time in over twenty centuries when it was the only form of Christian institutional organization. In this model, there were bishops (overseers or superintendents) who were the successors of the apostles, deacons (ministers or servants to the churches), and elders (presbyters or priests).

Refinements of this pattern occurred over the decades of the second century. The bishops claimed and assumed ever greater authority over the priests, ministers, and lay people in their geographical areas (usually cities) called "dioceses." Thus, a hierarchy was emerging. Eventually, from the fourth century onward, the bishops gathered together and took counsel in efforts to resolve disputes and formulate patterns of belief and practice that were intended to be obligatory on all Christians. These gatherings were called ecumenical councils and their participants intended to reach decisions for all Christian churches. Theirs was the aim of expressing the catholic (universal) faith of all Christians. From the outset, however, the authority of the bishops to make such binding decisions was questioned and denied, particularly by the proponents of views that were rejected by the councils. The issues that gave rise to such disputes have through the centuries proved to be those which have consistently provoked Christian thinkers to reflection. In that sense the councils set much of the agenda for Christian theology through the centuries. Some of those issues are examined in Chapter 5. The emerging alliance between the emperors of the Roman Empire and various Christian leaders in itself provided an important impetus toward attempting to unify Christians under the banner of a single organization and a unified set of beliefs. As the Empire is one, so, the emperors argued, should the religion endorsed by the emperors be one.

Although the Empire disintegrated over the centuries, the ideal of unity it bequeathed to the church outlived it. Predictably, in the absence of effective emperors in the West, especially after the capital of the Empire was moved in the fourth century from Rome to Byzantium, or Constantinople (now called Istanbul). The position of Bishop of Rome assumed an increasingly significant leadership role, not only in affairs of the church but also in political realms. That office over the centuries came to be regarded as the supreme bishop over all other bishops— the Pope.

Part of the story of the emergence of the Pope as the supreme bishop of Western Catholic Christianity lies in the adoption of Latin as the official language in the western churches. This happened over several decades in the second and third centuries. Tertullian (c.160–c.220) was the first theologian to write in Latin. Until then Greek had been the language of Gentile Christianity. (Jesus spoke

Aramaic and early Christians had to be multilingual.) All the books that came to be included in the New Testament were written in Greek, as were the theological reflections of most of the first two centuries. As for the Orthodox churches of the East, Greek usage continued to be the case, even after the Western Roman churches adopted Latin as their official language. Of course this complicated the theological debates of the great councils. Some participants thought and spoke in Latin, even if they knew or understood Greek. Concepts and ideas expressible in Greek were often extremely difficult to express adequately in Latin—and vice-versa.

Over the centuries the problem became more acute. The year 1054 was the date of the decisive separation between the Orthodox churches and the Western church.

The contraction of the former Roman Empire, as it suffered losses of land and people over the centuries, also contributed to the ascendancy of the Bishop of Rome repeatedly to claim and quite often to exercise supremacy. The conquest by and assimilation of the Germanic peoples into the Empire in the fourth century A.D. was a factor. The weakness of effective influence of emperors was another. The rise of Islam in the seventh century and its achieving a remarkable series of conquests of former territories held by Rome was another. Islam took over especially in the eastern provinces and along the southern shores of the Mediterranean as far west as Africa, and it eventually spread even up into western Europe as far as Spain where it would remain until the fourteenth century. The former glory of Rome was contracted into a much smaller geographical area. But, paradoxically, without the protection and power of the Roman Empire as an ally, Christianity in the West, often with the Pope leading the way, developed and even flourished as it had not previously done either originally within Judaism or subsequently under the Romans. The Muslim conquerors, deeply respectful of all "religions of the Book," did not typically abolish Christian communities and churches. Those groups were, however, severed from their prior political environment and developed their own forms of Christianity under conditions in which they were a minority religion. Papal decrees could make no effective difference under such circumstances.

The story of Christianity in time and space, however, encompasses far more than the story of the Catholic church or even of all the churches together. The heretics, the schismatics, the cultural expressions which were often ignored and sometimes condemned, but which in any case were typically marginal to normative Christianity must somehow all be kept in view. As the Creed affirms, Christianity is "one, catholic, holy, and apostolic." But that was more often an aspiration than a reality.

Over the thousand years and more between the fifth century, which was marked by the collapse of the Roman Empire in the West, by the last two of the great ecumenical councils (see Chapter 5), by the work of St. Augustine, by the papacy of Leo I (d. 461); and the reformation of the sixteenth century, one must distinguish between the internal story of church Christianity and the evolving relationship between Christianity and its socio-cultural contexts. In the East, Christianity was subordinate to the Emperor enthroned in Constantinople. From time to time, those emperors used language identical to that employed by Popes in the West to express their sense of control and authority over church affairs. Though problematic, the term "Caesaropapism" still most adequately expresses this. The Bishop of Constantinople was clearly subordinate to governing civil authorities, and this pattern continues until today in the Orthodox churches of the East. In sharp contrast stands the tension in the West between the secular and the spiritual authorities, which today we consider under headings of church and state. The uneasiness of the dynamic situation in the West has been manifested from time to time by Popes aspiring to exercise full control, as in the case of Innocent III in the thirteenth century (see above), and again in efforts by emperors and kings to subordinate the church in a manner similar to the Eastern pattern.

The issue of Christianity's relational patterns to the societies and cultures in which it has gained a following is one of great complexity (see Chapter 7). Christianity ranges from being the official religion of the Empire (fourth century) to being a persecuted minority religion, as it has been from time to time and in various places. Such changes in status raise a complex of questions that perplex political philosophers no less than theologians. Should religious concerns and convictions guide the actions of political leaders, or is theirs the task of governing well, even if that requires holding personal religious convictions in abeyance or rejecting the counsel of one's religious leaders? Is religion best served when its leaders concern themselves with political affairs and attempt directly to influence them? Such issues will obviously be more or less acute, depending upon the form of civil government. Tyrants, dictators, and sometimes monarchs and emperors are often loathe to concede the appropriateness of religious "interference" in their realms, and, typically, they relegate religion to rather tightly compartmentalized roles. Or, alternatively, they elevate their own responsibility to include leading the religious institutions, as well.

In democratic states, however, the issues fall out in different patterns. One, as in England, is to have a state church but to tolerate all other religious expressions. Another, as in the United States, is to build a separation between church and state and constitutionally to guarantee freedom of religion. The effect of the latter is to attempt to insure the non-interference of government in the affairs of religious institutions and the restriction of political influence exercised by religious bodies to that of only one voice among others attempting to influence public policy.

Given the seriousness of the issues just indicated, it is important to understand the differences of relational patterns among the various forms of Christianity, and their governmental contexts, especially the differences between East and West. One series of events in the Western church will stand symbolically to demonstrate the tension there. In the process of establishing the Holy Roman Empire, particularly through the establishing of a centralized governmental control over an extensive European Empire, Charlemagne encouraged ecclesiastical reform and a revival of scholarship in a movement often referred to as the Carolingian Renaissance.

On Christmas Day in the year 800, Charlemagne was crowned the first "Holy Roman Emperor." Did Pope Leo III actually place the crown on his head, thereby demonstrating the Christian leader's authority even to make emperors? Or did, as some accounts have it, Leo hand the crown to Charles the Great who then placed it on his own head, thereby demonstrating that the Empire was subordinate to no one and to no institution? The ramifications of these questions took centuries to be answered.

Papal claims to superiority in the earthly realm were extensive. Emperors, kings, and princes, were equally adamant in denying their subordination to the church. Civil authorities claimed the right and the responsibility to have a decisive say in the selection of ecclesiastical leaders in their areas, even to the point of some emperors demanding the recognition of their authority to choose the Pope. The name of this conflict was the "Investiture Controversy." The name derives from disputes regarding who had the right to invest whom with the authority of their office. Finally, after decades of struggle, the church forged out the freedom to select and invest its own leaders with the symbols of their office. But in spite of excessive claims sometimes made, with the exception of Innocent III (1198–1216), the remainder of the Middle Ages is a story of the ebb and flow of achieving an accommodation in which secular leaders came to power through hereditary, military, and political machinations in the secular realm, and ecclesiastical leaders were put in office through processes developed within the church.

Running through the story of the schism between the East and West and the struggles of the Western church to achieve independence from secular power is the office of the Papacy. The cast of characters is too extensive and the intricacies of the plot are too complex to reduce it to a few paragraphs. The highlights which follow should alert the interested reader to the existence of a vast literature on the subject which can be referred to by those interested in the larger story.

The doctrinal base of the rise of the papal office traces to the passage in a Gospel:

> You are Peter, and on this rock I will build my church, and the powers of death will not prevail against it. I will give you the keys of the kingdom of heaven, and whatever you bind on earth shall be bound in heaven, and whatever you loose on earth shall be loosed in heaven. (Matthew 16:18–19)

This "Petrine doctrine," coupled with the idea that Peter was the missionary founder of the Christian church in the city of Rome and that he was crucified by Nero in 64 A.D., combined to support the claim by subsequent bishops of Rome to be the first among equals in relation to all other bishops. When Pope Leo I was so successful in formulating the doctrine of "one person in two natures" for the Council of Chalcedon in 451 (see Chapter 5), the first of a series of remarkable successes in advocating what became the orthodox belief of Christians was scored by the bishops of Rome. Next, Pope Gregory I (590–604) fully embraced St. Augustine's theological position. This both enhanced Augustine's influence for a thousand years into the future and also clearly aligned the papal office with that towering champion of orthodox theology. Gregory's personal integrity and his theological orthodoxy consolidated the supreme authority of his office. To be Christian in the West, in spite of the disrepute of many of Gregory's successors, required obedience to the Bishop of Rome. Nicholas I (858–867) promulgated a famous document "The Isodorian Decretals" which purported to be an authoritative assemblage of all the decrees and decisions made up to that time by all previous Popes. It included the claim to ownership of vast amounts of geographical territory, which helped solidify the claims by the Pope to secular authority in conflict with emperors, kings, princes, and feudal lords.

Two other Popes tower above the others in recounting the ascendancy of the Papacy. Gregory VII (1073–1085) was deeply influenced by monasticism (see below) and by a determination to purify the corruption of the church and its clergymen. He sought, unsuccessfully, to reunite the divided Western and Eastern churches. He forbade lay investiture, reserving that right and responsibility only for ecclesiastical officials. His was an extraordinary and great reign. Then the zenith was reached under Innocent III (1198–1216). For the first and last time, papal theory was matched by papal action, authority and practice. Christendom was more nearly reunited under him than had been the case for more than a century. The remarkable accomplishments of Innocent III, however, were diminished and finally lost by his successors, none of whom was able to combine the gifts, insights, and effective authority of this remarkable Pope.

By the fourteenth century, Western Christianity endured the spectacle of the remove of the Papacy from Rome to Avignon in France and back again to Rome all within a few years, and consequently having at one time two Popes, each claiming legitimately to be in office. In reaction, there arose the "Conciliar Movement" that aimed at establishing ecclesiastical councils as the supreme authority for Christianity. Arising from within the church, this was the most serious challenge ever to have confronted the Papacy. If, as the conciliarist theorists insisted, Popes are subordinate to councils and are obliged to accept and implement the decisions of councils, then papal supremacy is a lost cause. In spite of extensive efforts in the fifteenth century to establish conciliar control of church affairs, the effort ultimately failed.

Centuries later in the first Vatican Council (1869–1870), the dogma of Papal Infallibility was promulgated. This symbolized the victory of papal over conciliar authority, although, ironically, it came as a decree of a council—but it was a council carefully orchestrated by a very powerful Pope. In the centuries between the papacy of Innocent III and the first Vatican Council, however, the restriction of papal authority to ecclesiastical matters had been clarified, as Popes exercised less and less effective influence in the realm of secular politics. Nation states and the theories of "divine rights of kings" combined to separate political from ecclesiastical affairs. That was a major issue in the Reformation of the sixteenth century, to which we shall come a little later.

MONASTICISM

Already in the third century, a movement had emerged that was parallel to but in many respects antithetical to the path taken by developments in the larger church expressions of Christianity. It was monasticism. Solitary individuals retired to the desert or to mountaintops to pursue the disciplines of contemplation.

Alternatively, and almost concurrently, other small groups of people were withdrawing into communities devoted to mutually supporting each other in efforts to live out their lives committed to loving and serving God. Through several centuries of development and disproportionate influence on the affairs of church Christianity, first in Eastern areas and eventually in the West, monasticism took clearer shape and form.

The formalization and regulation of the extremely diverse expressions of monasticism from the third to the fifth centuries was achieved in the early sixth century by Benedict of Nursia (c. 480–550). He formed communities, the most famous being Monte Cassino, and in 529 A.D. promulgated the *Rule of St. Benedict* that ordered the life of the monks, men and women, in the several monasteries that recognized his authority. Poverty, the giving away of all one's property; chastity, the renunciation of desire and an exaltation of selflessness; and obedience, submission to the duly constituted authority of the abbot, the leader of the community, were the ideals and the vows to which all who became full participants were required to submit themselves.

The courageous move into the desert by early monastics exemplified in the life of St. Anthony expressed a widespread, though seldom so dramatically acted upon, sense that ordinary Christianity inadequately represented the power of Christianity. The monastics did not typically suppose themselves to be superior persons, in fact they were characterized by their humility, but they often did believe that ascetic, disciplined lives were more consistent in aspiration with the Jesus story expressed in the Gospels and with the story of God's relationship with humanity as told in the Hebrew Bible (see Chapter 5). Untold and unimaginable possibilities awaited them in the desert in contrast with the fixed and determinate experiences promulgated in the church.

The monasteries, under the rule of St. Benedict and its few accepted successors, combined the disciplines of work, study, and prayer with a systematic division of labor to provide the basic needs of each member. Building, maintaining, and cleaning dwellings and planting, cultivating, and harvesting food were dominant forms that the work discipline required. Property was held in common and work was for the common good. Not surprisingly the monasteries not only flourished, they prospered. No other institution in medieval society in the East or West came close to being able to recruit, motivate, and support such devoted participants. In one respect, then, monasteries established a model of human organization that other institutions could emulate—as did several Popes in successive efforts to reform the secular clergy in the ninth to twelfth centuries. In this respect, the monastic movement was highly influential beyond its numbers of adherents and participants. But was it simply co-opted by the larger church? Did it lose its soul as it succeeded? Monastic reform movements indicate that the monasteries themselves were as susceptible to corruption, venality, ambition, and innumerable other human foibles as were the institutions to which they objected.

Monasticism was fundamentally transformed when the mendicant-orders (from the Latin, *mendicare,* "to beg") were created, the two most prominent of the thirteenth century being the Franciscans (from St. Francis of Assisi) and the Dominicans (from St. Dominic). These officially approved groups enjoyed freedoms that included papal protection of their members anywhere they traveled in Christendom. Traveling from place to place, they differed from early monastic communities which were stationary and represented retreat centers for the communicants. They were susceptible to the economic and governing structures in the locale where they were founded whereas the later mendicant orders were answerable to the Pope alone. The culmination of this development was reached in the sixteenth century when the Society of Jesus was created by papal decree in response to a petition by St. Ignatius Loyola. The Jesuits became and remain a powerful order in Catholicism, both in terms of the intellectual accomplishments of its membership and its influence on ecclesiastical affairs.

The power of monasticism derived from the commitment of those who joined orders in devotion to the ideals of the particular communities. Discipline and devotion typically enable people to accomplish much, and the monastics recognized this. Whether in scholarship, in agricultural development, in psychological insight, in political effectiveness, or any number of additional undertakings, the monasteries and convents were influential in a fashion disproportionate to their numbers. Spiritual growth and religious insight important beyond the confines of the orders were characteristic of them. But monasticism was not without its critics, who described them often as reclusive and renunciatory. As upholder of views often countering dominant trends and forces, monastics are always susceptible to objections from persons who were not called to that vocation and lifestyle.

No clearer arena of concern speaks to the tension between monasticism and generally held views than the practice of celibacy. From earliest Christian times there were some who were convinced that what Freud would later call the ubiquitous sex drive was the greatest impediment to spiritual maturation. From that perspective, the highest form of devotion was expressed in a sublimation of sexuality. The redirection of those energies to the service of God and humanity was the aspiration of the celibates—and to a remarkable degree was lived out by exemplary practitioners. Residing in this practice are far-reaching theories and judgments regarding human nature and the valuation of human sexuality. The traditional Catholic view, still promulgated by the Vatican, is that sexuality is primarily for the purpose of procreation to perpetuate the race. Pleasure and ful-fillment are unacceptable as ends of intercourse and love-making, though, as in-cidental means, they are tolerated. The regard for celibacy as a higher human achievement, and since the Middle Ages as a requirement for priesthood, is but one index of this swirl of issues. The Eastern Orthodox and Protestant churches have never imposed celibacy as a requirement for ministers and have seen sex-uality generally in a much more positive light. A few—very few—Christian think-ers through the long centuries have extolled sexual love as one of the means by which to give expression to and find the experience of drawing nearer to God. Christian monasticism in its demands for celibacy has been one of the sources prodding Christian thinkers to confront this complex of issues.

The contours of medieval Christianity are full of things that will arrest a person's attention. The Crusades of the eleventh to the thirteenth centuries, the Inquisition, the rise of literacy and the translation of the Bible into the languages of the peoples, the extensive conflict between secular and ecclesiastical authorities, the participation of the Christian churches in economic, artistic, literary, and philosophical developments—any one of these or another dozen matters has pro-vided materials for innumerable scholarly books.

Here, it must suffice to say that in Western medieval Christianity, the ex-tension of Christian thought and activity into the whole range of social and cultural activities occurred to an extraordinary degree. Sometimes designated as "the medieval synthesis," this accomplishment set the pattern to which subsequent generations have often looked back.

REFORMATION

Semper Reformandum (a Latin phrase meaning "always reforming") is an idea re-current in Christianity's history. Only one period, however, has been called the "Reformation Era." It was the period from 1500 to about 1650. The accumulated pressures of the previous several centuries joined to force a massive eruption in the body of Christianity. Tension between religious and political alliances was one high pressure arena. Papal authority against the ecumenical councils as the decisive authority in Christianity was another. Materialism as opposed to spir-ituality was yet another. And at the center of the cyclone appeared a remarkable individual, Martin Luther.

Luther was born to hard-working parents who gave him a fine university education aimed at his becoming a lawyer. Suddenly, a religious experience con-vinced him to become an Augustinian monk instead. In 1507 he began his study of theology, particularly focusing on the Christian Bible. In the midst of his con-certed effort to fulfill the obligations of monastic life and his continuous failure to experience the forgiveness and peace promised by such a disciplined life, Luther began to question whether contemporary religious teachings and practices were even compatible with, let alone appropriate to, what he found in the Bible. His initial efforts to open official debates within the church regarding certain of its practices were slow in coming to fulfillment. Finally in 1521 he publicly denounced the Popes and the later councils (after the first four). The grounds had shifted from specific practices and teachings to the foundational issue of authority: by whose authority? In the face of the Catholic appeal to tradition as expressed in papal and conciliar teachings, Luther appealed to Scripture alone as being authoritative. He insisted that Popes and councils had been mistaken, in fact, and were always open in principle to wrong-headedness and hard-heartedness. Only Scripture, in his view, had the authority to speak of, for, and to genuine Christian faith and understanding. Such was his call to reform. From the Catholic perspective, this was heresy. Luther was condemned by the church as a heretic and outlawed by the secular authorities.

Virulent controversies erupted between Luther's supporters, initially in the Germanic provinces of the Holy Roman Empire, and the defenders of traditional Catholic understandings in other portions of Europe. Theological faculties, councils of the church, monks, nobles, kings, and emperor took sides. Other reforming groups arose within Catholicism acknowledging that changes were required but confident that the church's resilience would prove sufficient to achieve what was needed. Anti-Catholic reformers appeared who were sympathetic with much of what Luther was doing and saying but who adapted the reform movement to the differing conditions in their home territories—Zwingli in Zurich, and John Calvin in Geneva, both in Switzerland, were the most prominent.

Yet other more radical anti-Catholics, and also anti-Lutheran and anti-Reformed (Calvinist), exploded onto the scene. Part of the radicalism of those exhibiting this spirit resided in their diversity of theory and practice. But in one respect they held a common view: Luther and the other moderate reformers were, they believed, inconsistent in failing to advocate the more radical socioethical views to be found in Scripture. For example, in 1526 the Germanic peasants revolted against the oppressive practices of their noble overlords. Luther's unambiguous condemnation of the rebellious masses earned him the support of the law-and-order nobility and the disdain of the peasants and their leaders, who were convinced that Luther lacked consistency in his reading of Scripture. That incident suffices to indicate the greatest difficulty in granting supreme authority to Scripture: namely, whose reading of a document that permits a variety of interpretations is to be accepted? Luther, Zwingli, and Calvin agreed that familiarity with Hebrew and Greek languages and long study of commentaries and texts were requirements for rightly interpreting the Bible. But even they did not always agree on the meaning and importance to be attached to specific texts (see Chapter 5, page 106).

When the radicals among the reformers appealed to their conviction that theirs was the authoritative interpretation because it was led by the same Spirit that had originally inspired the writers of those texts, they felt utterly confident that theirs was the true, right understanding of the Bible. The conflicts, often bloody, between the moderate and radical reformers and their followers—not to mention between the Protestants and Catholics—over the long Thirty Years' War is tragic testimony to the result of people, mostly sincere and honest, giving allegiance to different authorities. Neither the Catholic appeal to the authority of tradition nor the Protestant appeal to Scripture sufficed to find peaceful resolution of disagreements. Another basis for common life, some decided, must be found.

CHRISTIANITY AND THE ENLIGHTENMENT

In the latter years of the Reformation Era as religion was the nominal focus of devastatingly destructive war between contentious fanatics, other winds were blowing in European society and culture. Renaissance humanistic scholarship was developed in the emerging universities, and philosophical and scientific thinking were also developing. Both often offered severe criticisms of long-cherished theological beliefs and opinions. Voyages of discovery in the fifteenth and sixteenth centuries had led to the realization that Europe and the eastern Mediterranean areas were not the only places in the world where thriving cultures—and other religious traditions besides Judaism, Christianity, and Islam—were to be found. Opening trade routes with India and the Orient created visions of economic expansion that had been unimaginable during the rigors of the Middle Ages. Technological adaptation of scientific discoveries began to revolutionize, at least for the monied, upper classes, life in the growing urban centers. To these centers, the masses began the long march of migration in pursuit of better economic opportunities than were to be found in rural areas. Political theorists developed views of secular governments that subordinated or, at least, reduced the importance of religious institutions in affairs within and among the nation states. In sum, the world was rapidly changing and religion was being assigned a role alongside other institutions—governments, educational institutions, economic institutions, independent legal systems and centers of jurisprudence, and health care institutions. This very impulse to compartmentalize social life was contrary to the totalizing aspirations of religion generally and Christianity specifically.

Behind these developing impulses lay the most important challenge to Christianity, namely, the increasing appeal by many persons to the autonomy of human reason. The very name of the period from the mid-seventeenth century into the early nineteenth century, "the Enlightenment," indicates something of this change. Through the long centuries from the earliest decades of Christianity to the Middle Ages and the Reformation, faith and reason had been thought of as complementary, but whenever conflict between them appeared, reason was subordinate to faith, regardless of the authority upon which faith was based. In the new era, defenders of human rationality challenged that long-held, cherished belief. In Germany, France, and England thinkers prominent in the history of philosophy—Descartes, Locke, Hume, Leibniz, Herder, and many others—began to proclaim that rationality is that definitive capacity of humans to arrive at self-evident truths of nature and society, and of religion. Claims of revelational truth were increasingly subjected to the critiques of logic and discursive reason. Reason was offered as a trustworthy court of appeals with the ability to adjudicate what manifestly had not been and, in principle, could not be resolved by appeals to revelation whether as preserved in tradition or presented in the Bible.

Theories of innate, natural religion were offered to replace revealed religion. No dogma nor doctrine was immune from such reflections. The divinity of Christ, the triune nature of God, miracles, the inspiration of Scripture, the historical veracity of the Gospels and the stories in the Old Testament—these were but a few of the topics that received the attention of the critics of Christian theology. Few defenders of the system that had developed over the centuries arose who could persuasively respond to the critique. Christianity, both institutionally and theologically, was under assault in a way and to a degree never before experienced.

Two developments, however, are noteworthy. First, there was a move within Christianity, more prominent in Protestantism but not absent in Roman Catholicism, to shift the appeal to the will and emotions rather than to the intellect. In Germany the name of this movement was Pietism. Under the leadership of Philipp Spener (1635–1705), a turn was made from what that theologian regarded as lifeless, arid theological orthodoxy to the inner religious life of spirituality. House meetings were instituted where Christians prayed together, studied the Bible for its insights into their experiences, and studied other texts for spiritual insight. Spener regarded this move as a reform movement of Lutheranism, not as a separatist activity. Official institutional Lutheranism, however, rejected it and Spener and his followers were forced to continue independently.

The turn inward to an emphasis on religious experience and devotional discipline and practice was enormously influential, especially during the Enlightenment. Pietism influenced or was, at least, the precursor of such movements in England as that of the Quakers and Methodism, the largest and most enduring of the expressions of this kind of Christian life and understanding. Later in America, the Revivalist movement also was a perpetuation of this impulse within Christianity. Behind these manifestations of essentially the same impulse was the sense that all along Christianity was much more something to experience and live than it was something to believe with the intellect. Thus the emphasis lay on the will and the power of emotions to move the will. Pascal's famous comment "The heart has reasons of which the head does not know" and his appeal to "the God of Abraham, the God of Jacob and not of philosophers and men of science" was an apt summary of this impulse. Experience rather than reason, and also rather than tradition or a simplistic reading of the Bible, is the authority upon which this expression of Christianity is founded.

A second change followed the critical philosophy of Immanuel Kant (1729–1804) in Germany. He was a rigorous, vigorous thinker who became convinced and argued strenuously in voluminous writings that human rationality, magnificent as it is in generating knowledge, is limited in scope. Knowledge results, Kant argued, when sense impressions stimulated by the external world are processed through innate categories of human understanding, preeminently space and time. Humans only "know" that which is located in time and space. For Kant this conclusion was not destructive of religion. To the contrary, by showing the limits of reason and knowledge, Kant thought he had made room for faith. The challenge of his philosophy was not to faith but to theology insofar as it had come to regard its truth as a form of knowledge. Kant was decidedly a believer in God; he was equally convinced that no proof could ever demonstrate God's existence with the certainty of knowledge. Human beings simply are not equipped to "know" such things. Theologians and philosophers since Kant have had to take his thinking into consideration. More than coincidentally, Kant was the son of a clergyman in the pietistic tradition. However, his sophisticated philosophical work had little impact on institutional Christianity in spite of his influence on theology.

MODERN CHRISTIANITY

As Christianity, theologically on the defensive and institutionally embattled with the other institutions of culture, emerged into the nineteenth century, there would have been many reasons to suspect that it was to decline as a force in Western culture and in the larger world. Such was not to be the case. The nineteenth century was the period in Christian history when it grew most rapidly as a world religion and when it, at least in some respects, became more influential in the regions of the world where it had long been established than ever before.

The missionary movement of the nineteenth century extended Christianity's influence in every continent of the globe. But the religious wars of the sixteenth and seventeenth centuries and the transformation of Western society during the eighteenth century, particularly in the form of the rise of democratic forms of government and in the political revolutions in France and America, left their impact on Christianity as it engaged in missionary activities. The nineteenth century Western missionaries were apostles not only of the Gospel message but also of social action. Educational, political, philosophical, economic, medical, and agricultural values were transmitted as Christian missionaries tirelessly worked in South America, Africa, India, China, and Japan, not to mention among native Americans and immigrant European communities in America.

European, British, and American Protestant denominations were tireless in establishing missionary societies through which they procured the funding and personnel to undertake "great things for God." Every continent and most countries were targeted by one or many such groups to receive the "good news" of Christ. The tireless, caring efforts included a familiarization by the missionaries with the folkways and indigenous religious practices of the natives and a learning of their language in order to translate the Bible. For Protestants, it was essential to make the Bible accessible. Invaluable information was accumulated regarding the diverse societies and cultures to which the missionaries went.

Missionaries of heroic proportions emerged in the stories of the expansive century. Driven by their conviction that they were doing God's work and fulfilling the vocation of Christianity that had been established in its foundings, these people exhibited a devotion and commitment that was exemplary. The generally acknowledged father of the modern Protestant missionary movement was the Englishman, William Carey (1761–1834). He went to India in 1793 and lived out his life there working to promulgate the Christian message, under the motto, "Expect great things from God and attempt great things for God."

Christianity has never completely succeeded in displacing any of the other religions that have universal aspirations and that were already established in the societies to which the missionaries went. India, for example, remains predominantly Hindu. Most of the Arab nations are still committed to Islam. What Christianity did accomplish, however, was the conversion of significant numbers of individuals or tribal peoples to participation in church Christianity of one kind or another. In the process, the Christian Bible was added to the spiritual resources available to every nation; people around the globe have been enabled, or forced, to respond to the social and cultural values of the West, conveyed by the missionaries as a part of their understanding of what it means to be Christian.

Throughout the century of expansion, Christian theology was undergoing its own transformations. After the assaults of the Enlightenment by the champions of rationality and science, the nineteenth century saw even greater challenges to cherished Christian assumptions. Four thinkers symbolize these challenges—Charles Darwin, Karl Marx, Friedrich Nietzsche, and Sigmund Freud.

Charles Darwin's (1809–1882) work as a naturalist, along with the thought of several nineteenth-century geologists, combined to suggest that human life was a part of the grand evolution of life forms over millions (billions?) of years on the planet. These ideas countered the Christian views regarding the unique supremacy of human beings in the scheme of creation by God and the notion that the earth is only a few thousand years old. This set of scientific explanations undermined the confident Christian view that humanity enjoys a special place in the natural order. Its effects were more of a profound, psychological kind than a logical kind, reaching into Biblical and theological thinking with consequences still not fully worked out.

Karl Marx (1818–1883) was a revolutionary socialist theorist, who, as an economic thinker, replaced the particular, individual Messiah of Christianity with an impersonal, universal historical process. His critique of the subjugation of the masses and his vision of the achievement of a "classless society" echo the early Christian expectation of the "Kingdom of God." Human effort rather than divine intervention, however, was to be the source of this coming utopia.

Friedrich Nietzsche (1844–1900), the brilliant German philosopher, represented many thoughtful persons when he proclaimed: "God is dead, and we have killed him." His was not only a critique of the failure of Christianity and religion generally—and no critic has ever been more devastating than he was—it was a critique of a science, a philosophy, and a historiography that had disenchanted the universe and cut humanity off from any secure, dependable faith by which to live. Nietzsche's was a unique but not an eccentric voice. He has no disciples, but many fellow travelers in modernity. He stridently, insistently, called attention to the abyss and called for a superhuman courage to live meaningfully in a world that is absurd.

Finally, Sigmund Freud (1856–1939), the father of psychoanalysis, developed the ultimate challenge not only to Christian theology but also to traditional philosophy and modern scientific thinking when he came to the view that humans are unavoidably subject to unconscious drives, over which they can rarely successfully exert control. In this, the import of his work was similar to that of Darwin's—humans are a part of natural process, distinguishable but not separate from any other form of animal life. Again, the uniqueness of human existence was radically called into question.

Under this siege, Christian thinkers in the nineteenth century were, with few exceptions, ill-equipped to respond. Some adopted the posture of accommodation supposing with excessive optimism that Christian theology could incorporate any valid insights from whatever quarter without becoming totally compromised and co-opted by those insights. In very general terms, this was the strategy of theological liberalism. Others simply withdrew from intellectual engagement into a religious quietism or activism with the general attitude that faith is far more a matter of how one lives and what one does than a matter of what one thinks. Still others counterattacked by insisting that Christianity does possess the eternal truths once revealed by God in Christ and that the modern atheistic or agnostic opinions were no more to be respected or given credence than had been the ancient ones against which Christianity had emerged victorious. Such latter strategy was, obviously, the conservative position, one extreme version of which was Protestant fundamentalism. Defenders of these views spoke with great passion in the face of such challenges. But then and now, theirs was a minority voice, despite the claims of evangelical speakers today.

A few major theological and ecclesiastical voices do stand out from the nineteenth century. Towering above them all was that of the German theologian Friedrich Schleiermacher (1768–1834). He was deeply influenced by the philosophy of Kant, especially Kant's efforts to demonstrate the limits of human reason. Schleiermacher developed a view that the chief connection between God and humanity is through feelings and experience. Faith in his view is "the feeling of absolute dependence" by human beings upon God. He realized that all religions may serve to engender such feelings and that Christianity could not be held to be the only true religion on those grounds. It could, however, be the clearest and best of the religions, and he regarded it as such. As a professor of theology and as a preacher in a church throughout his adult life, he tirelessly worked to reground Christian thinking in a way that made it far less vulnerable to any intellectual attacks that might be offered. His achievement was very influential. But, alas, his successors and heirs to his approach were rarely as gifted and as sensitive as he.

Protestant Christianity expanded through attention to experimental religion as in Methodism, missionary activity, revivalism, and social concerns. Theologians in the Protestant churches rarely matched the needs of the time for influential voices to calm the storms within or for persuasive authors to respond to the critics without.

Roman Catholicism participated in the transitions of the nineteenth century largely by consolidating itself as the institution of continuity and stability amidst the storms of modernity. A few illustrations will suffice. First, as nation after nation adopted a posture of independence from overt religious influence in the affairs of government, the Catholic Church was left unclear regarding the ways it could influence the course of world historical events. As the walls of separation were erected between the secular and the spiritual authorities, centuries of alliance and theory were being overturned. Popes and emperors had long disputed, since Constantine in the fourth century, which enjoyed supremacy in the West; emperors and kings had controlled the bishops in the East; elector princes allied with Luther in Saxony; the governing council of Geneva was essentially led by Calvin; Henry VIII decreed himself sovereign head and protector of the faith of the Church of England—all of these remind us how radical the notion of separation of state from direct, official involvement by the church really was. A retreat was necessitated by events which the church had been powerless to prevent or to alter substantially. The response that seemed clearest, even if more of an affront to all non-Roman Catholic Christians, was the declaration in 1870 by Vatican Council I that: "The Roman Pontiff, when he speaks *ex cathedra* (that is, when fulfilling the office of Pastor and Teacher of all Christians—on his supreme Apostolical authority, he defines a doctrine concerning faith or morals . . .) is endowed with that infallibility, with which the Divine Redeemer has willed that his Church—in defining doctrine concerning faith or morals—should be equipped."[2] If the Pope could no longer officially influence secular authorities, it seems the Church was determined to say that in the spiritual realm regarding ultimately important matters—faith and morals—nobody else can challenge the Pope's authority, because God through Christ has so decreed.

Second, in the realm of theology the Roman Church appealed to its wealth of great thinkers from the tradition. The work of the thirteenth-century giant Thomas Aquinas, whose grand theological achievement had been the basis for most of the decrees of the Council of Trent (1545–1563), was further elevated by papal decree in 1879. It was as if to declare that in the realm of theology, the best has already appeared. In short, the basis for an official theology adequate to withstand anything by which modernity might assault the church intellectually has been formulated by that great Doctor of the Church. Variations on Aquinas's themes might be necessary, but no substantial differences from his thought would be tolerated. A major step in the direction of proclaiming one theological system

---

[2] Cited in Henry Bettenson, *Documents of the Christian Church*. London: Oxford University Press, 1943, pp. 381–82.

as supreme had been the famous "Syllabus of Errors" by Pope Pius IX in 1864. That Pope identified the major "errors" that seemed increasingly to guide the spirit and temper of modernity. It is totally unacceptable and not even to be entertained, the last thesis stated, that the "Roman Pontiff [the Pope] can and ought to reconcile himself with progress, liberalism, and modern civilization." In political theory, economics, education, and most clearly in matters of religion, modernism has erred fundamentally. Against modernism Rome stood staunchly opposed. The liberal temper of the times and later of the movement in Catholic theology called "modernism" was totally unacceptable to the Roman Catholic Church hierarchy.

The realities of the nineteenth century—an increasing secularism that relegated religion to a role in the areas of faith and morals combined with expansive church forms of Christianity—bequeathed an agenda to twentieth-century Christianity. There was no greater problem than the diversity of practices and understandings within Christianity, at least in the minds of many thoughtful Christians. The "ecumenical movement" was the response those people devised. At its heart, this movement aimed to discover and to articulate for all that which holds and binds Christians together regardless of their institutional loyalties and differences. Great conferences were convened to which representatives of all Christian groups were invited. The World Council of Churches, founded in 1948, was largely a Protestant effort, but Roman Catholic observers have been present at every one of the meetings. Reciprocally, when Pope John XXIII convened the second Vatican Council (1961–1965) observers from all other Christian groups were invited and informally participated in the debates. Around the globe, church mergers have been consummated that resulted in overcoming differences between groups and creating new entities—the Church of South India, the United Church of Canada, and so on. The net effect of success in those cases has been to stimulate explorations between other groups—Anglicans and Methodists in England; Roman Catholics and Lutherans in several countries.

The impulse toward reconciliation between factionalized Christians is real today in a way unmatched in centuries. However, the drive toward unity has another side that cannot be ignored. Like all human expressions, ecumenism carries within it the possibility of onesidedness. Much of the understanding of the genius of Christianity has been seen to reside in its diversity of understanding and expression. It may be that if this diversity is lost in the drive for unity, then the creative dynamic that has powered Christianity would be subverted. Reconciliation need not mean a world reduced to uniform gray, rather *ecumenical* (from the Greek, *oikoumene,* "the inhabited world") unity can be a dynamic interplay between contrasting views.

The story of theology in the twentieth century is more complex. Within Protestantism two figures epitomize the struggle. Rudolph Bultmann (1884–1976) and Karl Barth (1886–1968) were widely influential thinkers. Bultmann relentlessly pursued New Testament studies through a program he named "demythologizing." The liberal spirit of the nineteenth century combined with the long-standing Protestant commitment to the authority of Scripture were the motivating forces in his voluminous writings. How to express the Gospel in terms intelligible to modern humans was the challenge he accepted. Theologizing has been demanded from *within* Christianity by no scholar more forcefully than by Bultmann.

By contrast, Karl Barth, in even more voluminous writings, insisted that the Christian Church has a unique message to proclaim that demands fidelity to God's word in the Bible, even when that requires rejecting the cherished beliefs promulgated by science and philosophy and particularly by modern political theories and practices. Far more sophisticated and much more profoundly insightful than most conservative and fundamentalist preachers, Barth attempted to recover the wisdom embedded in the tradition of Christian thinking and to offer it as the Christian alternative to modernity's rush to what Barth thought is certain destruction.

Both strategies were extremely well served by great learning and superior intelligence in these two cases. Their examples and influence gave a burst of confidence and creativity to Protestant theology in many mid-twentieth-century circles.

Similarly, the freshness of Pope John XXIII and his calling of Vatican II (1961–1965) was characterized by his impulse to throw open the windows of the Roman Catholic Church to the breezes of modernity and to enable the church to confront contemporary issues in new and creative ways. Traditionalists were resistant and subsequent Popes have not shared the same enthusiasm, but a burst of theological creativity by Roman Catholic thinkers has resulted. The outcome of this activity is as yet uncertain.

Two other facts that have impact upon Christianity today, and as it moves into its future, require mention. First, and most obviously, the world under the impact of the technological revolution of the past two centuries has had to deal with forces never before confronted by humanity. The nuclear age inaugurated in 1945 has irreversibly altered the possibilities to be dealt with for the survival of sentient life. The religions of the world have to respond to such changes and all of them are being increasingly recognized as offering resources of greater or lesser potency to contribute to the quality of life. This has forced a greater awareness of religious pluralism and the variety of worldviews offered by those religions. Christianity shares, willingly or not, in this larger ongoing story.

Second, the study of religions as a scholarly undertaking within colleges and universities, as distinct from study under the auspices of a particular religious institution, is affecting religious life and understanding of Christians as certainly as that of the believers in other traditions. Anyone reading this book is participating in this movement. The understanding of Christianity in its cultural context, as explored in a classroom, in comparison with similar studies of Judaism, Buddhism, Islam, Hinduism, and other traditions, continues to emerge. That there will be different interpretations, however, does seem unavoidable and as necessary now as throughout the long history of Christian theologizing.

The panoramic movement of Christianity through time and across space, encircling the globe, was for many the sure proof of God's action in it. Catholic Christianity has consistently proclaimed that, for holding truth for the longest uninterrupted span of centuries, Orthodoxy and Protestantism—although offering significantly different faces of Christianity—have surely never displaced it. Perhaps St. Vincent of Lerins had a deep insight.

countercultures

Throughout its history, Christianity as a tradition has understood and tried to define itself in terms of its relatedness to other traditions and movements, as often within Christianity as outside it. Like other religions, Christianity defines itself in its relationship to other worldviews, other ways of being. The other ways internal to the Christian world may be described as "countercultures."

THE EXISTENCE OF COUNTERCULTURES

There are at least two ways to understand the idea of a counterculture. Most obviously, a counterculture is an independent culture that arises and forms itself in opposition to a larger, dominant culture. Then, there are individuals or loosely joined groups of individuals who, although not constituting a "culture" as such themselves, do indeed constitute a counterculture. Both these ways will be examined, in the first instance through the examples of the communities that evolved from the visions of Simon Magus, Marcion, and Peter Waldo and in the second instance through the relationships between orthodox Christianity and Christian mysticism as it came to expression with Meister Eckhart and St. Teresa of Avila.

Historically, countercultures and people movements that go counter to established cultures have been described as "radical," "dissenting," and "heretical." Of course, these descriptions can only arise from within the culture that is countered. In other words, these descriptions are applied by the upholder of

Religious Camp Meeting. Photo courtesy of The Whaling Museum, New Bedford, Massachusetts.

the *orthodoxy* of Christianity (from the Greek, *ortho,* ''right'' and *doxa,* ''opinion'') to that which offers another perspective and thus constitutes a potential threat to the coherence and cohesion of the established worldview. However, there are other ways to consider that which runs counter to orthodoxy. Perhaps the tradition's own descriptive terms can give access to it.

The dialectic can be described as that between orthodoxy and radical, dissenting, or heretical perspectives. Yet each of these words contains its own kind of dialectic. *Radical* (from the Latin, *radix,* ''root'') speaks of an extreme movement of change that proceeds *from* the root and at the same time reaches *into* the center or ultimate source of that which it counters. *Heretical* (from the Greek, *hairesis,* ''taking a choice'') implies being able to choose. A heretic can *hold* a doctrine that is at odds with the orthodox church and can *reject* a doctrine. Radicals and heretics are often reformers, those whose vision can renew a tarnished tradition, even as something new is manifested.

Radicals, heretics, and reformers are all *dissenters,* those who differ in thought and feeling, those who are nonconformers. But it is only from the orthodox perspective that dissent is in opposition in a warring sense. After all, nonconformist is not necessarily for or against the *conforma,* the common form or image. It is different.

Shifting the metaphor, it could be said that dissenters present counterpoints to the commonly accepted doctrines of orthodoxy. As this musical analogy suggests, dissent adds an accompanying melody to that which is already given, opening to the possibility of plural melodies that are not static but moving. Dissent offers melodies that are related, yet independent.

So, a countering movement may be one of dialectical relationship. *Counter,* from the Latin *contra,* means "against," as in the sense of standing over against. It can also mean "opposite" and "retaliatory," and it can further mean "reciprocal" and "complementary." Like melodies harmoniously interwoven yet independent, like lovers against each other in an embrace where intimacy arises through their individual differences, "countering" can be imagined as a transforming en-counter.

To be named a heretic in the earliest centuries of Christianity was not something to be borne lightly. Heretics, so named by defenders of orthodoxy, were subjected to scathing criticisms and denunciations. In the later centuries of the Middle Ages, they were subjected to the Inquisition and were tortured, and often put to death by burning. Such reactions clearly indicate the fear and threat that heretics provoked in their attackers. They were most frequently accused of being the instruments of Satan and their determined refusal to capitulate to their attackers was cited as evidence of their evil madness. From their own perspective, however, the heretics were passionately committed to the experience of God in their lives and in their thinking and understanding. Thus, the heretics most often were insistent witnesses to a powerful transformation that had occurred in them and that they dared not deny or surrender. They were cast to play out the contrapuntal role in Christian history.

St. Augustine cautioned in the fifth century: "Do not think that heresies could have arisen from a few beggarly little souls. Only great men [sic!] have brought forth heresies." To study Christianity today thus requires attention to what ecclesiastical leaders from the beginning would have totally eliminated from the historical record, but never succeeded in so doing.

In the New Testament there are many insights that have been ignored or forgotten, or both, by ecclesiastical leaders. One of the very wisest is the story of the Jewish leaders who gathered to consider the case of the Apostles. On the first occasion after Peter and John were arrested for preaching the message of salvation through Christ, the priests, scribes, and elders questioned them and forbade them to teach or speak in the name of Christ. To that, Peter and John responded: "Whether it is right in the sight of God to listen to you rather than to God, you must judge; for we cannot but speak of what we have seen and heard" (Acts 4:19–20). After their release, they continued their "heresy" and the leaders of the Jews were deeply perplexed. Their authority had been unambiguously challenged. What was to be done? A great teacher among the council named Gamaliel advised: "Men of Israel, take care what you do with these men [the Apostles.] . . . for if this plan or this understanding is of men, it will fail; but if it is of God, you will not be able to overthrow them. You might even be found opposing God!" (Acts 5:35, 38–39). The Apostles were released, confident that they were justified in their work and that they were following the lead of Jesus, that supreme Jewish heretic, whose steadfastness had led him to the Cross. But the wisdom of a Gamaliel was ignored by Christian leaders who rather than make a place for outsiders became the anxious defenders of the orthodox way.

Much of what is known of heretics is told in the records of their orthodox critics. Little wonder, then, that they appear so negatively. If, however, one reads through the accounts to learn what was unwittingly preserved in them, a different image of heresy from what the orthodoxists thought they were presenting may emerge. One of the most striking recognitions is that charges of heresy date to the very beginning of Christianity. Further, until the modern period, heretics were named and charged in every generation. Although any particular heretic was specific to the time and place in which she or he lived, there are some discernible common themes characteristic of them whenever and wherever they appeared.

First, the questions to which they respond are perennial. (And often the responses they offer later become the dominant response.) Second, at the outset, many a heretic aimed to call the church's attention to what it had ignored or forgotten. Thus, to understand orthodox, church Christianity requires insight into the views of the heretics as surely as into those of the insiders. Third, the heretic is passionate about what experience has led her or him to believe. Fourth, by their own understanding and experience, Christian heretics are Christians as much as those who were compelled to deny that. The heretics present one or another of the interpretations of Christianity that were repressed by the orthodox mainstream. Thus, the heretics often discovered dimensions of Christianity that were unseen or unappreciated by other Christians. Finally, heretics were often willing to face even physical death in addition to the denunciation of the orthodox, rather than submit. In an echo of Peter and John, heretics have often said that their trust is wholly in the God upon whom they must steadfastly and ultimately depend. Lacking the wisdom of a Gamaliel, church leaders often went to harsh extremes to silence what they heard as a demonic dissonance that fundamentally threatened the clarity of their monotone. Rarely, however, were the heretics silenced, and, often in death, their counterpoint to orthodox doctrine swelled to the proportions of a great fugue.

IN THE BEGINNING WAS HERESY: SIMON MAGUS

In the book of Acts, there is a story of a man named Simon who had been a magician among the Samaritans before the advent of Christianity. It is said of him that he possessed great power and gifts that amazed those who heard and saw him. But when the Gospel of Jesus Christ was proclaimed amid those same people, many converted, among them Simon Magus. The next movement in the story has been often told as the sure sign of Simon's incorrigible heresy. When he saw

John and Peter laying their hands on people and the Holy Spirit coming upon those people, Simon wanted to share in their power. He offered a sum of silver for their secret of power so that he, too, might be able to invoke the Holy Spirit through the laying on of hands. John and Peter were appalled, and Peter is reported to have replied to Simon: "Your silver perish with you, because you thought you could obtain the gift of God with money! You have neither part nor lot in this matter, for your heart is not right with God. Repent therefore of this wickedness of yours . . . " (Acts 28:20–22).

From such a story was born the view that to Simon Magus belonged the dishonorable name of the father of heresy in Christianity. That bears further investigation. Why did heresiologists ("hunters of heresy") for centuries feel so compelled to remind the orthodox of Simon Magus? What was his offence?

As the stories tell, Simon Magus was a man with the power to amaze others before he even heard of or became a Christian. It was reported that he had studied Arabic–Jewish magical medicine in Alexandria, where he had become familiar with pre-Socratic Greek philosophy, as well as with magical medicines. This is an important clue to understanding the charges leveled against Simon by heresiologists over the century. From their perspective, he was infected by a worldview of earlier Greeks, and more conventional early Christian thinkers found it appalling that anyone would imagine any connection between Christianity and pagan thinking.

Among the manifestations of his presumed effort to bridge Christian faith and Greek philosophy was the view attributed to him that saw a connection between the mythical figure of Helen (of Troy and elsewhere in the Greek stories) and Mary Magdalene in the Christian stories. Both female figures presented the human search for redemption of souls alienated from their source and seeking reunion with the "Infinite Force." In one respect it is impossible to know whether Simon held such a view, since the only writings on which such a judgment can be based were shown to be by "Simonians" a century later. From another perspective, that scarcely matters because the figure of Simon is archetypal. A fundamental pattern of a particular way of understanding is present in this figure. Simon's way reads Christianity mythically, imagistically and metaphorically. His literalistic opponents regarded that way of interpreting as heretical, whoever may have been first "guilty" of enacting it. The defenders of orthodoxy could not abide a way of imagining Christianity that even remotely suggested that other revelations of the Gospel's claims might have appeared in other cultures and other traditions. The Gospel's uniqueness was one of the claims made in its behalf by its devoted missionaries, and they felt the work of spreading the "Good News" was deeply threatened by imagining that the Greeks might have foretold even a similar, let alone the same message.

One of the recurrent ways of discrediting heretics has been to accuse them of immorality on the presumed (if often blindly selfrighteous) view that orthodox belief will more nearly guarantee the moral life. Simon, his critics have charged, was doubly immoral. First, he is presented in the story in Acts as having offered to buy the power from Peter and John with a payment in silver. No mention is to be found of the fact that there was a widely practiced exchange in Hellenistic culture of paying for a shared secret. Instead Simon was charged with having been so confused as to imagine that God's gift could be bought. Throughout the Middle Ages the term "simony" was used to designate any effort to buy ecclesiastical privilege and office. Simon's mistake echoed infamously through the centuries.

Second, Simon was accused of sexual libertinism. And further, his followers were believed to have practiced idolatry, reputedly by worshipping before a statue of Simon. This charge was factually disproven in the sixteenth century when a statue of an altogether different person was discovered precisely on the spot where the one of Simon had been supposed to stand. However, historical proof is less important than the heresy which it was held to demonstrate: spiritual arrogance. It was charged that Simon had proclaimed himself to be God. From the orthodox perspective, his lack of humility and extreme pride were the ultimate offense.

In the movement from a relatively uncomplicated story in the book of Acts through the accounts of Simon's dissident heretical teachings and the recounting of his life by the heresiologists over the centuries, some of the workings of the orthodox imagination appear. With increasing complexity, more details were recalled about Simon the further the teller of the story was from the time in history when he was said to have lived. Less emphasis was placed on Simon as an historical personage as he came to represent the image of "the heretic" in most of its unacceptable forms. There is a remarkable similarity between the creating of legends regarding Simon as the originator and father of heresy, and those surrounding the figure who is, from the orthodox perspective, the antithesis of heresy—Jesus the Christ figure.

MARCION

Partly because more of his life story is known than was the case regarding Simon Magus, Marcion (c. 85–160) is a more focused target for the defenders of orthodoxy. The issues he raised continue even now to occupy the thinking of some of the most significant Christian thinkers.

Until he first became prominent as an effective, influential teacher in Rome, little was known of Marcion, and that, in large measure, is still the case. One story tells that he was the son of an obscure Christian bishop in one of the provinces. It is known that he organized new churches based upon certain theological ideas, that he incorporated several of the practices and some distinctive emphases common to other Christians into the organization of his churches, and that he was prominently an object of the sharp attacks of major heresiologists for several centuries.

As a theologian, Marcion had one overarching idea. It was that the God revealed by Jesus Christ is the supreme God whose nature is pure love. This God, Marcion passionately believed, was completely unknown before the advent of

Christ. This God he named ''the Stranger'' whose radical otherness Jesus revealed. In this, the views of all other religions were challenged including, most disturbingly, the religion of Israel. The God witnessed to in Jewish scriptures, Marcion argued, is indeed the creator of the physical, material universe, and he rules by law and demands obedience. Furthermore, he is wrathful in his punishment of all who disobey his commandments. The stern cruelty of the creator God depicted in the Jewish Bible was, as Marcion viewed it, impossible to reconcile with the image of God revealed by Jesus, the pure unbounded redeeming God who loved without limit.

Certain other ideas flowed from Marcion's primary distinction between the creator God and the stranger God. Humanity in its bondage to the flesh and to impossible laws yearns for salvation from it all. The message of Christianity, as Marcion experienced and understood it, was that in a totally unexpected way the stranger God had made his love known through Christ and had thereby released those who heard and accepted the message from their bondage. It was a vision born out of religious experience, and Marcion deeply believed that it was a message completely unknown prior to its revelation in Christ.

From his passionate experience Marcion came to certain fateful conclusions regarding the other Christian voices of his own time. If, he asked, Christianity is a totally new dispensation of revelation, why are Christian leaders so adamantly attempting to place themselves within the development of the Jewish tradition? Why are *they* distorting and corrupting this wondrous gift that has been graciously given to them? His answer was that the Catholic church leaders—and all others who held views different from his interpretation of Christianity—were false apostles and teachers. These, as Paul had admonished, were to be rejected, whatever the steps required to do so (Galatians 2:4). There was a conspiracy of distortion of the Gospel being perpetrated by the churches' leaders. The most obvious sign of this was the legalism into which Christianity was being drawn by its most prominent leaders. To Marcion no clearer or surer sign of the deterioration of insight and understanding was needed. In Marcion's view, the Christian church, scarcely a century old, required a reformation!

Marcion's clarion call for a return to the original revelation of the stranger God in Christ makes clear that he did not imagine himself to be an innovator in any sense. For him, the corrupt leaders of the church were the distorters and deceivers, even if they too claimed only to be perpetuating the Christian message. In the year 144, a gathering of Christian leaders in Rome expelled Marcion from their fellowship. How different might the history of Christianity have subsequently been had there been a Gamaliel at that meeting. What were the views that led to Marcion's expulsion?

The distinction between the two Gods, the creator and the stranger God, was primary. Further, Marcion's effort to provide a body of sacred writings for Christians was a decisive matter. In his years of work leading up to 144, Marcion had engaged in a careful study of the Jewish scriptures and concluded that *none* of them was relevant to Christian faith. With one fell swoop Marcion dismissed the only Bible Christians at that time had available to them. Many, of course, found such a judgment to be far too radical and totally unacceptable. But, there was also Marcion's effort both to provide a body of sacred writings that he knew of and to evaluate them critically. In the end, he was left with only an expurgated version of the Gospel of Luke and carefully selected portions of ten of Paul's letters to churches. This collection was the Bible that Marcion offered to Christians. It was a shockingly bold move on his part. Never to that time had any Christian leader attempted to assemble a Bible and to cloak its writings with divine approval. That slender collection of works, Marcion had declared, is adequate and sufficient witness to the stranger God's pure love, and it is the only testament Christians can authentically accept. In arriving at that point, Marcion believed that Paul had more clearly than any other author understood the radicalism of the Christian revelation, and that he, Marcion, was faithfully following Paul in every important theological respect.

The audacity of the impassioned Marcion scandalized his contemporaries in Rome, but the idea of a Christian Bible had been unavoidably placed on the agenda of the Christian church. If Marcion was wrong, it was required that an alternative be offered, and over the next two and more centuries that process occurred. But it is indisputable that a heretic was the first Christian to propose that Christianity must have its own Bible. Suffice it to note that without Marcion's initiative, that might never have occurred or might have occurred quite differently.

After his expulsion by the Roman Christians, Marcion determined to call a new, faithful church into being—one that would be truly Christian. He wrote a work called *Antitheses,* no copy of which is now extant, that became the focus of many of his opponents' attacks. Through those assaults, some of the content of the book has been preserved as they used the technique of presenting passages from it in order to demonstrate its errors and false teachings. His writings and his deliberate founding of an alternative and rival church compounded the charge of heresy against Marcion. His churches' perpetuation at least into the seventh century and the continuing interest of scholars in his ideas even until today are testimony that Marcion was a formidable figure.

In the Marcionite church there were some features common to Catholic churches. The order of worship was similar. The rituals of Baptism and Eucharist were retained. Bishops, elders, and deacons presided, but laymen could also function as priests and women could even administer baptism. However, the ethical practices differed more markedly. In his thorough rejection of materiality as the work of the lesser creator God, Marcion called for radical spirituality. Sexual activity was completely banned. Marriage was not permitted. Only single people or married people committed to living apart could be baptized. Fasting from meat and wine was a part of the discipline of membership. These radical Christians expected persecution and were admonished, as the Apostle Paul had done, to be prepared to be martyred at any time. Such practices were ill suited to perpetuate a church of which they were the foundation for very long. Thus their continuation into the seventh century is even more noteworthy.

Marcion, perhaps more than any other figure in the second century, insured that Paul's place in the Christian tradition would be prominent. Many other church leaders were by then inclining toward ignoring Paul, but Marcion changed that. To be sure, none of the orthodox leaders would agree with Marcion's claims rightly to have understood Paul, and they thus were obliged to come to their own interpretations. But nobody after Marcion has been able to ignore or dismiss Paul's role in deeply shaping Christian self understanding.

Marcion and the Marcionites served to deepen orthodox reflection in ways it is hard to imagine would have happened without such challenges. Three recurrent issues will indicate the profundity of difference between his critics and this passionate soul. First, Marcion was profoundly unhistorical in his thinking. The novelty of Christ was his message and its integrity led him to deny any predecessors, most especially Judaism. He was not an antiSemitic racist, but he was decidedly anti-Jewish, and, one suspects, he would equally have been opposed to any attempt to argue for Jesus' being a part of any other tradition, whether gnostic, hellenistic, or whatever. In rejecting any ties of Christianity, as he interpreted it, with Judaism and its sacred writing, he denied himself and his followers the rich store of resources borne by that tradition. That Jesus appeared to be a Jew was for him accidental and irrelevant to the heart of his message and revelation. Orthodox Christianity, by contrast, has determinedly insisted that one of the greatest evidences supporting the claims of Christianity is that its stories are historically based. Little wonder that Marcion was so threatening to them.

Second, in differentiating between the creator God of the Jews and the stranger God of Jesus, Marcion was a metaphysical dualist and was undeniably fostering a basis for a polytheism that stood in stark contrast to the monotheism of orthodoxy. That was for them intolerable.

Finally, but no less importantly, Marcion in his dualistic thinking and rigorous antimaterialism was led unavoidably to dismiss and denigrate the natural world and any revealing power it might possess. The cruelty, capriciousness, and arbitrariness of nature in its destructive aspects was enough for him to characterize its creator in similar terms. In contrast, orthodox thinkers regarded nature in its beautiful, sustaining aspects as testimony to its creator being the same God as the Father revealed in Christ. Of course, the dark side of the natural world still remained, but now it became translated into the perennial and deeply troublesome "problem of evil."

Marcion is one of the great figures of Christian history. He countered orthodoxy in fundamental ways and risked offering a radically different view of Christianity. As every serious heretic before and after him, he steadfastly appealed to his experience of truths ignored, forgotten, or suppressed by orthodoxy. His contrapuntal notations provide a haunting theme, long after his countercultural institution passed from the scene. One of the greatest historians of Christian dogma remarked: "There is a greater difference between Christianity before and after Marcion than between the Western Church before and after the Reformation."[1] No amount of opposition or denunciation succeeded in silencing his insights or his passionate defense of them.

THE WALDENSIANS

From Marcion in the second century to Peter Waldo in the twelfth to thirteenth centuries is a leap of milennium. But more than merely 1,000 years is at issue in glancing at the Waldensian movement, which ultimately led to an independent Christian church that survives even until today in Italy despite repeated persecutions from ecclesiastical as well as from political leaders. There are some profound differences between Simon Magus in the first century, Marcion in the second and Peter Waldo in the twelfth. But some features they share, one of them being the insistent, persistent demonstration that "official" church Christianity never exhausted the believable and persuasive interpretations made possible when the message of Jesus Christ was let loose upon the world.

The story begins about 1170 in Lyons, France, when Peter Waldo happened to hear a storyteller at a fair recount a Christian legend of a figure named Alexius. In that story, Alexius personified an ideal of humility and poverty in his effort faithfully to follow Christ. The story profoundly affected Peter Waldo, who, as it happened, was a prosperous businessman. He had acquired wealth through unsavory exploitation of others' misfortunes. He was not at the time a religious man, but somehow the legend penetrated deeply into his heart and soul. Nor was he well educated, but he turned to local clergy for help in gaining some familiarity with the Bible. He persuaded them for a fee to translate several books of the Bible into the vernacular (common) language of the day. The hearing of that story was a fateful encounter that led him to study the Gospels deeply.

In response to what he read and because of his meditations, Waldo took a tentative step. He read the Gospel admonitions to the wealthy to care for the widows and orphans and the generally less fortunate, and he instituted a modest relief program among the people in Lyons in deepest need. But still his conscience troubled him. He was then moved to a radical step. He provided for his wife's and his two still-unwed daughters' future and went into the streets giving away all his money. The ideal of voluntary poverty, reminiscent of the monastics (see Chapter 2), inflamed him. He determined to live upon the charity of others. He had no interest in founding a monastic order or living in one place. Rather, his was an idea of enacting Jesus' admonition to the disciples, as recorded in the Gospels, to go into the world and proclaim the love and utter dependability of God. He felt this as a direct call from God to him, Peter Waldo, to make present again what had disappeared from Christianity.

---

[1] Adolf von Harnack, *Marcion: Das Evangelium von Fremden Gott.* Leipzig: Hinrachs, 1921, p. 247.

Roving preachers who totally trusted that God would provide for their minimal material needs rapidly arose in response to Waldo's example. The Bible, largely unknown to lay people at that time, was proclaimed in the streets by otherwise uneducated men and women. The response was extraordinary, especially, if not exclusively, from the lower classes. As they heard Waldo's message and saw him living as he preached, significant numbers joined him and began to do likewise.

The church's privileges were, its leaders came to believe, being radically challenged by this movement. Waldo, by contrast, viewed his and his followers' responses as efforts to conform to the life called for by the Gospels and were incredulous when church officials sought to block their undertaking. The Archbishop of Lyons banned their preaching. Waldo at first accepted the ban, but soon, conscience-stricken, he moved out of the diocese and resumed his work.

When the Lateran Council was convened in Rome in 1179, followers of Waldo petitioned the Pope to review their work and to give papal approval that would permit them to preach throughout the Christian world. This act alone makes it clear that neither Waldo nor his followers initially had any desire to break from the church. Rather, they sought to live out one aspect of the Gospel that had been lost or forgotten. Although he recognized the piety and sincerity of these lay people, Pope Alexander III was convinced that the priesthood was the proper channel for communicating the Christian story to the world. He, accordingly, commanded Waldo and "the poor men of Lyons," as they were by then called, to cease their missionary preaching.

Waldo was again thrown into a deep spiritual conflict. The highest authority of the church had now confirmed the local archbishop's injunction against him and his followers. But he deeply believed that he and his followers were obeying the mandate of the Bible. What to do? Peter's and John's words to the council recorded in Acts 5:35, 38–39 cited above (see page 41) echoed in his soul: "We must obey God, rather than men." This, it seemed to Waldo, was exactly the choice he faced, just as Luther would in the sixteenth century, as in fact have all Christian rebels. When the church puts itself above what people believe God demands of them, the church leaders have to be resisted and disobeyed. That choice, from the church's perspective, immediately marks one as heretic. Reluctantly but determinedly, Waldo made the choice. A new church was born in that choice.

In their preaching and missionary work, the Waldensians had no theology to support the message of their understanding of "the Law of Christ." They were in that respect, naive and innocent. But in the area of morality, they were passionately committed to the Sermon on the Mount as the guide to the Christian life. After the forced break with the Catholic church, the Waldensians became even more severe critics of church teaching and practice. Older heresies were unknowingly revived, one of them being Donatism (see Chapter 5), the view that the validity of the sacraments depended upon the moral purity of the priest. The movement spread from France to northern Italy and to Germany.

The violence of the church's efforts to control and eradicate the Waldensian movement increased the more unyielding the Waldensians proved themselves to be. The fervor of their conviction empowered a fierce stubbornness in them to refuse to capitulate to the church's authoritative claims. In the days when the church had initiated crusades against the "infidel" Moslems, it was startling but not surprising that the same militaristic mentality was turned against the heretical Christians. In both cases, whether the threat was from outside or from inside Christendom, the power and the insecurity of church leaders encouraged violence against its opponents.

For their part, Waldensians in their belief that truth was on their side stood unyielding. Martyrdom to them was a kind of confirmation of their fidelity to the Gospel—as they understood it. Willing to sacrifice everything to stand up for their perception of Christianity's claims, the Waldensians until today are testimony of the moral power that enables those who commit themselves utterly to tell and live the truth. It is we who must add the qualifying phrase "As they see it" to the truth. For them, however, it was not "the truth as they saw it"; it was the whole truth and nothing but the truth.

Simon Magus, Marcion, and Peter Waldo are prominent figures in the parade of Christian heretics. They differed in the particulars of their beliefs, but scarcely in the passion that fired them. They countered the larger culture in different ways, but had in common their refusal to grant that Catholic church Christianity was uniquely gifted to mark a single beat to which all must then march. All believed that God, not the Pope, is the ultimate authority and that fidelity to God's plan takes precedence over the church's rendering of it. The story of Christianity's movement through time is a rich and powerful one, vitalized by the unceasing dynamic between orthodoxy and heresy, insiders and outsiders, point and counterpoint, as each bears witness to her or his experience of the Gospel message. Eternal themes are played out and given life through the countless improvisations of countering cultures.

MYSTICISM

Throughout the history of Christianity, the mystics have been among the ones to play the counterpoint to orthodoxy's melody. They are also those who have sought to turn Christianity toward an image of the relation between humanity and God as that of a lovers' encounter. For their pains, mystics have often been branded as radicals, heretics, and dissenters. And in the deepened understanding of those descriptions, they have indeed been all those things—and more.

The term "mysticism" might suggest a counterculture but that is not the case because mysticism does not name a particular group in a particular time or place. It, rather, names a movement in the sense of a dynamic that has fired the hearts of individuals throughout history and in all religious traditions. And these individuals in some way often unintentionally find themselves countering culture.

Christian mysticism is directly connected to the ancient Greek mystery cults, the word itself rooted in the Greek *mystes* meaning "imitate" and in *muein* meaning "to close the mouth or lips." So by definition mystics speak out of a religious experience that is ultimately unspeakable. Many scholars have suggested that mystical experience lies at the heart of all religion and is the foundation of any of its institutionalised forms. In this sense, the relation of the vision of the mystic to orthodoxy will always appear as a radical questioning that recalls an establishment back to a founding experience. This is clearly a disturbing occurrence from the orthodox perspective. And yet, for the most part, the mystic does not seek to overthrow the tradition but rather to embrace it. Mystics are most often loyal to the established church and surprised by their tradition's rejection of them.

According to the *Oxford Dictionary of the Christian Church* a mystical experience is an immediate knowledge of God attained in this present life through personal religious experience. It is primarily a state of prayer in an experience of union with the divine that can be of permanent or short duration. The genuineness of the experience is given proof in the mystics themselves as they grow in humility, charity and love of suffering. Some theologians, especially Protestants, have named mysticism as "anti-Christian," or at least very highly suspect. The suspicion is that mystical experience is at root pantheistic and leads to self-deification, both of which, from a strictly orthodox position, are blasphemous. *Pantheism* sees everything as divine. From an orthodox Christian perspective, this can be seen as reducing God or as a containing of God by nature or creation. *Deification* sees human beings as divine, which for orthodoxy (although *not* the Eastern Orthodox Church) can be understood literally as human beings being made identical to God.

The tension expressed in the resistance of orthodoxy to mysticism on the grounds of its tendency toward pantheism and deification is a fundamental one. Briefly, it appears as the tension between first the Hebrews, then when they entered the promised land the Israelites, then after the diaspora the Jews and finally the Christians, and "the other nations," the Gentiles, the pagans. It appears as the tension between Yahweh and the Ancient Near Eastern Gods, between Christ and the Greek pantheon. Most concisely, it appears in the form of the first commandment "I am the Lord Your God, you shall have no other gods before me" and can be expressed as the tension between monotheism and polytheism. From the perspective of monotheism, this tension can only appear as a war to be won. But the mystics have another vision, as "heretics" they make another choice, one that can embrace this fundamental tension, that can view it as a creative dialectic mirrored within each individual soul.

By turning to the writings and lives of two great mystics, the dynamic of "countering" may further come to expression. Although bound by a common religious orientation, Meister Eckhart (1260–1327) and St. Teresa of Avila (1515–1582) express their experience at the foundation of that orientation in very different terms and out of very different contexts. Yet for both that experience is one of a deeply loving encounter with God, with themselves, and with others.

MEISTER ECKHART

Meister Eckhart, a Dominican friar and perhaps the greatest speculative mystic, has indeed had the words radical, heretic, and dissenter lodged against him. And yet, from his perspective, his work was from within and for the body of the church.

Meister Eckhart gained most renown as a great preacher and teacher, and he was also a reformer of his own Dominican Order. Unlike other scholastics, he spoke and wrote primarily in German, his native tongue, as well as in Latin, so that his insights might be available to all who heard him.

At the heart of Meister Eckhart's teaching lies the union of the soul with the Godhead, through the divine spark of the soul that has the same ultimate grounding as the Godhead. Likening the divine spark to a castle of the mind, Meister Eckhart warns that there can be no union—God cannot enter the castle— so long as he is God. Only by stripping off all attributes and characteristics can God become the Godhead who is the spouse of the soul.

For Eckhart, the Godhead lies beyond all discursive thought and description and paradoxically can only be known through ignorance. As he says:

> Let it be called ignorance, or want of knowledge, still it has more in it than all knowing and understanding without it, for this outward ignorance lures and draws you away from all understood things and even from yourself.[2]

Stripped of all the attributes given to a creator God, the Godhead appears as Darkness and Formlessness, as neither this nor that, neither Father, Son, nor Holy Ghost.

The darkness of the ground of the soul is the place of union with the Godhead. And at the same time, the fruit of that marriage breaks forth in the mystical birth of the Son as the divine word, as the deification of the experiencer. In his own words, in the essence of the soul:

> Here God enters the ground of the soul. None can touch the ground of the soul but God only. Mark now the fruit and use of this mysterious Word and of this darkness. In this gloom which is his own the heavenly Father's Son is not born alone: thou too art born there a child of the same heavenly Father and no other, and to thee also he gives power.[3]

And again:

> The soul who is in the here and now, in her the Father bears his one-begotten Son and in that same birth the soul is born back into God. It is one birth; as fast as she is reborn into God, the Father is begetting his only Son in her.[4]

---

[2] *Meister Eckhart,* Raymond Bernard Blakney, trans. New York: Harper & Brothers, 1941, Sermon 1, p. 102.

[3] Blakney, p. 102.

[4] *Meister Eckhart,* Edmund Colledge, trans. Toronto: Paulist Press, 1981, Sermon 83, p. 206.

In this eternal dialectic of the birth of the Son and the soul lies Meister Eckhart's vision of the relationship between the divine and humanity. It can be described as ''deification'' in which the soul becomes one with God. Again in Eckhart's own words:

> When the soul being kissed by God, is in absolute perfection and in bliss, then at last she knows the embrace of unity, then at the touch of God she is made uncreaturely, then, with God's motion, the soul is as noble as God is himself. God moves the soul after his own fashion. God contemplating creature gives it life; creature finds life in contemplating God. The soul has intelligent, noetic being, and therefore where God is, there is the soul and where the soul is, there is God.[5]

And to know the divine ''without image, without semblance, and without means'' ''I say, God must be very I. I very God, so consummately one that he and this I are one is, in this is-ness working one work eternally.'' This sounds unmistakably like an elevation of humanity to deity and an emptying of deity into humanity.

As noted earlier, ''deification'' presents great problems for Western orthodoxy. When the dialectic of continual birth or becoming is forgotten and replaced by a literal reading in which the human being is identical to God, this teaching evokes charges of pantheism, idolatry, and blasphemy. And to his great sorrow, this is what happened to Meister Eckhart. He was called before an archbishop's court to answer charges of heresy. But from his own perspective, his teachings in all their deep radicalism were offered for the sake of Christian faith. And to that end, he was prepared to overstep the boundaries of an orthodoxy that had become hidebound. In his own defense made before the church leaders, he pointed out that in condemning him they were really condemning the church fathers and even the Bible itself and that they themselves might be proved to be heretics! To the charges, he replied, ''I may err but I may not be a heretic—for the first has to do with the mind and the second with the will.'' He had no intention of destroying the religion to which he had devoted his life. But in 1327 his appeal to the Pope in Avignon was denied. That is the last that is heard of Meister Eckhart alive. In 1329, Pope John XXII condemned him posthumously as a heretic.

Consequently, the teachings of Meister Eckhart were not widely sought after and scholars consider him to mark the end of the speculative mysticism of the Middle Ages. Along with Plato and Aristotle, both of great importance in the thinking of Meister Eckhart and of many mystics and theologians of the Middle Ages, was the figure of Dionysus the Areopagite, or Pseudo-Dionysus, as he was also known. This early Christian mystic and theologian combined Christian teachings with the language of the Greek mysteries. His works, especially *Mystical Theology,* were deeply influential throughout the Christian tradition, and for ten centuries were taken as authoritative, as their author was believed to have been

---

[5]Colledge, p. 207.

the convert of the Apostle Paul (Acts 17:34). Later, doubt was cast on this, and one suggestion made is that he was a fifth century Syrian monk. In his works, he speaks of God as "divine darkness" and even more beautifully as "the Superessential Radiance of Divine Darkness," an image taken up in all its radicalism by the great mystic St. John of the Cross (1542–1591). The way to union with the divine is the way of negation, that opens through "not-knowing" and "ignorance" to a God that is beyond all attributes and is even the negation of them. This then was the beginning of the *via negativa* trodden so carefully by Meister Eckhart.

Despite the lack of attention to his works, the insights of Meister Eckhart were carried forward in those mystics who followed after him, particularly Blessed John Ruysbroek, Henry Suso, and John Tauler. However, their emphasis moved away from the intellectual and philosophical and into what became known as the religion of the heart. The thought of Meister Eckhart is considered by some scholars to be a precursor to the Reformation.

Like all other reformers, Meister Eckhart was, as we have seen, a threat to established religion. As reformer, he sought to return both his own monastic order and each individual soul to the experience of emptiness that shakes all foundations, of darkness so deep that its radiance shines, of being stripped to nothingness in union with a Godhead beyond all categorization. The radicalism of his vision brought forth a new articulation of religious experience that was particularly Christian. He chose to move inward from the outer expressions of Christianity and to speak out from his heart. He chose to speak out in a way that brought him up against thoughts and actions that had become unyielding. But, as suggested earlier and as echoed in Meister Eckhart's own words, his dissenting was not merely opposition to orthodoxy. It can also be imagined as an encounter, an embrace that sought to return the Church to the radical vision of love proclaimed in the founding stories of the Bible. His counterpointing can be heard as the notes that both break up and amplify the monotone of orthodoxy into a dynamically moving melody of plurality.

ST. TERESA OF AVILA

The ambivalence of the place of mysticism in relation to orthodoxy is especially clear with the figure of St. Teresa of Avila. During her lifetime and in subsequent centuries, she evoked great devotion from her followers. She is also considered by many scholars to be an exemplar of Christian mysticism in the way that she was able to balance a life of contemplation with periods of intense activity in the world. St. Teresa was a devout, obedient, and loyal servant of the church and yet she, like Meister Eckhart, found herself repeatedly "up against" the authority of the established order. She had to struggle constantly to carry out the work to which she felt herself called by God, namely, the reforming of her own monastic order. She met violent resistance not only from within the Carmelite Order itself but also from the whole weight of the ecclesiastical authority of the Catholic church, extending to the Pope, and even from secular provincial rulers. Yet, her efforts to renew the Carmelite Order by returning it to its founding ideal of poverty were dedicated to the strengthening of the church. They were part of the Counter-Reformation, moves of the Catholic church to shore up its foundations in the face of the Protestant Reformation then sweeping through Christendom.

Prior to the event, some discussion had occurred concerning the reform of the Carmelite order among Teresa and her companions. But in 1558 she received her divine command. She describes in her *Life*[6] how the Lord ordered her to take up the task of the reform and promised he would be her guiding strength. The new house was to be named St. Joseph's. Not until 1526 did she receive support to set up this first house of what was to become known as the Discalced (barefoot) Order of the Carmelites. Their move was a return to the strict discipline of poverty under which the order had originally been founded in the image of primitive Christianity. (See the account of the Waldensians above.) During the course of the next twenty years, Teresa endured great hardships as she undertook the establishing of many new houses. She held firm under the pressure of Rome and found herself caught in conflicts between papal authority and the rulers of the Spanish provinces in which she worked. Several times she found herself in disgrace. She was even at one point branded apostate and excommunicated and ordered into reclusion for carrying out her reform.

Some of the most terrible conflicts occurred within the Carmelite Order itself, between the Calceds who were content with the way things were and the Discalceds who were not! The power was on the side of the established order, and they engaged in many tactics of harassment and violence. St. John of the Cross, another great Spanish mystic and an ally of St. Teresa's and others engaged in the reform of monasteries were kidnapped and held captive. St. John was held for nine months in a prison cell, and many feared for his life, as the dangers of poisoning were very real. St. Teresa appealed to the king for his safety. In the midst of all this upheaval, Teresa had to convince both the Calced Order and the Pope that a separation was needed. Finally, in 1580, papal authority was given for the Discalced to be officially recognized as a separate Order but not until 1593 were they recognized as a fully independent Order.

All the while, St. Teresa was guided by her visions and voices trusting in her own inner "knowing" rather than in the outward forms of ecclesiastical authority. And yet, at the same time she placed herself obediently under the direction of her confessor. His instruction included that she write down her many experiences and insights. The description of her active life as a reformer and founder is recorded in *Foundations*[7] while her autobiography is entitled *Life*.

Born to a wealthy family in Avila, Spain, Teresa enjoyed a privileged early

---

[6] *The Complete Works of St. Teresa of Jesus* (3 Vol.), E. Allison Peers, trans. and ed. Volume 1 is "The Life of the Holy Mother Teresa of Jesus."

[7] Peers, Vol. 3: "Book of the Foundations."

life, which she renounced at twenty-one when she entered the Carmelite Convent of the Incarnation in Avila. The story of her life is very moving as it recounts her intense joys and pains. It tells of the conversion experience at age forty before a statue of the Suffering Christ; of the ecstatic moment in which she was pierced through the heart by an angel with a fiery lance; of her many visions and locutions and most especially of the experience of her mystical marriage to Christ. For example, in the early years she received a locution which told her "I wish you now to converse not with men but with angels" and then in 1572 she saw a vision of Christ appearing to her and showing her the nail in his hand, promising that she would be his Bride and never be apart from his love.

As well as for her work as a founder of an order, Teresa is renowned for her spiritual writing. She developed a psychology of prayer that has repeatedly been drawn upon by scholars and interpreters since that time. Perhaps the most illuminating and best known example of her works is contained in the *Interior Castle.*[8] Here she describes, through the metaphor of a transparent crystal castle, the seven levels of prayer and the necessary trials through which the soul must pass on its way to the center where she experiences the mystical marriage with Christ. Teresa writes:

> I began to think of the soul as if it were a castle made of a single diamond or of very clear crystal, in which there are many rooms, just as in heaven there are many mansions.[9]

Teeming with images that overflow from each of her "levels," the castle of St. Teresa stands in contrast to the stark emptiness of the "inner castle" of Meister Eckhart. But for both, the preparation for entry is an arduous process of stripping away psychological attachment to the world of things and to language of possession in order to fall into a mysterious world of erotic image and metaphor. Like Meister Eckhart, St. Teresa is overwhelmed by the recognition that the experience of union out of which they speak defies all rational explanation and discursive description. In her own words:

> What God communicates here to the soul in an instant is a secret so great and a favor so sublime that I do not know with what to compare it, . . .[10]

She further meditates:

> This "centre" of our soul, or "spirit", is something so difficult to describe, and indeed to believe, that I think, sisters, as I am so bad at explaining myself, I will not subject

---

[8] Peers, Vol. 2: "Interior Castle," pp. 187ff.

[9] Peers, Vol. 3, "Interior Castle," First Mansion, Chap. 1, p. 201.

[10] Peers, Vol. 3, "Interior Castle," Seventh Mansion, Chap. 2, p. 335.

you to the temptation of disbelieving what I say, for it is difficult to understand how the soul can have trials and afflictions and yet be in peace.[11]

Out of this experience she turns to the poetics of likenesses:

[In the spiritual marriage] it is like rain falling from the heavens into a river or a spring; there is nothing but water there and it is impossible to divide or separate the water belonging to the river from that which fell from the heavens. Or it is as if a tiny streamlet enters the sea, from which it will find on way of separating itself, or as if in a room there were two large windows through which the light streamed in: it enters in different places but it all becomes one.[12]

In the end, she cries out ecstatically:

The soul cannot help uttering "O life of my life, and sustenance that sustaineth me!" and things of that kind. For from those Divine breasts, where it seems that God is ever sustaining the soul, flow streams of milk, which solace all who dwell in the Castle; . . . [13]

In a saying that expresses her recognition of her release into the play of metaphorical language, St. Teresa warns her readers against literalisms that will reduce all to the pursuit of merely the truth of reason:

These comparisons make me smile and I do not like them at all, but I know no others. Think what you will; what I have said is the truth.[14]

The truths that St. Teresa struggled to articulate drew her and her followers into a controversial position. During the early years of her visions and locutions, Teresa experienced great anguish as she tried to discern whether they were indeed from God or from Satan. And during her turmoils some interpreted her experiences as demonic and denounced her works to the Inquisition. In these responses, we can hear the echoes of the charges made by the orthodox church against Meister Eckhart: pantheism and deification, idolatry and blasphemy. The mystical vision ever finds itself "up against" the established order.

Even after Teresa's death in 1582, the tension and ambivalence continued. As her books were made available there was even greater veneration directed toward her but still some rallied against her. Francisco de Pisa, one of the doctors of the church, was to call her ignorant and in error. A few fanatical friars branded her a heretic; one took her books five times to the Inquisition and finally to Rome

---

[11] Peers, Vol. 3, "Interior Castle," p. 338.

[12] Peers, Vol. 3, "Interior Castle," p. 335.

[13] Peers, Vol. 3, "Interior Castle," p. 336.

[14] Peers, Vol. 3, "Interior Castle," p. 338.

where he pressed charges for a dozen years until the repeated testimony of her orthodoxy and personal sanctity brought their persecution to a halt. In 1622 she was canonized a saint.

This extraordinary power that is manifest in the tension between mystic and orthodox, that both passionately repels and attracts, is very clear in the figure of St. Teresa. Not only did her life and works evoke great resistance but also extreme devotion. This aspect is wonderfully illustrated by the stories surrounding her death and the period following. Before and at her death, her body exuded a mysterious fragrance that became so powerful that it penetrated the whole building of the convent in Alba where she had been visiting. Within the year of her burial, her body was exhumed by an official visitation from Avila. Her left hand was cut off and placed in a sealed casket to be taken to Avila. Then later, the body was clandestinely exhumed and taken to Avila after the left arm had been severed and left at Alba. After a time, the body was again taken out and displayed with great reverence. Its preservation was considered a supernatural event. After the theft from Alba was discovered, the body was returned by order of the Pope. Five times the body was exhumed, mutilated and replaced. Parts of the body found their way to many distant places. When her body was publicly exhibited in the eighteenth century, what remained was uncorrupted but much of it was missing, including the heart which was held in particular awe since it was described as bearing the marks of its piercing by the angel's lance.

When the stories of Meister Eckhart and St. Teresa of Avila are looked at together, it is clear that mystical ways are anything but singular. Meister Eckhart's *via negativa* that leads ever deeper into the divine darkness continuously culminates in a mystical marriage at the most interior part of the castle of the soul. St. Teresa's way through the castle accumulates a profusion and a fullness of images as she moves toward the light at the center that does not dazzle but is a "soft whiteness and infused radiance" that delights the eyes.

For St. Teresa the darkness does not disappear in the vision of light, rather it is placed in vivid dialectic. She describes the darkness as cramped, suffocating places with a bottom covered in "slimy foul-smelling water full of vile reptiles." Although there was no light, it was not "mere" darkness, for seeing was still possible.

For Meister Eckhart the fruit of the mystical union was the birth of the soul in the Godhead and the birth of the Word in the soul, which came to expression through his great work as teacher and preacher. For St. Teresa the fruitfulness of her union was expressed through her many writings and the founding of a "new" order. The offspring of her marriage were "good works."

What then is the tension in the encounter between mysticism and orthodoxy? Each calls the other into question; orthodoxy challenges mysticism with history, tradition, and the transcendent otherness of God; mysticism presents orthodoxy with another way of seeing that emphasizes both the eternality and radical immanence of the religious experience at the heart of Christianity. Paradoxically, mysticism's loving embrace can shake the rigid foundations of an institution that has forgotten how it feels to speak out of the soul:

> The Lord said these words to me: "As it cannot comprehend what it understands, it is an understanding which understands not." One who has experienced this will understand something of it; it cannot be more clearly expressed, since all that comes to pass in this state is so obscure. I can only say that the soul feels close to God and that there abides within it such a certainty that it cannot possibly do other than believe. All the faculties now fail and are suspended in such a way that, as I have said, it is impossible to believe they are active. . . . The will must be fully occupied in loving but it cannot understand how it loves; the understanding, if it understands, does not understand how it understands, or at least can comprehend nothing of what it understands. It does not seem to be understanding, because, as I say, it does not understand itself. Nor can I myself understand this.[15]

CONCLUSION

Whether in the way of defying the ultimate authority of an institutional form of Christianity, as with Marcion and Peter Waldo, or in ways of working within the given structures of the church recalling it to forgotten experiences as suggested by the mystics, those named as heretics, dissidents, and radicals are a vital part of the story of Christianity. The act of countering culture has appeared in many different expressions in this chapter, all of which beckon the reader to avoid the seduction of thinking that any one vision or version of Christianity can exhaust its richness. Dissonance, contrapuntal melodies, and improvization—all these are re-soundings of the themes carried by the instruments of orthodoxy. The suggestion is that, when heard, the radicalism of their differences can deepen the understanding of all who "have ears to hear" (Matthew 11:15).

---

[15] Peers, Vol. 1, Chapter 18, p. 110.

christianity and the arts

A RICH AND VARIED HERITAGE

The expression of Christianity through painting, sculpture, architecture, music, and literature has produced a vast and diverse panorama of beauty. From unpolished paintings on the walls of Christian catacombs, mostly of the Good Shepherd carrying lambs, to the Sistine Chapel of Michelangelo or to *The Last Supper* of Leonardo da Vinci and to that of Salvador Dali, Christian faith has been the inspiration behind the painter's brush. In architecture, the same faith has produced visible results from the ancient basilica and the tiny cross-shaped churches of the Anglo-Saxons, to the soaring medieval Gothic cathedrals with their incomparable stained glass, to such modern edifices as the fantastic Church of the Holy Family in Barcelona, Spain, by Antonio Gaudi and the eloquent shiplike chapel at Ronchamp, France, by the influential architect Le Corbusier. In music, one need only mention Gregorian chant, Bach, and Handel; in literature, Dante and Dostoevsky.

Virtually every religion finds important expression in the various arts, just as it does in ritual and sociology; for religion is far more than ideology or intellectual worldview. It is both those conjoined with a wide spectrum of articulations in many areas of human ability. Part of the difference between a religion and a purely philosophical position is not only that the former has worship and elaborate social structures but also that it is much more likely to have inspired an impressive assembly of paintings, statues, buildings, poems, novels, and musical compositions which explicitly reflect its symbols and values. Christianity has certainly done this. It has probably expressed itself more fully in more artistic media than any other religion, though there are gaps: the Christian faith has employed sacred dance far less than Hinduism or Shinto, and the landscaped garden is far less a significant Christian art form than it is for Zen Buddhism.

Christianity is no exception to another matter, the complex and ambiguous relation of a religion to its artistic expressions. Some great Christian masterpieces have been produced by artists like Le Corbusier who were not personally believers, or who are only marginally so; at the same time, fervent faith on the part of its producers has not prevented innumerable instances of Christian painting, poetry, and music from being very undistinguished artistically.

A religion's art can sometimes reveal crucially important insights into the faith's essential experience, which are far less well conveyed through its bulwarks of doctrine and philosophy. On the other hand, what is often taken to be the artistic expression of a religion may actually have only an incidental relation to the latter's essence, being just a part of the same pluralistic cultural milieu as the religion. For instance, modern America and medieval Europe are predominantly Christian societies with high levels of church attendance, but only some of the art and letters of either has had any very intimate relation to specifically Christian concerns.

Independent artistic development in a religion seems generally not to emerge for several generations after its inception. Distinctive themes and styles in the visual arts are likely to be among the last aspects of the new faith to be unpacked. The earlier art of a religion will undoubtedly borrow heavily from the themes and techniques of the surrounding culture, even though those may be considerably indebted to other spiritual perspectives. As the religion and its art evolve over the centuries, often it is not easy to tell just how much the religion is influencing the culture, and the culture is influencing the religion. This is due to the fact that only in the later stages of some religions, Christianity being a prominent case, does it become possible to distinguish culture from religion. Art will commonly be the most creative point in the meeting of faith and culture.

For example, we can assume from the prevalence of shepherd figures in the catacombs that the Good Shepherd was a particularly important symbol in early Christian life—and yet we also learn that those pastoral representations were a very common motif in the art of the Roman Empire, and their Christian form is so similar to the pagan that often only the location tells which is which.

Here is a comparable but much more far-reaching issue. It has often been observed that traditional Christian art is usually more realistic and representational than that of most of the other great religions. Medieval and Renaissance Christs and Madonnas look like real men and woman, far more than do the stylized, symbol-laden, often multiple-armed gods of Hinduism, or the Buddhas and bodhisattvas of Buddhism. (In the arabesques of Islam, human and animal forms are rejected.)

Some have argued that this has to do with the Christian affirmation of ordinary humanity grounded in the centrality of the doctrine of the Incarnation, of God uniting himself with human nature in Jesus Christ, who was both human and divine. Undoubtedly much great Christian art is rooted in incarnational faith.

At the same time, we must recognize that realism in Christian art is also influenced by the marked realism of pagan Greco-Roman art. In fact, the more severe Christians of the first centuries considered the art of their day far too closely linked to idolatry or licentiousness to be of good repute. Much early Christian art, especially in the Byzantine East, strenuously attempts to spiritualize contemporary styles in a Christian way. Helpful to note is the realistic strand in Hindu sculpture which can be traced to Hellenistic influence.

These instances may give us pause before we fall into easy generalizations about the history and meaning of Christian art. Yet, with this awareness, a few statements about what much of it has in common can be made. Whether these characteristics are intrinsic to its Christian nature or grew out of elaborate interaction between Christian faith and non-Christian aesthetics is in the end beside the point. These characteristics are authentically Christian and have come to dominate the perspective of Christian art, even though some are certainly not exclusive to Christianity and may have initially been borrowed.

1. *Affirmation of creation.* Christian faith and art treats with care the created things of this world, from the faces of saints down, even though it perhaps centers less upon the natural world than such religious expressions as Taoism and Zen. But it sees human and natural creation as a stairway to God with all creation reflecting his glory, so there is no extreme rejection of representationalism either. Moreover, creation suggests, as does the Kingdom-of-God concept, a hidden structured order of the universe. If the universe was made by God, it must have been made well and correctly. Even though humanity may have so "fallen" as not to be able to see or understand the inbuilt structure without God's further help, still order remains. Thus, much of the literature influenced by the Christian tradition emphasizes as a basic theme the existence of a fundamental moral order, which individuals defy to their ultimate peril. Christian art, music, and architecture often possess a precise mathematical and geometrical pattern which seems to go against nature, as we ordinarily know it, but which suggests a grand design behind this present world. Hindu temples may often seem like strange biological growths, and Buddhist chant often sounds like the droning of frogs or insects, but Gothic cathedrals soar upwards in defiance of nature and gravity, and Christian music has a melodiousness unlike any sounds of the "natural," nonhuman world. Christianity affirms creation by existing in some tension with "nature" as it is. It seeks the veiled structures and aesthetic and moral order behind nature, which reflect the mysterious divine intelligence, and then it makes them explicit in art, architecture, music and literature.

2. *Affirmation of the human.* As the preceding comments suggest, Christianity and its arts put a special emphasis on humanity. In a real sense, human beings lie at the center of the religious vision, and Christian arts convey this message over and over. God himself is known through the human form created in the image of God and manifest paradigmatically in Jesus Christ. Nature becomes significant insofar as it serves or is at odds with the human mission on earth. For all our sinfulness, we are still, from the perspective of many Christians, the crown of creation and the vehicle of God's redeeming work.

The exaltation of the human form has led to the already noted human and historical realism; expressed through making people look like people rather than symbols and portraying historical events such as the Crucifixion of Jesus, which are so important to Christianity. (However, there is some highly symbolic Christian art, especially from the Byzantine world and the late Middle Ages in the West.) In such forms as architecture and music, the centrality of humanity is shown in the exaltation of human creativity, of the human discovery of order, as against the timeless and recurrent rhythms of nature. Christian art, then, characteristically wants to preserve the human and the historical.

3. *Affirmation of human suffering.* Honoring and even exalting the human and the historical means also accepting human suffering and death, for the human world as we know it is hardly a paradise, and history is, as much as anything, a chronicle of horrors and terror. Christianity is well aware of this, for it is supremely encapsulated in the Biblical narrative of the passion of Jesus.

Thus, Christian religious art thematically gives a central place to human suffering, especially emphasizing suffering inflicted by others rather than the self-imposed asceticism of Shiva or the Buddha. Suffering is primarily portrayed in representations of the passion and death of Jesus, but is also reflected in the sorrows of his mother Mary and the martyrdom of saints. Another major theme of Christian art, the mother-and-child grouping of the Madonnas, has many echoes from around the world, but the Crucifixion and the deaths of saints, with their torture and blood—scenes which grace the walls and altars of countless Christian churches—stand virtually alone.

Yet Christianity is not pessimistic. It balances emphasis on suffering with a vision as lofty and full of hope as the anguish portrayed is keen. For death is understood as the gateway to life. The Book of Revelation, after picturing the suffering of the Lamb and the terrible wars and plagues to torment humanity in the last days, ends with the descent of the heavenly Jerusalem, the ideal of paradise. Significantly, paradise is not nature idealized, but a transcendent city. A glorified humanity that thoroughly harmonizes on either hand with an accepting benign God and a sanctified nature is the splendid ideal, foreshadowed in Jesus Christ. This ideal is communicated in, say, the painting of the Nativity by Giotto with its marvelous sense of the transcendent in human flesh, and again it is so well expressed poetically in the lines of Richard Crashaw:

That he whom the Sun serves, should faintly peepe
Through clouds of Infant flesh: that he the old
Eternall Word should be a child, and weepe. . . .

That Glories self should serve our Griefs and feares:
And free Eternity, submit to yeares.[1]

Perhaps the paradisaical ideal of Christianity has never been more con-

---

[1] *Horae Mysticae*, Eleanor Gregory, comp. London: Methuen, 1908, p. 33.

cretely and movingly expressed than in the paintings of the nineteenth-century American "primitive" artist, Edward Hicks, a Quaker. His many versions of *The Peaceable Kingdom,* when "the lion shall lay down with the lamb," show these and many other animals living in harmony and fair children playing with them— "a little child shall lead them." In the background, to illustrate an historical event which might be said to represent the Kingdom in the world and point toward the ways of paradise, Hicks usually placed a cameo scene of William Penn making the covenant between his Quaker settlers and the Indians—the one treaty between Whites and Native Americans traditionally said to have been arrived at without bloodshed and never broken.

THE ARTS IN CHRISTIAN HISTORY

Throughout the long history of Christianity the visual and literary arts have provided touchstones for understanding how the Christian experience was interpreted, and the worldview in which it appeared. Each age has, for example, offered its own interpretation of Jesus himself.

The Christ of the early years of the Christian triumph and of Byzantium was the *Pantocrator,* ruler of the universe enthroned in glory, like the model of the Christian emperor in Figure 4.1. He was also the crucified one, but it was his resurrection and return to power and glory that was emphasized. Byzantine churches, such as the great cathedral of the Holy Wisdom (Hagia Sophia, sometimes erroneously called St. Sophia) in Constantinople (Istanbul), the greatest Christian church in the world until the fall of Constantinople to the Turks in 1453, were built on the model of the universe itself. The four-sided body of the cathedral, with the sanctuary to the East, was the earth, and the great overarching dome the infinite sky. There above, Christ, with imperial regalia surrounded by disciples like courtiers, was portrayed as enthroned in state; the earth was his footstool. An equally common theme was the holy Mother and Child, especially after the veneration of the Virgin Mary was given impetus by the Council of Ephesus (431), which declared her *theotokos* (from the Greek for "Birth-giver of God"). Mary was also portrayed seated in regal splendor, holding the sacred infant on her lap or to her breast, inexpressibly tender, wise, sorrowful, and sovereign all at once.

Byzantine art has rich colors and a serene majesty. Its figures are in spiritualized, formal poses, which suggest the eternal and cosmic truths of the Christian story. The Byzantine style is perpetuated in the icon, now an object of veneration everywhere in the Eastern Orthodox church. These icons, or holy images of God, Christ, and the saints, show that the Byzantine style is well suited, with its luminous eyes and transcendent hues, to present the immortal light behind the faces of Christ and his saints. This artistic tradition is highly conventionalized;

detailed rules must be followed regarding the pose and symbolic accoutrements of each figure. Each execution, as a ritual act of devotion by the artist, through its formality is understood to release the viewer into transcendent reality.

The Eastern church uses no sculpture in its sacred art. The prohibition dates from the so-called Iconoclastic Controversy of 725–843. During this time, several Byzantine emperors tried to stamp out use of images in worship on the ground they led to superstition and idolatry, despite their appeal for much of the lay public and many ecclesiastics. Finally a compromise emerged that permitted pictures but not three-dimensional statues.

The church in the West, however, developed a more varied and flexible art which included statues and paintings in several different styles. The first post-Constantinian churches in western Europe were modelled on the basilica, Roman courts of law that were rectangular buildings with a platform at one end where the magistrate sat behind a desk. This was transformed into the altar with perhaps a representation of Christ as judge of the world behind it. The ambiance fitted the taste of the early Western church, which was likely to emphasize the divine lawgiver aspect of Christ and his heavenly teachings.

Rome was not the only voice, however. On the western fringe of Europe, as was also the case in such eastern lands as Egypt and Ethiopia, peoples newly brought to Christ were expressing the faith in new idioms. The turmoil of the Dark Ages was not conducive to much large-scale building. However, works of ornamentation and illumination, evidenced in crosses and manuscripts, reached a high level of intricacy and beauty revealing much indigenous influence. The famous Book of Kells, from Ireland c. 700, presents the Gospels illuminated with magnificent colors and tracery, both flamboyant and delicate, and baptizes the swirling shapes of the earliest Irish art.

The first great new style of West European art was known as Romanesque. Its exact origins are complex and much argued, though, as the name indicates, it has affinities with the Greco-Roman tradition. The style emerged with the re-establishment of a relatively stable society after some centuries of upheaval, and it was dominant in the eleventh and twelfth centuries. Thus, the monk Raoul Glaber wrote about 1048: "In the years that followed the year 1000 we witnessed the rebuilding of churches all over the universe, but especially in Italy and Gaul. Even if there were no need for it, each Christian community resolved to build sanctuaries more sumptuous than those of its neighbors, as if the world, anxious to cast away its rags, wished to dress in a beautiful white robe of churches."[2]

Romanesque architecture varies considerably from place to place. Its most characteristic feature is the use of the semicircular "Roman" arch for windows, arcades, and doors. The interior is often a half cylindrical "barrel vault" or is

---

[2] Cited in Jean Hubert, "Romanesque Art," in *Larousse Encyclopedia of Byzantine and Medieval Art,* Rene Huyghe, ed. London: Paul Hamlyn, 1963, p. 261.

supported by massive piers. Often the interior exfoliates into a complex arrangement of small chapels and side aisles. Windows are few and little more than slits. The church gives an overall impression of mystical darkness together with fortress-like security.

Sculpture and painting are closely related to architectural requirements. Romanesque renditions were designed to fit precisely into geometrically defined niches or walls. They often had a brilliant realism in detail, for sculptors (little Romanesque painting has survived) were highly adept at lending character to the face of a saint or demon. Yet the figures stand rather stiffly fitted into, say, a bas-relief of the Last Supper which must conform to the semicircle of an arch above a door. Christ in majesty, a favorite subject, appears as a remote, magisterial figure humanized by his saints and apostles.

Moving forward through history, Christian art and architecture produced from about 1150 to 1500 is termed Gothic. In the Gothic world, we can see the breakthrough of a new, more confident and soaring Christian spirit. The massively walled churches and monasteries of the Romanesque and allied schools suggested emphasis on the church as rocklike citadel, a vision appropriate to its role in the often embattled early Middle Ages; in the Gothic ages it is also beginning to become the center of a newly expanding human consciousness. Instead of the boxy Romanesque towers built like battlements, the Gothic cathedral raises immense spires toward Heaven and the infinite; the round porthole at the rear of the Romanesque cathedral becomes the Gothic edifice's great Rose Window, its ray of color splashing out in all directions of the compass.

The spiritual thrust of Gothic architecture expressed through its soaring spires rested upon monumental achievements in engineering. The remarkably light and uplifting quality of its structures came into being through such new techniques as the ribbed vault, the pointed arch, and the flying buttress. Gothic represents, then, spiritual and technical progress moving hand in hand—for the last time, in the view of some commentators.[3]

Like the architecture, Gothic painting and sculpture reflect a trend toward clarity and warmth. While still formal by modern standards, new discoveries of human variety and tenderness are unmistakable. Much of what is new in Gothic, especially late Gothic, such as its portrayals of Christ, the Blessed Virgin, and the saints expresses the medieval trend toward devotionalism. This warm, loving approach to the worship of Christ and the saints was promoted by the Franciscan and Dominican movements (which began in the thirteenth century). St. Francis, for example, was said to have made the first Christmas creche, while St. Dominic received the first Rosary from the Blessed Virgin. The devotionalist sense of warm love toward the infant and the crucified Christ and toward Mary and the saints, called for art able to offer all the nuances of anguish and love. Among the greatest

---

[3] For a fascinating fictionalized and lavishly illustrated study of medieval cathedral-building techniques, see David Macaulay, *Cathedral*. Boston: Houghton Mifflin, 1973.

exponents of the new painting was Giotto di Bondone (1266–1337), whose figures begin to display lifelike postures and emotions and whose settings show a "realistic" treatment of space.

These are the themes of the next great period, the Renaissance, followed by the Baroque, in the seventeenth and eighteenth century. It is a time of mixed meaning, so far as the relation of art and Christianity is concerned. On the one hand, this was the great age of the rediscovery of classical and secular topics in art, and even in religious art perhaps the greatest emphasis is on technical and human features. On the other hand, when the vast expansion of skill and vision that the Renaissance unleashed is applied by its great masters to religious subjects, as when Michelangelo painted the Sistine Chapel and Leonardo da Vinci *The Last Supper,* the result is a treatment at once monumental and sensitive that cannot but give new life to the viewer's inward image of God and Christ. In Michelangelo's Sistine ceiling, God imparts the gift of life to Adam with a majestic divine vigor that goes beyond the contemplative mood of medieval art and suggests the renewed vigor of the Renaissance itself. For all its anthropomorphism, it presents a somewhat more modern view of God as energy and historical force. In Leonardo's *Last Supper,* the painter gives us a Christ serene and radiant surrounded by disciples, each of whom is a quite distinct human personality. Here the Renaissance man's pride in his distinctive personality is reflected, yet Christ still remains the master of such a gathering of forceful individuals.

Renaissance and Baroque architecture is resplendently represented by St. Peter's Cathedral in Rome, largely designed by Michelangelo and his school. The papal cathedral is a magnificent tribute to the boldness and skill of Renaissance designers and artisans, and to the munificence of Renaissance patrons, particularly Popes of the fifteenth and sixteenth centuries. Baroque architecture is notable for its monumental quality, the revival of certain classical elements, such as columns and capitals and exceedingly rich but rigorously geometrical ornamentation, and quality that reached its height in eighteenth-century Rococo.

As the style spread throughout Europe and the New World, Baroque acquired national characteristics. Its Spanish and Portuguese forms, with the flat but lofty curve-topped facade and the lavishly pillared and ornamented reredos (an ornamented screen) behind the altar, are reflected in countless Latin American as well as Iberian churches. German Baroque and Rococo is noted for an extreme decorativeness, which, making much use of stucco, exudes a strikingly light, airy, joyous quality. English Baroque, on the other hand, emphasized the severely classical side of the school, and culminated in the Georgian or Palladian style, perhaps best represented in America by numerous New England colonial churches.

Within these edifices, Christian music since the Middle Ages has followed a course quite as divergent as that of the visual arts. From medieval plainsong came the polyphonic masses of the Renaissance, the work of composers such as Palestrina and Gabrieli. By the eighteenth century a new world of music, still largely religiously inspired, emerged in the oratorios and chorales of composers like Handel and J.S. Bach. Yet the music of these centuries betrays a process no less discernible in painting, sculpture, and architecture since the Renaissance: although the initial statements of these early modern innovations, whether in visual or audial media, are characteristically religious, the sacred gradually becomes more and more overwhelmed by the secular in all these forms. Thus, it would have to be said that since around 1800, at the latest, the proportion of truly significant and original painting, sculpture, music, and architecture that is distinctively and unambiguously identifiable as Christian is small in comparison with medieval or even Renaissance creations.

In volume, of course, the creation of artistic works intended as Christian in the nineteenth and twentieth centuries has not been small. Innumerable churches have been built and hymns composed. But most of it has been derivative, either from earlier periods of Christian art, as in successive classical, Gothic, Baroque, and even Romanesque and Byzantine "revivals," or from the artistry of the surrounding secular world, as in the Romantic masses of Schubert and Berlioz. Only a few exceptions, such as the brilliant artistic visions of William Blake or the marvelously unique churches of the devout Gaudi, obviously join deep Christian inspiration and expressive genius. What meaning this proportional diminution is to be given, the reader may ponder.

We turn now to an area of Christian artistic expression which we have not yet explored, namely the literary arts. Significant Christian literature is that which either expresses consummately the Christian vision of an established Christian culture or which explores new facets of the images in the mirror that Christianity holds up to human life. (By "literature" is meant, in this context, fiction and poetry.) If the nineteenth and twentieth centuries have been relatively dry ones for Christian visual and musical arts, literature that can be understood as Christian has flourished. Writers of the first rank, from William Blake, Emily Dickinson, and Fyodor Dostoevsky to Graham Greene, W.H. Auden, and Flannery O'Connor, have been deeply affected by the Christian experience and have produced work that profoundly wrestles with it. The secularization of the modern world has not driven religious-minded writers from the field, but has forced new and deeper searches for meaning by those of unclouded eye who also know the power of the Christian symbols.

Christian literature has generally employed the dominant genres of its day—saga, sonnet, epic, or novel. But it is distinguished by its symbolic content and the questions it raises. The figure of Christ, the one whose resurrection redeems through suffering, may well be central, either symbolically or actually, and the rest of the traditional Christian cosmic order, with its heaven and hell, may be hinted. The work may explore the extremes of human glory and degradation, and emphasize the demand that choices be made in a universe with a hidden but real moral order that imposes abiding significance on each choice made.

Apart from hymns such as those of Fortunatus,[4] we have little Christian fiction or poetry from the early Christian centuries. Only with the emergence of national languages in the early Middle Ages does distinctive Christian poetry and fiction appear. Very often it is among the first fruits of a new tongue. In Anglo-Saxon there appears, along with essentially pre-Christian works like *Beowulf,* a powerful Christian statement like that of "The Dream of the Rood," to be discussed later.

The supreme Christian literary product of the high Middle Ages is considered by scholars to be *The Divine Comedy* of Dante Alighieri (1265–1321). No less than a Gothic cathedral, this work gives form to the complex and transcendent medieval vision of reality and the meaning of human life. Dante shows us graphically Hell (Inferno), Purgatory (Purgatorio), the earthly paradise, the Limbo of good pagans, and finally Heaven (Paradiso), where his guide is the beloved and radiant Beatrice, whose motive power is the Love which moves "the Sun and the other stars."

As in the other arts, the Renaissance shattered the medieval window into many pieces, but some of them still glowed brightly with faith in the face of humanism. In England, John Donne (1572–1631) and George Herbert (1593–1633), among others, expressed in intricate verse forms the joys and torments of introspective souls whose worldviews were still shaped by the classical Christian cosmos. That cosmos in Puritan format was magnificently articulated in John Milton's (1608–1674) epic *Paradise Lost.* He, no less than Dante, captured a universe of Christian meaning and his own age's spiritual vision and struggle.

The day when an entire culture's experience would be caught in Christian language was rapidly closing, however. Writers of subsequent centuries could not assume that in speaking in a traditionally Christian way they spoke a language common to all. Out of their individual experience, they sought to express eternal truths. In William Blake (1775–1827), Christian images such as Jerusalem as an earthly paradise stand in contrast to the harsh new world being wrought by industry and commerce, and the meaning of the tradition was refocused by an array of new images.

Perhaps no modern novelist's understanding of Christianity is more discussed than that of the profound and paradoxical Russian writer Fyodor Dostoevsky (1821–1881). Dostoevsky's is a world in which all objections to God and

---

[4] The attractive Christian Latin poet and bishop of Poitiers Venantius Fortunatus (c. 540–600) wrote such poems as *Pange lingua* (translated as "Sing My Tongue the Glorious Battle") and *Vexilla regis* ("The Royal Banners Forward Go"), which are still widely sung today as hymns. These verses magnificently express the militant, triumphant spirit of the West European Christianity of his day. As the old Roman Empire dwindled, the newly victorious church, under Christ the new sovereign, saw itself the more holy inheritor of the still powerful Roman mystique of marching armies, imperial grandeur, and world dominion. But, ideally, the armies were now peaceful missionaries. The grandeur became spiritual and the dominion one of faith and love; of this transition Fortunatus sang. Not a few writers noted that *Roma* reversed is *amor*, love.

Christianity are fervently and forcefully argued. The sadistic abuse of innocent children, which, as he was well aware occurs far more often then we like to contemplate, calls in question every argument for the existence of a God of justice. Yet in an alternative world without God there is no order; all is permitted. Dostoevsky could not resolve this dilemma intellectually, yet in searching toward an answer he repeatedly employs Christlike figures of innocence who suffer and yet end up strangely victorious. Readers are led to feel that the mystery of the cross holds more about such deep matters than can ever be put into words.

Many other names and titles could be cited with Dostoevsky. But rather than multiply them, let us examine in more detail two selected examples of Christian literature from other sources. Both are poems, both are by English authors, but they come from periods in which the relation of Christianity to culture was very different.

The first example is "The Dream of the Rood," by an unknown Anglo-Saxon author of around the eighth century. (The earliest complete manuscript, found in Italy in 1822, is from the tenth century, but some lines from an earlier version are inscribed on the runes of an eighth century stone cross at Ruthwell in Dumfriesshire. *Rood* is an old word that means the "cross." The symbol of the cross was very important to Anglo-Saxon Christian piety. Ornamented crosses of exquisite workmanship, and fine boxes or reliquaries for wood believed to be pieces of the True Cross survive from the age of this poem. In the poem, the Cross of Christ itself speaks to the poet in a dream and relates its story. Here are some selections from "The Dream of the Rood":

> *Lo, I will tell the best of dreams*
> *that came to me dreaming in the midst of night*
> *when living men had sought their rest.*
> *It seemed that I saw that noblest of trees*
> *aloft lifted, wound with light,*
> *brightest of wood; all that beacon*
> *was flooded with gold, and gems stood*
> *fair on the earth beneath; there were five more*
> *up on the crossbeams. The Lord's angels all gazed upon it*
> *fair throughout creation —that was no felon's gallows—*
> *but there beheld it holy spirits,*
> *men upon earth, and all this noble creation.*

* * *

> *Wondrous was the victory-tree, and I stained with sins,*
> *wounded with wrong. I saw the tree of glory*
> *clad with honour, shining joyful,*
> *girded with gold; and noble gems*
> *had worthily clasped their Maker's tree.*

Yet through that gold   I could see afar
the struggle of poor ones,   when it first began
to sweat on the right side.   I was all troubled with sorrows,
fearful was I for the fair sight;   I saw that eager beacon
change its raiment and colour;   now it was bedewed, wet,
stained with blood poured out;   now wound with treasure.
Yet I, lying there   a long while,
gazed heart-repentant   on the Healer's tree,
until I heard   that it spoke aloud;
it uttered words,   that best of wood:

"It was long ago,   I yet remember,
that I was hewn down   at the wood's end
torn from my place.   They took me there, strong foes,
they set me up as a gazing-stock,   bade me lift on high their felons.
Men bore me on their shoulders,   till on a hill they set me,
many foes fastened me there.   Then I saw mankind's Lord
swiftly come with courage,   for He willed to mount on me.

Then dared I not,   against the Lord's word,
bend or break,   when I saw
the earth trembling.   I might there
have felled all my foes,   but I stood fast.
Then He stripped Himself, the young Hero,   that was God Almighty,
strong and firm-hearted   He mounted the mean gibbet;
noble-hearted in the sight of many   He would set free mankind.
I shook when the Prince clasped me,   but I durst not bow to earth,
fall to the ground,   but must needs stand fast.
A rood I was raised aloft,   I lifted the mighty King,
Lord of Heaven,   I durst not bend.
They drove me through with dark nails,   on me the marks are plain,
wide wounds of hate.   I durst not harm any of them.
They mocked us both together.   I was all wet with blood
poured from the Man's side   when He had sent forth His soul.
There on the hill   I underwent
many bitter things.   I saw the God of Hosts
sorely stretched out.   Darkness there
had wrapped in clouds   the Ruler's Body,
its fair radiance.   A shadow went forth
wan under clouds.   All creation wept,
bewailed the King's death,   Christ on the rood.
But there came from afar   eager nobles
to Him all alone;   I beheld all that.

Sore was I troubled with sorrows,   but I bent down to the hands of the men
humbly, with hearty will.

Lo, He has honoured me,   the Prince of glory,
over all trees of the wood,   He, the Keeper of Heaven,
even as Almighty God,   for mankind's sake
honored His Mother,   Mary herself.
the most worthy   of all women.
Now I bid thee,   my beloved one,
tell of this sight   to other men;
unveil in words   that this wood is glorious
since God Almighty   suffered on it
for the many sins   of all mankind,
and for Adam's deed   done long ago.
There He tasted death,   yet the Lord arose
with great might,   so to help men.
Then He mounted to Heaven;   thither shall He come
into this middle-earth   to seek mankind
on Doomsday,   the Lord Himself,
Almighty God,   and His angels with Him.
The Son was victory-fast   in His far-going,
mighty and enriched   when He came with many,
a spirit-army,   into God's kingdom,
The Almighty Lone-Wielder   was bliss to the angels
and all holy ones   who ere in heaven
dwelt in glory,   when their Ruler came,
Almighty God,   where His homeland was.[5]

This poem celebrates the confident faith and triumphant mood of a Christian culture on the way toward becoming established in Anglo-Saxon England and throughout the British Isles. During the seventh and eighth centuries, Roman Christianity was still expanding, turning once more to the British Isles with a double task of converting the pagan Anglo-Saxons and regularizing the older Celtic church which had been in place since Christianity first came to those northern shores. All of these influences appear through the magnificent language of the poem as they unite to tell the story in a way that is clear and surely founded on faith undimmed by ambiguity. The faith expressed in this poem may perhaps appear naive and unphilosophical to us, heirs of the Enlightenment, but it was felt with power by a people still consciously close to such primal veins of feeling as heroic myth, honor, and loyalty.

The faith so beautifully expressed here presents the image of Jesus Christ

---

[5] Excerpted from *Word-Hoard*, Margaret Williams, trans. and arr., London: Sheed and Ward, Ltd., 1946, pp. 206–212. Reprinted by permission of the publisher.

as the preeminent epic hero greater than Beowulf or Queen Boadicea or even the god Thor with his hammer and the undefeatable Lugh with his all-conquering spear. Christ has power mightier than the great goddesses associated with war and battle, those such as Epona represented as a white horse or the triple goddess of the Celts named in Ireland as the great queen Morrigan imaged as a white horse and endowed with a hateful laugh and as Macha, also a horse figure, who carried humans to the Otherworld, and as Badb, the goddess of battlefields and death, who enticed warriors to fight and die and was often represented as a crow or raven. Christ had ventured far on a great heroic quest, risking all. He had undergone pain unflinchingly at the hands of cruel foes and in the end had defeated and over-turned their power. He had achieved victory through wielding a greater and more powerful weapon—his willing sacrifice. This was the sort of courageous strength the warrior people of the North could understand and respect. Christ had shown it superbly and had well earned the right to be Master.

A still deeper and happier mystery also glows through Anglo-Saxon Chris-tian poetry. Christ is not only a human hero, but God Almighty, too, even as the ultimate enemy behind the dark shadows over earth is nothing human, but rather is Satan. The Christian struggle here below then becomes an engagement in a cosmic battle. The epic is of infinite dimensions, yet centered on the starkness of the wooden Cross.

Next we shall look at some lines from *Auguries of Innocence* by William Blake (1757–1827). Blake, poet, painter, and prophetic visionary, was profoundly steeped in Christian lore, but saw both Christ and the world differently from the author of "The Dream of the Rood." They shared the fundamental idea of a universe essentially ordered, yet often alienated from the source of its order, and in which the suffering of Jesus is the touchstone for interpretation and rectification of this situation. But the contrasts between the two poems mark the varied mean-ing of Christian vision between the early Middle Ages and the modern world whose glories and horrors Blake, as he watched the machine age painfully emerg-ing around him, saw more clearly than most.

Blake came from the sort of Puritan tradition that took the Sermon on the Mount seriously as a model, and in its light he was a radical social critic who saw no essential difference between political and spiritual oppression, between the tyranny of money, class, and outmoded tradition, and the inner tyrannies that enslave one to confining ideas like jealous gods in the mind.

Against all these despotisms, Blake saw Jesus Christ representing freedom. He represents freedom precisely because he is in the flesh, and not abstract spirit, light, or idea. For Blake true human freedom could only be found where we are, in the flesh. "The flesh is eternal delight," he once wrote—whereas reason, dog-mas, and philosophies entrap what is meant to be free. This meaning of Christ is subtly but powerfully suggested in the last four lines of the poem printed below.

Blake saw in the world around him new dangers to real fleshly freedom. He saw the Industrial Revolution producing a mechanized world that could reduce humans to standardized machines like the ones they operated. But he also saw a new freedom, or potential for freedom, in a revolutionary age.

For Blake, faith meant seeing all things just as they are, in flesh, in life and death, in the interrelatedness of all of creation. Faith is the direct seeing that perceives heaven in a wild flower and hell in the unjust suffering of a single mistreated child or animal. Unfaith or doubt is seeing while blinded by the glaring lights of reason or ideology untempered by feeling. Any injustice can be rationalized; mind and body and spirit and flesh become alienated from the perspective that prefers to manipulate machines or abstract ideas rather than dwell in the concrete world of enfleshed delights and pains.

William Blake's Bible illustration of a woman taken in adultery.

In this sense, the following poem is about faith and doubt in the modern world, a world beset by doubt and false light, but in which clues to the substantial reality and its morality can be seen in even the smallest signs, in the tiniest animals, by those who see through rather than with the eyes, and who, like Christ, are willing to dwell in human form. Here are some selections from *Auguries of Innocence*:

> *To see a world in a grain of sand,*
> *And a heaven in a wild flower;*
> *Hold infinity in the palm of your hand,*
> *And eternity in an hour.*

> *A Robin Redbreast in a cage*

Puts all heaven in a rage;
A dove-house filled with doves and pigeons
Shudders hell through all its regions.
A dog starved at his master's gate
Predicts the ruin of the state;
A game-cock clipped and armed for fight
Doth the rising sun affright;
A horse misused upon the road
Calls to Heaven for human blood.

He who mocks the infant's faith
Shall be mocked in age and death;
He who shall teach the child to doubt
The rotten grave shall ne'er get out;
He who respects the infant's faith
Triumphs over hell and death.
The babe is more than swaddling-bands
Throughout all these human lands;
Tools were made, and born were hands,
Every farmer understands.
The questioner who sits so sly
Shall never know how to reply.
He who replies to words of doubt
Doth put the light of knowledge out;
A puddle, or the cricket's cry,
Is to doubt a fit reply.
The child's toys and the old man's reasons
Are the fruits of the two seasons.
The emmet's inch and eagle's mile
Make lame philosophy to smile.
A truth that's told with bad intent
Beats all the lies you can invent.
He who doubts from what he sees
Will ne'er believe, do what you please;
If the sun and moon should doubt,
They'd immediately go out.

Every night and every morn
Some to misery are born;
Every morn and every night
Some are born to sweet delight;
Some are born to sweet delight;
Some are born to endless night.
Joy and woe are woven fine,

A clothing for the soul divine;
Under every grief and pine
Runs a joy with silken twine.
It is right it should be so;
Man was made for joy and woe;
And, when this we rightly know,
Safely through the world we go.

We are led to believe a lie
When we see with not through the eye,
Which was born in a night to perish in a night
When the soul slept in beams of light.
God appears and God is light
To those poor souls who dwell in night;
But doth a human form display
To those who dwell in realms of day.[6]

[6] From *The Poems, with Specimens of the Prose Writings, of William Blake,* with prefatory notice by Joseph Skipsey. London: Walter Scott, 1888, pp. 208–13.

beliefs

Legend has it that the twelve Apostles met together and gathered the beliefs central to the Christian tradition into a formula of faith. Known as the Apostles' Creed, this formulation recounts the characters and events that give image to the experience of faith that is distinctly Christian. It will be presented later in this chapter.

THE NATURE OF CHRISTIAN BELIEF

The first word of this recounting, for which the formulation is named, is *Credo* (Latin for "I believe"). Belief then is not merely a proposition to which one gives intellectual assent. It is grounded in an act of "believing" that is a reaffirmation in every instant of the faith experience. The various expressions in which statements of belief are formulated are attempts to articulate an experience that moves the one so experiencing it to speak in a way that might be shared with others. The first words of the Nicene Creed are "*We* believe." The shift from the singular to the collective pronoun indicates an expression of shared experience.

Scholars have attempted to describe the religious experience, and one such expression proclaims that "*a strange, 'Wholly Other' Power obtrudes into life.* Man's attitude to it is first of all *astonishment* and ultimately *faith.*"[1] It is an experience

---

[1] Gerardus Van der Leeuw, *Religion in Essence and Manifestation.* Gloucester, Mass.: Peter Smith, 1967, Vol. I, p. 681.

that turns one around and radically changes one's perspective, one's orientation. "Credo" can be heard as the cry of the reborn. The source of power and the depth of the experience of believing is well attested to in the central texts of Christianity. Belief, when also remembered as "believing," is at the heart of Christian self understanding:

> Jesus said to her, "I am the resurrection and the life; whoever believes in me, though he die, yet shall he live, and whoever lives and believes in me shall never die. Do you believe this?" She said to him, "Yes, Lord; I believe that you are the Christ, the Son of God, he who is coming into the world." (John 11:25–27)

Uniting head and heart and thought and action, the complexity of belief involves the calculating intellect that coolly reasons out the connections between one doctrine and another and also the firing passion and emotion that ignites moral courage. Belief involves living one's life, as well as reflecting upon that life. The saints and martyrs, who live exemplary lives that move others to follow as best they can, are to be considered along with the great theologians in attempting to understand the inclusive notion of "belief" in Christianity. Some of the greatest thinkers in the world have been challenged to reflect deeply on the most far-reaching and all-embracing issues confronting people—life, death, joy, sorrow, sin, salvation, damnation, the natural world, social order, justice, goodness, evil, suffering, and so on. When such issues engage a thinker and stimulate her or him to formulate responses to them that are informed or inspired by foundational Christian stories, they produce theology. In the interplay between experience and reflection and between story and theology, belief comes to expression.

St. Patrick's Cathedral. Photo courtesy of Ken Karp.

Few religious traditions—perhaps none—have so prominently stimulated and exalted theology to the degree that Christianity has done. Lurking next to this exaltation of the importance of belief has been the recurrent temptation to forget its dynamic nature and to suppose that if one set of beliefs is "right," then all others must be "wrong." For, if there is supposed to be a direct link between what a person thinks and how that person lives, and if how one lives one's life is the proof or demonstration that one is truly a Christian, then ineluctably, some argue, everything hinges on what one thinks and believes.

But among Christians that sequence of connections is not universally accepted. There has consistently been a strain of Christian thought that believes God to be ultimately mysterious and not capturable by human thinking. From that perspective, human thinking can never "get it right." Thus only trust and faith in the mercy and grace of God, mysterious gifts that they are, mark any person as a Christian. The challenge to Christians holding this view is to love God and all people; to engage in rituals that collectively encourage trust and love; and to hear, learn, and tell those stories that collectively recount the lives of exemplary persons, living and dead. For such Christians, belief means being continuously formed and informed by stories that re-present Christianity to every generation.[2]

Characteristic of many Christians is the conviction that the foundational stories recount events that happened in time and space, i.e. that they are historically based, and in that particular sense are "true stories." However, the distinction made here between stories of this kind and those of other types—legends, sagas, epics—is not to be confused with myths. Myths are true stories, regardless of the genre in which they are expressed. Their truths cannot be reduced to that which is historically actual. Myths, as expressions of belief, tell what is true about the way things are in Reality. They tell of the creation of the religious world. Christian myths take the form of history or history-like stories.

In recognizing the central importance of stories, Christianity joins all other religious traditions in the regard it has for narrative modes of communicating its most cherished experiences and ideas. Stories are foundational; reflections upon stories, when given systematic expression, mark a crucial shift in form from that which expresses itself in and through narrative to that which expresses itself as conceptual treatise, essay, or extended argumentation. Despite the formal differences between storied communication (which is most prominent in parables, Gospels, homilies, and sermons) and closely reasoned treatises (which give expression to doctrines and dogmas for theologians), both are ultimately founded upon stories. These consist of the God story and the Jesus stories, and, subsequently, the stories of saints and sinners affected by the God and Jesus stories. To understand the fact and the prominence of belief in Christianity, then, surely requires one to be familiar with the foundational stories.

---

[2] See the account of the Waldensians in Chap. 3.

THE GOD STORY

A story of beginnings, stretching back to the time before time, was adopted by Christianity from Judaism. The book of Genesis, the first book of the Bible, begins with the words: "In the beginning God created the heavens and the earth." The story then accounts for everything in the universe: sun, moon, stars, earth, sky, water; plant life, animal life, and then "in our image, after our likeness" humanity. All that is comes from God and nothing is or could be of which God was not the source. Then, as if to say to any who might not have recognized it as a myth, the book of Genesis in its second chapter tells a different story of the experience of beginnings. Separately or together they tell, and implicitly admonish, all who would become a part of this story: We believe in God as "the creator of heaven and earth," the one without whom the world and all that is in it are meaningless and make no sense at all, or, at best, a quite different sense.

From such a beginning as just recounted, the God story moves through one mighty act after another. The chief energy for the drama continues to be the interactive relationship between God and those people who understand their lives to be characterized primarily by their relationship with God. Such vignettes are highlighted in the following selections. The story of the relationship between God and his creation begins in the Garden of Eden with Adam (Hebrew for "man," "earth") and Eve as the figures of archetypal humanity. The story of the "Temptation," "Fall" and "Expulsion" from the Garden is played out against the backdrop of paradisiacal existence in which all is at one with God.

Adam and Eve committed the "original sin" of disobedience: they ignored the divine threat of death for the sake of acquiring knowledge that would make them Godlike. And for this they were expelled from the Garden and sent into the world. Cursed forever to toil and suffer, they experienced alienation from God, from each other, and from the rest of creation. And in the recognition of their own mortality they were separated from themselves.

This story of "beginnings," placed at the beginning, sets the pattern for the whole of the rest of the story as it is played out in the Bible. For the narrative unfolds as a series of quests, to return to the Garden existence of atonement (etymologically: at-one-ment) with God, creation, and themselves.

And yet, as events unfold, the quality of the "Garden" takes on shades of ambivalence, perhaps suggesting that the story of "beginnings" offers more than one way to imagine an ending. Paradise is also the Promised Land, and in the Book of Revelation, "Jerusalem," the heavenly city, becomes the holy bride that descends at the end of history to sanctify all creation in divine union. And in the writings of the Apostle Paul, the kingdom of heaven is located nowhere else than in the heart of every believer. These archetypal themes that set forth the fundamental ways of being human in the world may be read and interpreted in a variety of ways.

In one such reading, the Adam-and-Eve story seems to focus upon the problem of ''seeing.'' When the fruit of the tree of the knowledge of good and evil is eaten, the eyes of both are ''opened.'' Having divine wisdom, they become ''like God.'' The price exacted for that is death, which is played out as banishment from the Garden, lest they eat of the fruit of the tree of life and become immortal.

The images indicate a shift in the way existence is ''seen.'' Prior to eating the fruit, all creation is at one with God; afterward, a radical separation takes place. Yet, viewed another way, just as the fruit of good and evil flourishes on the same tree, so a paradisaical existence of oneness is, *at the same time,* the terrible recognition of human mortality.

The suggestion might be that seeing ''like God,'' or seeing one's life as mirroring divine (archetypal) likenesses that reflect existence in terms of an immediate relationship to the divine is, *at the same time,* to undertake a long, hard, and painful journey in search of God. Understanding oneself as ''Godlike'' is not the same as believing oneself to be identical with God. Paradoxically, divine and human ''likeness'' depends upon remembering the difference within the similarity.

In and through images one may discover that, paradoxically, along with the terror and agony undergone by Adam and Eve and every other person, as each is cursed and cast out of the garden of innocence and into history, there is simultaneously a blessing of being returned to the place one has never left. To eat of the fruit of the tree of knowledge, to suffer through a desert exile, to be torn upon the cross, and to be devastated by apocalyptic holocaust is concurrently to be turned inward into the dwelling place of God in the heart and soul.

Each image speaks of a radical shift in perspective and a new orientation of consciousness. The Garden of Eden as it tends to become literalized, is ''left behind'' and relocated in the heart. Demanding hard and painful work, this move is into an imaginative ''seeing'' where the play of existence is *between* joy and sorrow, union and separation, life and death.

Immediately, the depth of the ambivalence of humanity's place upon the earth is re-created in the story of Cain and Abel, the sons of Adam and Eve. Within the movement of this story, the tension that is the relationship between God and creation is mirrored in the relationship between individuals and the psyche of each person is revealed in a new metaphor: that between farmer and shepherd. Echoes are heard in the tension between settlement and nomadic wandering, and eventually between priest and prophet. Cain slew Abel. Out of jealousy, the farmer destroyed the shepherd, whom he saw as the chosen one. As a result, Cain was cursed and ''cast out'' from home and the divine presence to wander as a fugitive and vagabond. And yet, in a way similar to covering the nakedness or exposed vulnerability of Adam and Eve with the skins of animals (signifying perhaps the recognition and acceptance of the bestial part of human nature), God placed a protective mark upon Cain, to mark him even in his wanderings and isolation as within God's love (Genesis 4). The story of heights and depths continues in the image of the destruction of a world fallen into ways that had separated the people from God. For forty days and forty nights it rained. Only Noah and his family survived the deluge by being carried in a wooden ark—they and a pair of creatures of every kind in creation. The waters subsided and left the earth newly created, as in the original creation story. Yet, this time a rainbow appeared as a perpetual covenant between God and humanity (Genesis 6–9).

Still, this is not the end of the story. Again there is a rising up and a falling down, this time carried in the image of the "Tower of Babel." Important to note here perhaps is that the images appearing in the stories are both universal and particular. A paradisaical Garden, primordial parents, serpents, apples, warring brothers, flood, and tower are all themes that appear in the mythologies of many traditions, very notably in the stories of the peoples of the Ancient Near East, the birth-place of the Hebrews.[3] Yet, the interpretation placed on these themes is at the same time in many ways particular to the changed context in which the people of the "new story" found themselves.

The Tower of Babel, symbolic of the center of the world, was being constructed to reach up into the heavens. The people living in the unity of a single language overstepped themselves and sought to take the place of God. Like Adam and Eve, they were cast out, this time scattered over all the face of earth, their language divided into a multiplicity of tongues incomprehensible to each other. And they were forced to cease building the city and to wander (Genesis 11).

Yet, out of the confusion of tongues, a call was heard that carried the potential to still the babel; perhaps to hear many tongues as one voice and at the same time one language as many tongues. Abram, from the city of Ur in Mesopotamia, was called by God to leave his country, his family and his father's house to go to a new land that the Lord would show him: the Promised Land. The recognition and acceptance of God's call effected a radical reorientation in the lives of those involved and was symbolized by a change of name, as it is today in baptism (see Chapter 6). Abram became Abraham and Sarai, his wife, became Sarah. Their heretofore barren union now blossomed like a desert after the rain. In their old age, Isaac was born and the Covenant between God and humankind was reestablished. The promise was given that from their union and its perpetuation in Isaac many nations would come forth and be characterized by a special Covenant relation and the land of Canaan would be given to their descendants forever (Genesis 12).

But, true to life, the story did not end on that happy note. In fact it began all over again. Temporarily, Abraham and his company occupied the land of Canaan, but famine drove them into Egypt and into the testing that awaited them

---

[3] Much work has been done in the field of history of religions in collecting and interpreting universal themes manifest in mythologies and rituals. The work of Mircea Eliade is particularly important perhaps especially here his *Patterns in Comparative Religion,* Rosemary Sheed, trans. New York: Meridian Books, 1958 and *The Myth of Eternal Return or, Cosmos and History,* Willard R. Trask, trans. Bollingen Series XLVI, Princeton, N.J.: Princeton University Press, 1971. Also helpful for themes especially common to the ancient Near East are J. B. Pritchard, *The Ancient Near East* (2 vol.), Princeton, N.J.: Princeton University Press, 1958, and S. H. Hooke, *Middle Eastern Mythology,* Baltimore: Pelican Books, 1963).

there. All through their movements, demands were made, but none so full of horror and anguish as that put to Abraham after their return to the Promised Land. Abraham understood God to require of him the sacrifice of Isaac: the return to God of all that had been given. In an example that speaks to all times and places, the story presents Abraham as sufficiently trusting God to obey the command—and miraculously, having shown his fidelity, as being spared the terror of killing his only heir and, symbolically, the hopes of the Hebrew people (Genesis 22).

The story moves through the book of Genesis to subsequent generations; to Jacob and Rachel, to Jacob and Esau, to Tamar, and to Joseph and his dream interpretations. Each image echoes the themes laid down "in the beginning," each recounting the hardship and the prosperity of a people bound in a Covenant of trust with their God, as they forget, fall away, and are returned to the terms of that Covenant. The book ends with the Hebrews (wandering peoples), as they came to be known, living in plenty in Egypt.

Again, as with the Garden of Eden and the Promised Land, a time of plenty is the beginning. As the second book of the Bible reveals, the plentitude became oppressive. The Hebrews found themselves as slaves in bondage to their "hosts." The book of Exodus recounts the story of God's raising up of Moses as leader of the oppressed Hebrews. Moses gathered the people and, under cover of darkness, led them out of slavery through the Red (or Reed) Sea, which miraculously parted to let them pass, but fell back upon and destroyed their pursuers. Resembling the story of the parting of the waters at the moment of creation, the dividing of the Red Sea marks the passage of rebirth through the "exodus" into a renewed covenantal relationship with God. The events of this sacred time are commemorated in the Jewish annual feast of the Passover. This feast appears in the Jesus story as the last meal Jesus shared with his disciples prior to his arrest, trial, crucifixion, and resurrection. Later, this same time of year came to be commemorated by the Christian church as Eastertide.

Once freed from the prison of Egypt, the Hebrews did not find themselves delivered into the abundance and fecundity of the Promised Land, the "land of milk and honey." Rather, they found themselves being led into the desolation and drought of the Sinai desert. For forty years they wandered, being tested and tried in the heat, like ore to be purified. (In the Jesus story, Christ enters the desert for forty days and nights of ordeal. Recalling also the number of days of the deluge, the number forty appears significant in these stories.) At the beginning of the time in the desert, the Ten Commandments of God, the laws by which the Chosen People were to live, were given to Moses, etched by fire into tablets of stone. Afterward, the tablets were to be carried in a wooden ark wherever the people were led.

The basis for life on earth for those participating in the God story is caught up in the first commandment: "You shall have no other gods before me" (Exodus 20:3). Nine other commandments follow to explicate what is entailed by this basic, foundational commandment. In a sense, the laws of the Hebrews served as their theological formulations, inasmuch as the law explained and conceptualized the story of God's relationship with the people. One such formulation is recorded in the book of Deuteronomy (from the Greek meaning "second law," the word denotes a repetition of the law of Moses). Known as the *shema* (Hebrew for "hear") it is a central focus for Jewish worship. It begins "Hear, O Israel: The Lord our God is one Lord; and you shall love the Lord your God with all your heart, and with all your soul and all your might" (Deut. 6:4–9). All else is to be understood in the context of and encompassed by this commandment.

Some later theological reflections on the story transform the commandments into inviolable laws; other reflections seek to express the conceptual generalizations thought to be implicit in the stories and take the form of doctrines or dogmas. Through the centuries, Jews have favored the former and Christians have chosen the latter. Both, however, depend upon the stories themselves.

After Moses came Joshua, the great military leader, who is presented in the story as the one who rallied the Hebrews to repossess the Promised Land. But the Hebrews repeatedly "fell away" and were brought back to themselves through great adversity. Other great leaders arose, including Deborah the prophetess. Known as judges, their vocation was to redeem the people. The "Song of Deborah" voices the tension beautifully (Judges 5) as does the story of Samson and Delilah (Judges 14–16). The motif of a "Messiah," an "Anointed One" chosen to lead the people to possess the Promised Land, is recurrent in the subsequent vignettes of the God Story.

Soon however, tired of the minimal social and political structures, the people demanded that the "anointed one" be a king for them, that they might be "like all the nations" (1 Samuel 8). And in great tension with the desert nomadic ideal established in Exodus, a series of kings arose: Saul, David and Solomon. As Israel became mighty and splendid, those figures eventually came to represent the same desire as the eating of the forbidden fruit in the Garden and of the building of the Tower of Babel.

In due course, the Israelite kingdom fell. Its conquest by the Assyrian peoples resulted in the loss of memoried influence of a large proportion of the people—the "ten lost tribes of Israel." Later, the Babylonians conquered and captured large numbers of the remaining people, called Judeans, who lived in the Southern Kingdom. Prior to and during the Babylonian captivity, among the Israelites and Judeans persons called prophets arose and, in varying sociocultural circumstances, recalled the special relation the people had with Yahweh, God.[4] No calamity was so great, no trial so severe, but that some prophet saw in it a chastisement of the people by God and thus as evidence of God's love. No challenge to such confidence was greater than that which confronted the Judeans while in captivity to the Babylonians. "How can we sing the Lord's song in a strange land?" was their cry (Psalm 137). Without benefit of temple, aliens cut off from

---

[4] Yahweh or YHWH a transliteration of the Hebrew יהוה, a very ancient compilation at least as old as 850 B.C. Known as the tetragrammaton, the word since at least 300 B.C. has been considered by the tradition to be too sacred for utterance. Hence it is articulated as "Adonai" and translated as "Lord." In the sixteenth century, this became known in its bastardized version of "Jehovah."

their homeland, how were they to worship? The temple had been destroyed, the center of their world demolished. Yet, the power of the stories of God's covenanting with the Hebrews was such that those Judeans found ways to accommodate their religion to unprecedented sociopolitical conditions.

When the Persians defeated the Babylonians and allowed those Judeans who wished to do so to return to Judea and to begin to rebuild Jerusalem and the temple, some, convinced as they were that their religion no longer required them physically to be in Jerusalem in order to worship Yahweh, chose to remain in Babylon. This dividing of the ways resulted in some Jews being in dispersion (*diaspora*), who from then on felt free to migrate to foreign places as opportunity allowed or need required them. Yet there were others who felt required to return and remain in the Promised Land and at the temple as the necessary way to remain faithful to their God. This division, recalling that rift between Cain and Abel and symbolic of many others, subsequently, was crucial for Christianity, as will be indicated below.

As one empire after another arose to prominence in the last five centuries before the appearance of Christianity, the land of Palestine (some of which is Israel today) was under a series of subjections to foreigners. Alexander the Great's conquest established the Hellenistic Empire in the fourth century B.C. Later, the Palestinians succeeded for a brief period in winning their independence before the Roman Empire enveloped it again into its provinces. As conquest after conquest was experienced, the Jewish longing for a leader who would restore the glory of bygone times became acute and a Messiah who would be like the ancient kings anointed by God came to be expected, or at least desired. Independence from foreign control and domination was a major part of that expectation.

Christian Jews declared to their fellow Jews that in the person of Jesus, the Christ, the Messiah had come. How radically the Christian reinterpretation of Jesus as the Messiah shifted the image remains a point of debate, but it is echoed in the truism: Jews still await the coming of the Messiah; Christians are those heirs of Judaism who believe the Messiah has already come in the person of Jesus, the Christ, and that he will come again. In that appropriation of the image of Messiah, the inseparable connection between Christians and Jews was cemented from the beginning. And as Christians uncovered ways to interpret the Jewish foundational stories that are dependent upon the books of the Law, the Prophets, and the Writings, it was all but certain that Christianity must include those books in its own Bible. Named by Christians as the Old Testament, these writings gave Christians a way to appropriate the God story as their own "history," even as it remained the "history" of the Jews.

THE JESUS STORY

Christians, however, were and remain convinced that in one interpretation of the person of Jesus of Nazareth, the Messiah, the Christ, God had supremely acted to restore the old Covenant. In the stories of the miraculous birth, life, teachings and healings, and death and resurrection of Jesus, Christians found and find the embodiment of the ideas and ethical precepts in various combinations and emphases for their religious convictions. The writings that most directly and inclusively recount those stories are the four Gospels in the New Testament (the four, however, were selected from a considerably larger number, perhaps twelve or more that were written and circulated in the early centuries). In addition, other writings believed to bear the authority of the Apostles[5] were also regarded as crucial. Acts of the Apostles, letters to various churches from Paul, letters thought to be from other prominent Christians, such as Peter, James, and John and the Apocalypse of John (the Book of Revelation) came to be regarded as sacred writings and eventually were canonized as Scripture. These writings include stories and interpretations of the implications of the foundational stories. Some, such as Paul's letters to the church in Rome and to the church in Galatia have time and again in subsequent centuries been cited as critically important sources of and for theological reflection.

Thus, from the earliest stages until now, Christians have been storytelling peoples. The Old Testament and the New Testament are the repositories of foundational stories. Christians have been interpreters of the stories who have claimed their beliefs to be consonant with and explicative of those stories. Indeed, the twenty centuries of the history of Christianity[6] may be understood as the history of various interpretations of the scriptural stories. Not only familiarity with the stories, then, but also correct interpretation of them has been the ceaseless challenge confronting Christians through the centuries.

The God story, as Christians recount it, requires a confidence not only in God as the creative source—the Genesis stories and the doctrine of creation—but also in God as trustworthy at and beyond the end of everything. The Book of Revelation is the last book of the New Testament, and in it are recounted wondrous visions of a new heaven and new earth. As crucifixion is followed by resurrection in the stories of Jesus, so the end will, despite its apparent finality, be followed by unimaginable glory in the eternal presence of God. This story is one of the most beautiful and all-encompassing narratives to be found in any religious tradition.

THE JESUS STORY

The variety of Christian interpretations of the God story all depend upon the multiple interpretations of the Jesus story. This story is held by all who regard themselves as Christians to reveal the deepest and most abiding meaning of God in relation to the world and human existence. Anyone aspiring to be Christian

---

[5] See a discussion of the Apostles in Chap. 2.

[6] See Chap. 2.

is required to be familiar with, to understand, and to appropriate Jesus' life story because it is the center or hinge of history.

The diversity that has characterized Christianity since its beginnings is in large measure attributed directly to the variety of interpretations Christians have given to the Jesus story. Some regard him primarily as a great teacher, a Rabbi; others regard him as the culmination of the prophets of Israel. Both these perspectives emphasize his teachings and, in these views, Christianity tends to be regarded as the school of the heart and head. Those who learn their lessons are named Christians.

Others interpret Jesus, the Christ, as the incarnation of God in human form. This embodiment of God tends to be interpreted less in terms of the teachings given than in terms of the sacrifice of God to God. Incapable of making this sacrifice on their own, people require the sacrifice of a divine–human mediator. This motif undergirds the sacramental rituals that are presented in Christian patterns of worship.[7]

Still other interpretations of the Jesus story emphasize his having lived a morally exemplary life. True Christians promise to adopt the very highest in virtuous living to demonstrate their commitment. These different interpretations are not, of course, mutually exclusive and, typically, they will be found in various combinations and degrees of emphasis in different theologies.

It deserves to be carefully noted that the Jesus story provides the foundational structure for the patterns of Christian worship. In the most highly sacramental forms, this modelling can be seen quite clearly. The seasons of the Christian year hold the Jesus story to be central as they move from Christmas through Epiphany, Lent, and Easter. Preceded by Advent and followed by Pentecost, which mark the preparation for and the consequences of the coming of Jesus and the transformation of time, this way of dividing the calendar has its source in the Jesus story. Further, the occasional rituals—baptism, confirmation, matrimony, ordination, last rites—mark moments in the life of individual Christians that recapitulate events in the stories of Jesus, thus linking the individual as a microcosmic reflection to the universal drama of salvation.

THE IMPORTANCE OF THE STORIES

The centrality of stories for Christianity becomes ever more clear. Christian belief is founded upon the credibility of the God story and the Jesus story. For most people who regarded themselves as Christians in the centuries up to the Enlightenment in the West, it would scarcely have occurred to them to question the authenticity or credibility of those stories. The stories functioned to account for what was experienced, individually and collectively, even when the interpretations of

---

[7] See Chap. 6.

and meanings attributed to the stories markedly diverged. If today it seems naive to some readers and hearers to regard many of the Biblical narratives as being "true," such doubts seem only very infrequently to have beset ancient or medieval Christians. In the situation of religious pluralism of today, in which most persons are aware of religions alternative to their own, many suppose themselves to be accidentally Christians or mainly hereditary or cultural Christians. This often results in a kind of toleration and indifference, with the consequence that Christianity ceases to be radically significant to and for them. What is forgotten in such attitudes is that for millions of people, living and dead, Christianity has been experienced as formative, informative, and transformative. For those, it could never be a matter of indifference, even if they would be generous enough in spirit to respect and honor the religious commitments and convictions of adherents of other religions. For such committed Christians, it matters a very great deal not only *that* one believes but also *what* one believes.

CREEDS AS REPOSITORIES OF FAITH

Stories give expression to experience. Their retelling often occurs as translations into other forms as part of the unending quest for understanding. As we saw at the beginning of the chapter, a central mode of expression of the foundational beliefs of Christianity has been the Creed. A *creed* is a concise, authorized, formal expression of Christian beliefs, the classical instances of which are the Apostles' Creed and the Nicene Creed. Although the legend which tells of the twelve apostles gathering together and formulating the Apostles' Creed may not be "true" from the historical perspective, nonetheless, its importance and antiquity is great. It probably is traceable to a formula which was called "The Old Roman Creed or Symbol."[8] Its affirmations focus on the nature of God and on the universal (catholic) church.

Clearly, some person or institution must be regarded as having the authority to formulate, or at least to approve, such a creedal statement as authentic. The practice of using Creeds seems to trace to the early church in which candidates for baptism on Easter day would affirm their faith by reciting a Creed. It was a way of expressing to the congregation that the candidate's understanding was in accord with her or his participation in the ritual and subsequently in the community. Also, recitation or the exact repetition of particular words is recognized crossculturally as a symbolically powerful act. In the rhythmic resounding of the words, all time is recounted and is transcended. The words uttered in the present recount the past and tell of the future. They unite the believer with the community

---

[8] The Apostles' Creed in its present form is said to be first quoted by St. Pirminius in the early eighth century and is an elaboration of the shorter "Old Roman Creed" that had itself evolved from earlier, simpler texts that had survived for centuries and were based on Christ's threefold baptismal commands in Matthew 28:19.

of those faithful who have gone before and with those who are to come. They unite the one standing in the world of continual change with those who are partaking in eternity.

In its Christian particularity, the ritual recitation of the Creed itself was a way of identifying an individual and a community with the story of the baptism of Jesus and with the church's adoption of baptism as its primary rite of initiation into Christianity.[9] The words of the modern version of the Apostles' Creed are these:

> *I believe in God, the Father Almighty, creator of heaven*
> *and earth.*
> *I believe in Jesus Christ, His only Son, our Lord.*
> *He was conceived by the power of the Holy Spirit and*
> *born of the Virgin Mary.*
> *He suffered under Pontius Pilate, was crucified, died,*
> *and was buried.*
> *He descended to the dead.*[10]
> *On the third day he rose again.*
> *He ascended into heaven, and is seated at the right hand*
> *of the Father.*
> *He will come again to judge the living and the dead.*
> *I believe in the Holy Spirit, the holy catholic church,*
> *the communion of saints, the forgiveness of sins,*
> *the resurrection of the body,*
> *and the life everlasting. Amen.*

Even the idea and usage of Creeds is one index to Christian diversity. Many Protestant forms of Christianity have developed their own creedal statements to augment or substitute for the ancient creeds. The newer statements are often called "confessions of faith" or "affirmations of faith."

Note should also be taken of the place of Creeds in the Orthodox Churches of the East (Greek, Russian, Syrian, *et al.*). In doing this, however, one must recognize that the Orthodox Churches are opposed in principle to the authoritarian attitude so prominent in the Western churches, Protestant as well as Roman Catholic. As Brian Gerrish remarks, the Eastern Orthodox Church "contents itself with what are considered to be the bare minimum of essential dogmas and allows extensive freedom for the exercise of theological insight."[11] Further, he

---

[9] See Chap. 6.

[10] The versions of the Apostles' Creed and the Nicene Creed (see page 90) used in this book are those of the 1979 *Book of Common Prayer.* The wording differs somewhat from the older version perhaps most significantly in line 8, "He descended into hell," and lines 4 and 13 where "Holy Ghost" has been replaced by "Holy Spirit," as is also true in the Nicene Creed.

[11] *The Faith of Christendom: A Source Book of Creeds and Confessions,* Brian A. Gerrish, ed., New York: World Publishing Company, 1963, p. 259.

rightly observes: "Many Orthodox beliefs and practices . . . are sanctioned more by the liturgy than by special dogmatic definitions . . . This means that the liturgy itself constitutes a doctrinal norm for the Eastern Christian: *lex orandi, lex credendi.*"[12] The legalistic uses to which Western churches have inclined regarding Creeds and other theological formulations is foreign to the Orthodox Churches. They have not, however, been theologically stagnant; they have, rather, retained a much greater sense of the mystery to which all beliefs and their conceptual expressions are pointing and which none can capture.

If the Apostles' Creed was derivative from the "Old Roman Symbol," then the word "symbol" is significant in understanding some of the multiple meanings of any Creed. The formula may have served as a password for entrance to the community, or as a pact with God made by the initiate. The liturgical (ritualistic) use of creeds clearly suggests that, as was and is the case with every other element in a worship service, they are multi-meaningful. That is one of the characteristics that has helped Creeds survive centuries of changing circumstances of Christians who have recited them in many languages, in many cultures.

The other classical creed is called the "Nicene Creed." This creed was issued by the first Council of Nicaea (in modern Turkey), which met in 325. It was convened by the emperor Constantine to deal with the dispute over the doctrine known as Arianism that was dividing the church. The Arians held that the Son of God, incarnate in Jesus Christ, was created by God and therefore lesser than God, and had come into being later than God. The some three hundred bishops who attended the Council decisively rejected this view, affirming the essential unity of God the Father and God the Son by saying the latter is "of one Being with the Father." The Greek term *homoousion*, "of one being or essence," although not a biblical expression, was pointedly used instead of the Arian preference *homoiousion*, "of like or similar nature." This creed, then, served not only as a symbol of inward faith like the earlier Apostles' Creed, but also as a test of intellectual adherence to the statement of belief the majority of church leaders, and the Constantinian state, held was orthodox. It has a place in worship, however, as the creed generally used in the eucharist of the traditional liturgical churches. The text of the Nicene Creed is as follows:

> *We believe in one God,*
> *the Father, the Almighty,*
> *maker of heaven and earth,*
> *of all that is, seen and unseen.*
>
> *We believe in one Lord, Jesus Christ,*
> *the only Son of God,*
> *eternally begotten of the Father,*
> *God from God, Light from Light,*

---

[12] Gerrish, p. 300. "The law of worship is the law of belief."

true God from true God,
begotten, not made,
of one Being with the Father.
Through him all things were made.
For us and for our salvation he came down from
heaven: by the power of the Holy Spirit he became
incarnate from the Virgin Mary, and was made man.
For our sake he was crucified under Pontius Pilate;
he suffered death and was buried.
On the third day he rose again in accordance with
the Scriptures;
he ascended into heaven and is seated at the right
hand of the Father.
He will come again in glory to judge the living and
the dead, and his kingdom will have no end.

We believe in the Holy Spirit, the Lord, the giver of
life, who proceeds from the Father and the Son.
With the Father and Son he is worshipped and
glorified.
He has spoken through the Prophets.
We believe in one holy catholic and apostolic
church.
We acknowledge one baptism for the forgiveness of
sins.
We look for the resurrection of the dead, and the
life of the world to come. Amen.[13]

Perhaps enough has been said thus far to indicate that the formulation of belief or theology is, as Theodore Jennings has expressed it, "reflection on the Christian mythos."[14] "Mythos" as used in that definition, incorporates rituals, stories, symbols, and assertions that taken together serve to represent, orient, communicate, and transform human existence by re-presenting the sacred for a community of persons. Life is "life together" in a group that shares common convictions derived from honored stories and enacted rituals. The formulating of concepts into assertions that are regarded as both amplifying and explicating and remaining consistent with the stories, rituals, and symbols is a very appropriate description of the practice and aim of theology in the Christian community.

Theology is a human activity in the obvious sense that human beings do it. Although it has to do with an effort to give expression to and to understand the transformative experience of ultimate reality, theology is an effort of people—

---

[13] See note 10 on page 89.
[14] Theodore Jennings, *Introduction to Theology.* Philadelphia: Fortress Press, 1976, p. 2.

live, finite women and men. God does not, so far as we know, do theology. As a human activity in the broadest sense, anyone with an interest in doing so can reflect on the mythos of any religion, regardless of whether she or he is a participant in the faith community of that religion. To be sure, most theologians are members of the traditions upon which they focus their reflections. But in principle, that is not a necessary condition for reflecting on the Christian, or any other, mythos since the motive is to understand and to give expression to formulations that are consistent with the mythos.

DOCTRINE AND DOGMAS

Over the centuries, when theologians have reflected on the Christian mythos, certain issues have again and again demanded attention. The gatherings of bishops on the occasions that are called ecumenical councils have demonstrated Christianity's intense interest in formulating assertions consistent with the rest of its expressions. Virtually all Christians acknowledge that the issues debated in the first four such councils (Nicea, 325; Constantinople I, 381; Ephesus, 431; and Chalcedon, 451) were crucial. The Eastern Orthodox and Anglican churches also honor the decisions of the fifth, sixth, and seventh such councils. Roman Catholics regard the decisions of twenty-one such councils, the last of which was Vatican II (1961–1965), all to be decisive.

However, theology is not confined to the thought of the participants in some or all such gatherings. It goes on all the time when persons reflect on meanings of the Christian mythos. Nor is it the case that the "best" theologians were necessarily to be found among the conciliar participants, for some of the greatest theologians in the history of Christianity (see below) never participated in a council. But it is indisputably the case that the topics treated by the councils have time and again occupied the attention of theologians, many of whom articulated opinions that were strikingly in contrast to decisions of the councils. Ferment in theologizing, in fact, often precipitated the need for a new council to be convened to sort out the alternatives and to reach an appropriate resolution.

The aspiration to reach a resolution touches an issue that is always a concern in theology, namely, on what authority is a theological opinion proposed? Christians divide irreconcilably over the issue of authority. The concept of a council of bishops who claimed the authority to make decisions for all Christians was predicated upon their belief that the office of bishop can be traced directly to the Apostles. As the Apostles (except Paul) were the disciples of Jesus and knew him and his thinking most intimately, and as the bishops are the direct spiritual descendants of the Apostles, the decisions of the bishops are informed by their direct link to Jesus. Thus, their decisions have binding authority. This argument is formally known as the Doctrine of Apostolic Succession. In almost all churches governed by bishops today, some trace at least of this argument may still be found.

But Apostolic Succession is only one way of grounding the authority of the

Church. Other Christians have been persuaded from the beginning that no office guarantees the legitimacy of the opinions of the persons who may occupy that office. Such Christians believe that individual bishops and collections of bishops in council can make mistakes in their theological opinions as certainly as in other matters. Martin Luther (1483–1546) is emblematic of the resistance to the authority of bishops and of a church that supported such authority. Luther contended that only the Word of God, as witnessed to in the Bible, exerts binding authority on the minds and hearts of Christians. *Sola scriptura* ("Scripture alone") was his cry of refusal to submit to tradition-based ecclesiastical authority. Yet, the splintering of Protestantism into hundreds of denominational churches is testimony to the difficulty inherent in Luther's position. Fundamental questions are raised, such as: whose interpretation of Scripture is to be accorded authority?

The effects of such disputes over the authoritative status of certain theological assertions are manifest in the distinction between dogma and doctrine. A *dogma* (from the Greek, *dokein*, "to think") is an officially sanctioned belief or *doctrine* (from the Latin, *doctrina*, "teaching") that is regarded as so basic and central that to deny it is grounds for being expelled (excommunicated) from the church. Obviously, the very idea of dogma presupposes the authority of the church (through its bishops) to formulate statements of belief in a binding, indisputable way. Heresy (from the Greek, *hairein*, "to take, choose") is the name given to opinions held that are inconsistent with dogma. A person who denies the necessity of accepting a particular teaching in order to be a Christian, or who chooses another way, is subject to being condemned as a heretic. Predictably, Martin Luther was, in 1521, condemned as a heretic as a result of his adamant rejection of dogma and the authority of tradition. Since then, Protestant Christianity has by and large consistently denied that any church or theologian is capable of formulating dogmas.

The perspective of Protestant Christianity may become clearer by considering the word "Protestant" itself. Historically, the word "protestant" was first used to describe the German princes who participated in the Diet of Spires (1529) that came about in protest against an edict intending to crush the development of the Reformation in Germany. In the seventeenth century, the word referred to adherents of Lutheranism or Anglicanism and later came to include Puritans, Presbyterians, and others, who from the orthodox perspective, were dissenters. Later, the word came to describe any Christian not of the Roman Catholic or Eastern Orthodox churches. The term is rejected by many members of the churches of the Anglican communion.

Rooted in the Latin *protestantis*, Protestants etymologically are those who are continually protesting. They represent a formal objection; their existence is an ongoing remonstrance to a church that tends to become institution-bound and a theology that becomes rigidified. Further, the Latin *protestari*, "to protest," means to be a witness, to affirm the experience of truth. Thus, their name indicates that Protestants are those who bear witness to the ongoing experience of truth unmediated by a humanly constructed hierarchy that must always be subject to sin.

John Calvin. Photo courtesy of Musée Historique de la Reformation, Geneva.

Truth is, rather, directly experienced by the believer in her or his engagement with the word of God: *sola scriptura.*

Within the Protestant churches, the principle of "always reforming" applies no less to beliefs than to institutional forms and patterns of governance. Thus, most of them teach certain doctrines as patterns of belief, but they have historically been less rigid in testing the commitment of individuals to those beliefs as a condition for admission or continuation in the membership of the church. Rather, behavior inconsistent with the moral teachings of such churches has far more frequently been the basis for expelling members. This means that how one acts is regarded to be more important than precisely what one believes.

But here it is possible to hear the echo of a problem encountered by Protestantism as much as by Catholicism. It is the problem encountered whenever a vision becomes concretised into an institution. The dynamic between church and founding experience is forgotten. The stories that carry vision into history are replaced by doctrines that become laws to be taken only literally. Etched in stone by fire from the finger of God and placed in the Ark of the Covenant, the laws given to Moses were transportable. Although eternal, they were also moveable and thus had flexibility. But the stones of the law that in the beginning form the firm foundation of the temple or church tend to become petrified under the weight of the establishment built upon it. "Living stones" no longer breathe, laws are no longer moveable. Truth becomes the one truth to be understood in only one way, identically applicable to all believers in all times and places.

The different attitudes toward the authority, importance, and adequacy of beliefs stated as assertions and toward the centrality of "right action" is another index to Christian diversity. Yet within this complex of concerns, certain specific issues have preoccupied some of the most notable Christian thinkers through the centuries. There are assertions that for having been preserved for hundreds of years and believed by millions of Christians carry great weight and significance. We shall attend to several of them by way of suggesting how they are formed and the role they play.

Foundational for most Christians through the centuries has been a response to the question: Who was Jesus? Responses to that question reflect a variety of influences on any particular thinker who attempts to answer. Some, of course, emphasized the importance of the testimony of eye witnesses of Jesus' life and teachings. The several Gospel accounts were regarded as providing the basis for an adequate assessment of Jesus. But that presented a problem. Everyone knew that Paul had never seen or known Jesus during his lifetime. Yet, Paul had in several of his writings in the form of letters to various churches thought deeply and written very influential reflections on the meaning and significance of Jesus. Further, in subsequent decades of the first, second and third centuries, Christian thinkers often felt free to use the resources of Greek philosophy as well as the Jewish Bible in formulating their views of the meaning and significance of Jesus. Thus, there was, from earliest times, an implicit acknowledgment of the tension between regarding Scripture as ultimately authoritative and accepting the fact that thinking is always influenced by the sociocultural context within which it occurs. This is no less the case for theological thinking than for any other kind.

Christian thinkers in their estimates of Jesus and his importance recognized that the Jewishness of Jesus was a fact to be reckoned with. The most frequent way of responding to that was the assertion that Jesus was the fulfillment of prophecy within Judaism. Isaiah 53 was an oft-cited Jewish writing that to the mind of many Christian theologians had accurately foreseen the work of Jesus and of which Jesus was the final fulfillment:

> *Who has believed what we have heard?*
> *And to whom has the arm of the Lord*
>   *been revealed?*
> *For he grew up before him like a young*
>   *plant,*
>   *and like a root out of dry ground;*
>   *he had no form or comeliness that we*
>   *should look at him,*
>   *and no beauty that we should desire*
>   *him*

He was despised and rejected by men;
  a man of sorrows, and acquainted
      with grief;
and as one from whom men hide their faces
  he was despised, and we esteemed him
      not.

Surely he has borne our griefs
  and carried our sorrows;
yet we esteemed him stricken,
  smitten by God, and afflicted.
But he was wounded for our
      transgressions,
  he was bruised for our iniquities;
  upon him was the chastisement that
      made us whole,
  and with his stripes we are healed.
All we like sheep have gone astray;
  we have turned every one to his own
      way;
  and the Lord has laid on him the
      iniquity of us all.

He was oppressed, and he was afflicted,
  yet he opened not his mouth;
  like a lamb that is led to the
      slaughter,
  and like a sheep that before its
      shearers is dumb,
  so he opened not his mouth.
By oppression and judgment he was taken
      away;
  and as for his generation, who
      considered
  that he was cut off out of the land
      of the living,
  stricken for the transgression of my
      people?
And they made his grave with the wicked
  and with a rich man in his death,
  although he had done no violence,
      and there was no deceit in his
      mouth.

> *Yet it was the will of the Lord to bruise*
> *   him;*
> *he has put him to grief;*
> *when he makes himself an offering*
> *   for sin,*
> *he shall see his offspring, he shall*
> *   prolong his days;*
> *the will of the Lord shall prosper*
> *   in his hand;*
> *he shall see the fruit of the*
> *   travail of his soul and be*
> *   satisfied;*
> *by his knowledge shall the righteous*
> *   one, my servant,*
> *make many to be accounted righteous;*
> *and he shall bear their iniquities.*
> *Therefore I will divide him a portion*
> *   with the great,*
> *and he shall divide the spoil with*
> *   the strong;*
> *because he poured out his soul to*
> *   death,*
> *and was numbered with the*
> *   transgressors;*
> *yet he bore the sin of many,*
> *   and made intercession for the*
> *   transgressors.*

Without resorting here to commenting extensively on themes within this ancient Jewish prophetic writing, it should be clear that such a passage could be utilized by Christian thinkers to support an argument that Jesus was the culmination of what Jews had religiously awaited for centuries. The effect of this line of argument was an affirmation by Christians of the importance of revelation within Judaism, while at the same time claiming the finality of revelation in Christ Jesus. Similar kinds of arguments drew upon pagan sources to indicate that Jesus was no less the embodiment of what the pagans had sought, as well. Past prophecy and revelation had been fulfilled in Jesus; that was one common Christian response to the question of who Jesus was. These are instances, it must be clear, of Christian interpretation of materials that others, before and after Christians, interpreted in quite different ways.

Not only the mainstream (orthodox) theologians, but also those whose views came to be regarded as heterodox (heretical) appealed to sacred writings and sources available in the larger culture. Basic to selecting whatever resources were to be drawn upon, and, even more importantly, to how those sources would be interpreted, were the deepest religious beliefs of the thinker-interpreter. And, of course, giving expression to those deeply held beliefs was the task of theological reflection. Many theologians held that everything else hinged on two issues: the real humanity of Jesus and the unity of God. The previously discussed issue of authority was inseparable from these two, or from any other theological issues. Further, the claim that one view is correct and all others incorrect depends upon an appeal to some authority to legitimize that decision: the church's pronouncement, God's direct communication with the believer, religious experience or some other basis.

THE NATURE OF CHRIST

If Jesus were not fully human, he would not have experienced the limitations, trials, sorrows, joys that are all experienced by actual women and men. If he were not human, his suffering, passion, and death would not have been real in the way that humans experience them. If he were a spirit with only the appearance or outward form of a human body, his gifts to and his works in behalf of humanity would be less consequential or beneficial. Such were some of the assertions made by defenders of the real humanity of Christ against others, who, in their concern to express their belief in the divinity of Christ, felt compelled to deemphasize and sometimes even to deny the humanity of Christ. The latter thinkers were determined to safeguard their conviction that in Christ God was doing for people what they were incapable of doing for themselves. Only by divine intervention could salvation take place. The nub of the problem was how to give expression to the complex belief in both the full humanity and the full divinity of Christ, both of which have their foundation in the Jesus stories, in such a way as to avoid unintentionally slipping into one or the other viewpoint and thereby reducing the paradox to a literalism. The orthodox view of this matter was expressed in the Nicene Creed (see above).

The heresy most prominently rejected by the Council of Nicea (325), as we have seen, has been called *Arianism*. Arius was an extremely influential teacher in the late third and early fourth centuries. Beginning from a belief in the radical otherness (transcendence) of God separated from creation, including humanity, by an unbridgeable gulf, Arius doggedly held to the view that no creature could have participated in the being of God without changing God. And the unchangeability of God was and has remained one of the cherished beliefs of many Christians. In contrast, the passing of time changes the natural world and all that is in it, and most obviously humans are changeable. Thus, so the defenders of belief in an unchangeable God argue, no human being could participate in the being of God. The logic of this argument concluded that the "Son of God" was a created being and in that respect like all other creatures. The instrument through which God created the world and all the creatures was the *Logos* (Greek for "word" or "reason"). This creative agent is "higher" than humanity, by virtue of having always chosen to avoid sin, but "lower" than God by virtue of itself being the first of God's creatures. This subordination of the Logos to God and its elevation above humanity accomplished for Arius the double advantage of preserving both the belief in the unchangeable nature of God and the belief in the more-than-human nature of Christ. But another way of seeing this suggests that the manner in which Arius placed the Logos as mediator between humanity and God did not offer movement across the separating gulf but rather a widening of the abyss. If he is neither fully divine nor fully human, the Logos can participate fully in neither.

THE UNITY OF GOD

The larger context within which Arianism must be seen was the attempt by Christians to find a way to express their beliefs regarding the nature of God. All of this was to be seen within the context of the near universal practice among Christians of baptizing initiates into Christianity with the words: " . . . in the name of the Father, the Son, and the Holy Spirit," whatever they might believe as assertions regarding the meaning of those words (see the Apostles' Creed above). The trinitarian formula—Father, Son, Spirit—was what was required to be understood, as best they could find ways to do so. In their determination to preserve their belief in God the Father's unchangeability, Arians were forced to express their belief in the nature of Christ as derivative, and less than the nature of the Father.

What was really at issue in the orthodox Christian insistence on the trinitarian assertion regarding the three persons of the Godhead? At least a partial response to why the emphasis on the Trinity was so consistently made is caught up in a remarkable passage from the writings of Gregory of Nyssa (c. 330–c. 395). "The Jewish dogma [of monotheism] is destroyed by the acceptance of the Logos and by belief in the Spirit, while the polytheistic error of the Greek school is made to vanish by the unity of the [divine] nature abrogating the notion of plurality. . . . It is as if the number of the Trinity were a remedy in the case of those who are in error as to the One, and the assertion of the unity for those whose beliefs are dispersed among a number of divinities."[15] Christ, the divine and eternal Logos of God, had transcended Greek polytheism and Jewish monotheism and by countering the tendency to assert either the oneness of God or the multiplicity of the gods and thereby preserving the paradoxical nature of the divine had shed light on problems unanswerable from one side or the other.

A trinitarian belief required asserting the divinity of the Holy Spirit no less than that of Christ. However, the experience of the mystery of the Spirit is such

---

[15] Gregory of Nyssa, *Catechetical Orations* from *Patrologia Graeca* (Paris, 1857–1866), Vol. 45, pp. 17–20.

that assertions made regarding the third person of the trinity have remained more flexible than those regarding the nature of Christ. The Spirit's inspiration has, in fact, been claimed as the basis for enormously diverse forms of Christian practices and beliefs. Thus, an unchanging Father, a fully divine *and* human Son incarnate in Jesus of Nazareth, and a mysterious Spirit have traditionally characterized beliefs regarding the persons of the one God who is triune.

The doctrinal assertions regarding the nature of God and the incarnate Christ were so crucial because they were central to describing the saving effect or work of Christ. And in order to do that well, assertions regarding the condition of humanity that was to be saved were also required. Technically, the theological issues are *soteriology* (doctrine of salvation) and *anthropology* (doctrine of the human condition). One other inseparable doctrine is that pertaining to Satan (the Devil). Together these doctrines give a picture of Reality; to many they offer a map of the passageway through this life to immortality.

In the traditional Creeds the coming of Christ is invariably asserted to have happened for the salvation of all people. The corollary, repeated through the centuries, is that God in Christ did for people what they are incapable of accomplishing for themselves. Further, humanity is incapable, even though made in "the image of God" (Genesis) and only slightly "lower than the angels" (Psalms), because of sin.

Traditionally, "sin" describes the state of being separated or alienated from God, whereas "sins" are actions that arise from and express that condition of alienation. In ritual confessions of sin, although specific acts are repented, the deeper confession is for being a sinner; it is a recognition of being in a condition in which it is impossible not to commit sins. This archetypal human condition, as recounted in the God story and discussed earlier in this chapter, is brought to expression in the imagery of the Fall of Adam and Eve.

The readings of this story given by the theological tradition assert that by their exercise of will and response to temptation, they broke their relation with God, or rather so dramatically altered it that neither they nor any of their offspring could, by their own work and effort, restore themselves to that right (original) relation. In the story told in Genesis, it was a serpent which beguiled Eve and then Adam into disobeying God's instructions. And much of the Christian tradition has identified the serpent with Satan or the Devil, the Lord of darkness whose realm is the tormenting pit of Hell. The serpent is so designated by the tradition despite the fact that the story does not give it a name.

In cosmic scale, the human situation is then traditionally imagined as one in which God and Satan are engaged in eternal combat for mastery of the souls of all. Nor is it clear—until the coming of Christ, Son of God—who will win the war. Thus, Satan is an indispensable figure in traditional Christianity. Without him, it would be unclear why God had to do what he did in bringing salvation through Christ. Satan had, once and for all, to be vanquished.

Other branches of the tradition have also offered microcosmic interpretations of the fundamental tension that places both demons and angels within the soul of the individual where they are forever held in dynamic tension. Here the heights and depths of the founding Biblical stories are seen as the interplay of psychic states.

Although Christians insistently assert that through Christ salvation was made possible, there has never been a single doctrine that achieved a consensus expressing the meaning of salvation. Was it a cure for an otherwise incurable disease? Was it the provision of knowledge without which humanity is doomed to ignorance? Was it a fish hook by which humanity is lured from the clutches of the Devil? Was it a satisfaction of the conditions of justice that were necessary to be met if a just God were to readmit humanity to his company? Was it a ransom price paid to Satan who had kidnapped humanity and held it in bondage? All of these, and many others, were theories or images of salvation expressed at one time or another in the course of Christian theologizing.

Other occasionally popular ways of getting at essentially the same issue of salvation emphasized the work of Christ as a great teacher whose pupils learned from him the way back to God. Or, Jesus was extolled as the example of how humanity should live in relation to God, and thus as the one supremely to be imitated by Christians. But perhaps the most recurring motif is that of Christ, whose cruel death as a sacrifice restored humanity to the possibility of living reconciled with God. This view is the foundation of the sacraments of the Eucharist and of Penance.[16] Each of these images speaks of one face of the multifaceted nature of the divine. Throughout the tradition, problems have arisen when one aspect of divine nature has been chosen to the exclusion of all others; when God is reduced to one form, then worship becomes idolatrous.

Thus, human beings responsible for what they have become in complicity with Satan, but powerless on their own to repair themselves, have been visited by God the Son through whom salvation is made possible. This is one of the recurrent patterns of Christian belief and repeats itself with varying emphases.

Such beliefs, especially those that emphasize the role of Satan and the limitations on the capacity of individuals to achieve their own salvation, are severely challenged by widely shared presuppositions in today's scientific world. The work of two theologians whose ways of thinking have exerted enormous influence through long periods of Christianity, namely, St. Augustine and Martin Luther, show that both of them had in their day and age to deal with culturally dominated presuppositions that were impeding understanding of the Christian beliefs. Both were reinterpreters of their tradition.

St. Augustine (345–430)

Among the many persons who have reflected most deeply on the Christian story and whose reflections have been most influential on others, some twenty theo-

---

[16] See Chap. 6.

logians have been regarded as "Doctors of the Church" in Western Catholic Christianity. Augustine of Hippo, born to a pagan father and a Christian mother in North Africa, is one of the first four theologians who came to be regarded as a Doctor of the Church. The details of his biography, fascinating in themselves, include his education in rhetoric; his conversion first to the Manichean religion, then to NeoPlatonic philosophy, and finally to Christianity; his monastic, celibate lifestyle; his being forcibly drafted by the people to become a priest; his thirty-four years as a bishop in the city of Hippo; and his prolific literary career—each of these is worth extensive study. But in this brief account, attention can only be given to Augustine as a theologian of monumental influence and significance, and only a very limited number of his theological assertions can be explored.

St. Augustine's career occurred during the dissolution of the Roman Empire. The old was passing away and being replaced violently by the new. Anxiety was great and scapegoats were eagerly sought. As Christianity had only become a licensed religion early in the fourth century[17] and later in the same century come to be the official religion of the empire, it was hardly surprising that opponents of Christianity would seize upon the barbarian conquest of province after province of the Roman Empire as evidence of the weakness, deficiency, and falseness of Christianity. After all, they argued, Christianity's God was not strong enough to prevent the defeat of the Empire. This argument against Christianity was one that occupied Augustine over a long period of reflection (413–426) and culminated in his masterful work, *The City of God*. Few other writings by Christian theologians have exerted remotely comparable influence.

The major premise of the book is a belief in the necessity of distinguishing between the celestial city (City of God) and the worldly or terrestrial city (city of humankind). Given the pervasiveness and unavoidability of sin by and among humans, Augustine counseled faith in God alone. This world is constantly in flux and will pass away; the city of God by contrast is dependable and trustworthy because God is its providential sustainer. Belief in essentially this form of a "theology of history" prevailed among Christian theologians until well into the nineteenth century, when a secularized "philosophy of history" was developed to challenge it. Comparative study of the work of such philosophers as Marx and Hegel with that of Augustine suggests, however, that in spite of material differences of content, they still were expressing views remarkably compatible at a formal level with those of Augustine.

As the creator of a major genre of literature, Augustine is widely known for his spiritual autobiography, *The Confessions* (c. 399). As a story of his spiritual journey that recounts with astonishing candor his temptations and failures, it can be read as a subjective companion to *The City of God*. The individual, says Augustine in the *Confessions,* is as utterly dependent upon the grace of God for salvation and the forgiveness of sins as is the whole world, according to *The City of*

---

[17] See Chap. 3.

God. Both of these major writings can be heard to resound the archetypal themes of the God story and the Jesus story in language specific to their time and place.

The more technical (though not necessarily more profound or influential) theological writings authored by Augustine were often generated by controversies in the church. Thus, these writings are highly polemical. Three such controversies were especially important for the views they evoked from Augustine and for communicating a flavor of his thinking.

The first of the controversies arose concerning Manichean influences that were understood to be infecting the thought of some Christians. The focus of the debate was the problem of evil (or *Theodicy,* the problem of the justice of God). The Manichean view was dualistic. It held that an independent, coeternal evil force is forever combatting a benevolent God. The effect of this duality was, in Augustine's view, a belief in a force equal to (and potentially greater than) the power of God. Augustine's rejoinder was carried in the view that God is the source of everything, the solitary creator. Evil, then, is not an independently existing coequal power but, rather, is the absence or "lack of good," *privatio bonum,* from the Latin. Imperfect creatures, lacking in total goodness, do evil in the world by virtue of exercising free will, which in order to be free will has to be capable of choosing evil as well as good.

This particular debate is a highly abstract and metaphysical one, important in its own realm. But it might be helpful to imagine this controversy in another way offered by the *Confessions.* For Augustine, the world is not dualistically good and evil; all is within God. Evil or lack of goodness can then be thought of as turning away from this recognition. Evil is like blindness, loss of perspective, or unconscious forgetfulness. But, as in Augustine's own experience, in the midst of this darkness there is another "turn" or "con-version." Experiencing evil is bad, yet it can also lead us to want, and finally to recognize, the good. Like the "Prodigal Son" (Luke 18:11–32), one can return home to the place where, in the depths of his memory, one had always been. As Augustine remembers:

> *You were within me, and I was in the world outside*
> *myself.*
> *I searched for you outside myself and, disfigured as I*
> *was, I fell upon the lovely things of your creation.*
> *You were with me, but I was not with you.* [18]

The second, the *Donatist* controversy, was crucial for developing the doctrine of the church and its sacraments. Donatus was a bishop consecrated by schismatic bishops in Africa. These leaders had broken with the Roman church over the interpretation of the validity of sacraments administered by priests who had ca-

---

[18] Saint Augustine, *Confessions,* R. S. Pine-Coffin, trans. Baltimore: Penguin Books, 1961, Book X, 27, p. 231.

pitulated under persecution but who subsequently repented. It was the view of the Donatists that in order for a sacrament to be valid, the administrator (priest or bishop) must be "holy" in order to officiate at sacramental rituals. Like the "errors" portrayed in the stories of the Garden of Eden and the Tower of Babel, this view seems to suggest that holiness is a state that can be worked for and permanently achieved. Whereas, Augustine's more radical view was that the worthiness, or lack of it, of a priest or bishop was not the proper issue. Removing the possibility of confusing grace freely given by God with a human power, he argued that Christ is the true minister of the sacraments and that, so long as the intention of the priest was to do what Christ intended to do, the "validity" of the sacrament can be trusted. He argued further that God alone can judge the "holiness" of anyone, priest or lay person, and that since the subjective state of the priest is unknowable by anyone else, the issue must be focussed upon the objective character of the sacrament itself.

Augustine insisted that a sacrament is "the visible form of an invisible grace." Grace is made present through and in the sacrament because God in Christ has chosen that such shall be the case, he asserted. It is not because of the worthiness of the priest. Far more than a moral issue is at stake here. As the stories tell, Christ did not become incarnate because humanity deserved it; the Hebrews did not become the chosen people because they were the purest. Far from it. The pattern is of the "least likely" one being raised up as were Abraham, Joseph, Moses, and then Christ who was born in a stable and executed as a criminal. Grace cannot be earned; it is, rather, an immediate experience that grants a particular perspective on existence. For Augustine, provided only that the right matter (water for baptism, bread and wine for the Eucharist) is used in the right form (the priestly consecration) with the right intention, the sacrament is valid and does its work "in and through itself" (*ex opere operato*). The Church, further, was instituted by Christ to be the instrument through which the sacraments shall always be available to humanity. Deficient though the church as a human institution may be in many respects, sinful though its leaders and participants assuredly are, so long as the church provides the sacraments its reason for being is served. The Donatist heresy was condemned in a local council in Carthage in 411, but persisted in Africa until the seventh-century Muslim conquest.

The third controversy, named for Pelagius who attacked Augustine for one of the sentences in *Confessions,* focused on the human condition, i.e., on Christian anthropology. Of necessity, the *Pelagian* controversy involved the meaning of doctrines of the Fall, of Original Sin, and Predestination. The issues are so complex and detailed that even the most extensively informed students of this controversy sometimes disagree in their efforts to explain it. The following comments, however, express what is generally accepted. Pelagius contended that the sin of Adam in the Garden of Eden (Genesis 3) injured only himself and not the entire human race. Pelagius further insisted that newborn children are in the same condition as Adam was before he sinned and are capable, as he was due to free will, not to sin. Augustine insisted in reply that humans as originally created had certain supernatural gifts that were lost in the Fall of Adam. Consequently, after Adam each person necessarily suffers from an inherited moral disease and is liable for its consequences. God's grace alone can provide salvation from those consequences.

Pelagius rejected belief in Predestination (the doctrine which holds that God has preordained who shall and shall not be saved). Augustine affirmed belief in that doctrine. Officially, Augustine won the controversy and Pelagius was repeatedly condemned for heretical teachings. But innumerable Christians through the centuries have been closer to Pelagius in their beliefs on these matters than to Augustine. How can this controversy be understood in relation to human experience? Again, more than morality is at stake. In the story, the consequence of the Fall of Adam and Eve is mortality. Being in a state of sin, then, appears to be a way of describing the experience of finitude, of being "not-God." To insist with Pelagius that sinfulness or mortality is a choice is to deny experience, and to seek to make mortals identical to the divine. Couched in Augustine's language can be heard the full acceptance of finitude and the accompanying experience of grace that brings the knowledge of eternal life in death.

St. Augustine was a towering intellectual figure in the history of Christian theology and church life. Beyond the instances cited above and his involvement with the larger world historical events such as the Teutonic peoples' conquests of the Roman Empire, he made many other great contributions. He was a prolific expositor and commentator on Scripture. Scriptural authority was crucial in formulating his theological positions. He had a profound sense of the importance not only of what one believes but also of how one expresses what one believes. His training in rhetoric enabled him to employ an array of styles of discourse. He was as accomplished a narrator as he was a debater. His sensitivity to language, to eloquence, to poetry, and to aesthetics matched his passion for truth. The volume of his writing in the midst of his other involvements and commitments was enormous. His was a determination to attempt to achieve proportion and conformity between his beliefs and his devotion to the stories, the rituals, and the symbols of the religion that had claimed him and laid its demands for intellectual honesty upon him. Few Christian theologians before or since have so nearly accomplished that purpose as witnessed by the importance of his writings even today for those who seek a better understanding of Christian beliefs.

Martin Luther (1483–1546)

The Protestant Reformation of the sixteenth century in Germany erupted in an Augustinian monastery under the leadership of a monk named Martin Luther. Just as St. Augustine had in the fifth century, Luther experienced a radical turning point that he attributed solely to the grace of God. Just as Augustine has exerted influence on Catholic Christianity (as well as certain strands of Protestantism, including Luther and Calvin), so Luther has profoundly influenced Protestant Christianity. The formulations of many of his central beliefs were also produced in the heat of controversy with other theologians. But given the direction of Protestantism toward diversity, Luther's influence was and is proportionately far less upon the subsequent generations of Protestants than Augustine's was within later Catholicism.

Theologians within Protestantism have tended to be influential only within a closely circumscribed tradition. As one learns something of what Luther believed and taught as a theologian, it must be remembered that if a more rounded picture of Protestant Christian beliefs is desired, one must move out from Luther within Lutheranism, to Zwingli and Calvin in the Reformed tradition, to some of the radical reformers in the free churches, to Wesley and Methodism, and on and on. The hundreds of Protestant denominations in the United States are traceable to individuals or groups that typically split off from one of the other older branches of Protestantism. Often this was a result of disagreements regarding church governance and policies more than it was from disputes regarding theological beliefs. This suggests that theology is by no means the only source of friction and strife in the history of Protestant Christianity.

The preceding glance at Protestant diversity is appropriate in this section on Luther as it emphasizes the radicality of his break with Catholic Christianity. Against the cumulative weight of a tradition that was claimed by its defenders to stretch directly over 1500 years to Jesus of Nazareth and his disciples, Luther dared to stand. For Catholic Christianity, tradition has equal authority with Scripture for informing Christians of what was acceptable and appropriate belief.

During the centuries after the fall of the Roman Empire, the flame of literacy had been reduced to a flicker. The renaissance of learning, preserved largely in the monasteries, had occurred in the twelfth to the fifteenth centuries when canon law, medicine, and other studies had been instituted in the new universities and academies. But the overwhelming majority of the laity and many clergy were incapable of reading and understanding Scripture. The offices, practices, and institutions of the church, even the magnificent buildings themselves[19] were the major sources of the beliefs most Christians held during the Middle Ages. Formal theology had, of course, its towering exemplars: Anselm, Pierre Abélard, Peter Lombard, Thomas Aquinas, William of Occam, to list but a few. But the influence of their work was in large measure confined to that tiny minority of sufficiently educated thinkers who could engage their conversations. The masses of Christians were informed to whatever degree they attained by tradition.

Martin Luther, monk, theologian, professor, and, most importantly, Biblical scholar, became increasingly convinced that Scripture did not support, let alone agree with the tradition as presented by the priests, the bishops, the popes, and the ecumenical councils after Chalcedon (451). Standing before a tribunal of imperial inquisitors and ecclesiastical judges in 1521, Luther was asked to renounce the views he had expounded. He responded that unless he could be per-

---

[19] See Chap. 4.

suaded by references to Scripture that his views were mistaken, he would not recant. In the midst of the fire of trial, he announced that Scripture alone (*sola scriptura*) was the basis of the authority to which he was bound. He was denounced as a heretic for his insistence that councils could be and had been wrong in the past and that similarly popes were untrustworthy. He was facing imprisonment and perhaps execution when he was spirited away and hidden by a friendly prince. During two years of hiding, Luther's primary work was to translate the New Testament into the German language so that the people might have direct access to it and be better able to judge whether Catholic Christianity was adequately presenting the Christian message in its traditions. There was, of course, no doubt on his part. A reformation was essential!

The events of 1521–1523 were the climax of a process put in motion in 1517 when Martin Luther, Doctor of Theology, had offered a set of ninety-five theses to be debated regarding the sale of indulgences by representatives of the Pope. An indulgence was a transaction in which a person would make a cash contribution, and, depending on the amount, be encouraged to believe that one could reduce the time a deceased loved one would be required to spend in purgatory (the immediate place of trial after death and before eternal life with God). Luther denied the legitimacy of encouraging such a belief or engaging in the practice of selling indulgences.

There was nothing radical or novel in his proposing theses to be debated. That was standard procedure in theological and ecclesiastical circles. But the Pope's representatives were initially resistant to engaging in the debate. Finally, however, it was arranged in 1519, and, in the interim, Luther was gaining popularity among the masses of German Christians. The printing press had shortly before been invented. Luther's writings were rapidly printed and distributed. He was becoming a nuisance.

Luther was more and more convinced that the claimed authority of tradition was illegitimate. In 1521, he wrote three major theological treatises. One of them, entitled "The Babylonian Captivity of the Church," proclaimed among other things that the sacraments, except Baptism and the Eucharist, had no Scriptural basis. The church was imposing rituals on Christians that did not have equal bases to the two Scripturally authenticated sacraments. Although he judged those rituals to be valuable, especially Penance and Holy Matrimony, they were not equal in importance with the two that are Scripturally based. In "Christian Liberty," another of the 1521 treatises, he argued for the freedom that faith, given by God, generates in the lives of Christians. Now more than a nuisance, the force of his position was increasingly becoming a menace.

German church leaders impressed the seriousness of the challenge posed by Luther to the papal officers and upon the Holy Roman Emperor. Luther threatened not only the authority of the Catholic Church, but also the authority of the civil government that was allied with that church. When he was condemned as a heretic, he thereby simultaneously became an outlaw in the eyes of the imperial forces.

Although the date of the experience is a much debated question, it is indisputably the case that, through his deep study of Scripture, Luther had become impassioned by the belief that faith alone (*sola fide*) is what secures a "right relation" with God. He developed this belief into the doctrine designated as Justification by Faith. Luther had found that his most strenuous efforts to fulfill all the practices required of a monk and of a priest still left him uncertain and lacking in confidence that he was accepted by God. Subsequently, he regarded those efforts to have been a form of attempting to earn his salvation through his own efforts—righteousness through good works.

Many other persons, prior to, subsequent to, and contemporaneous with Luther, have been untroubled and confident when they have disciplined themselves to keep the ordinances of the church. But Luther was sick of soul and longed to get into a right relation with God. Finally, in a way similar to the ancient Hebrew prophets recalling the people to the desert, and like Jesus knocking over the money changers' tables, he came to believe that faith alone was all that could accomplish what he sought and that, no more than anything else he tried, could faith be achieved by his own efforts. Grace, the unmerited forgiveness and acceptance by God of the sinner, was the source of faith in those to whom God chose to give it. The person so blessed is justified before God through grace. Thus, there was an inseparable connection of beliefs: Scripture alone proclaims that only grace brings faith and that faith alone trusts God's Word. It is the Word that announces that through Christ God has forgiven sin and has accepted the sinner. Important to remember is that one never ceases being a sinner; one becomes a "saved sinner." The church's task, in such a set of beliefs, is not to provide the means of salvation, for no human institution is capable of that. Rather, the vocation of the church is to proclaim the Gospel (the good news) and to enact that same message in administering Baptism and Holy Communion.

Luther's beliefs spurred him to reformulations of many doctrines and led him to argumentative encounters with other reformers as certainly as with Catholic theologians. At one famous encounter, he and the Swiss reformer, Ulrich Zwingli, debated the meaning of Holy Communion (Eucharist). Emphasizing the promise inherent in the words "This is my body. . . . " that the Gospels report Jesus had spoken while eating the Passover meal with his disciples on the night before his capture, Luther's view was that in a mysteriously powerful way, Christ is always the "real presence" in the bread and wine of communion. Zwingli emphasized the other part of the sentence: "do this in remembrance of me." It was his view that as a memorial service, participants in Holy Communion are undertaking the sort of discipline that enables them to participate in the mind, heart, and life of Christ Jesus. In the language of post-Enlightenment modernity, Luther emphasized the objectivity of Christ in the sacrament, while Zwingli emphasized the subjective state required for the sacrament to work effectively in a Christian's life. After several days of discussion on this and many another theological questions, they reached agreement on virtually everything else, but had to agree to disagree on this basic issue. And the difference between "real presence" and "remembrance" is so basic and significant an issue because it touches the heart of the rift in the modern Western imagination: the dualism between faith and works, spirit and body, and ultimately between humanity and God. Ironically, Luther's insight had been to move beyond dualism into a creative dynamic between the polarities represented in this context by church and scripture. In important respects, the agreement to disagree has become one of the basic motifs in many of the relations between Protestant groups in subsequent centuries.

In emphasizing belief in the unique authority of Scripture, Luther and his contemporary reformers were immediately thrust into one of the greatest of difficulties that still persistently beset Protestants. Over centuries of struggle, Catholic Christianity had come to recognize that when people disagree on basic issues there is great value in having a type of "court of last resort" to which to appeal. This need was served by the view that "when Rome speaks, discussion ceases." In the Catholic system, the Supreme Pontiff (the Vicar of Christ, the Pope) has been put in place by God to speak the definitive Christian view regarding otherwise divisive questions of faith and morals. Protestants, by contrast, have regarded the elevation of any office as a move fraught with the danger of idolatry. The problematic issue, again, is that of authority in matters of belief and practice.

When Luther propounded his belief that the Bible testifies to the Word of God, he was making a subtle but crucial distinction. The Bible is not itself the Word. Rather, it testifies to the Word. In order to receive the Word, according to Luther, grace has to be given and faith is required. Further, familiarity with the Greek and Hebrew languages and deep study of the writings in the Bible plus commentaries on them by the great theologians of the past are both highly desirable. In short, Luther was not a simple-minded advocate of a view that one may simply pick up a Bible in translation, read it, and thereby properly understand it.

Many other Christians, otherwise deeply sympathetic with Luther's rejection of the authority of Catholic tradition, were convinced that Luther was unwilling to follow out the radicalism implicit in his own views. For many of them, adherence to *sola scriptura* required one additional belief if it is to be properly understood. Many argued that as the Bible was written by persons inspired by the Holy Spirit, it must be read by persons who are also Spirit-inspired. That alone will enable such persons to be confident in their understanding of the meaning of the words, passages, and books of the Bible. On this view, being God-led—not learning—is the requirement for an adequate reception of the truth conveyed by Scripture.

Thus, many of the splits within Protestantism in the centuries since the Reformation of the sixteenth century are directly traceable to matters surrounding the interpretation of Scripture. And it is not only the result of different interpretations of one portion or passage or word in the Bible but, more profoundly, of different interpretations of what the Bible is. If the Bible is testimony to the Word of God, then interpretation is a challenge that requires many gifts and hard work. If, by contrast, the Bible *is* the Word of God, then the primary challenge is to the will—it requires that one choose to believe it. In this latter view, lie the seeds of fundamentalism, which believes in the infallibility of Scripture, opening itself to the real possibility of idolatry of the word. In the former view, however, there is manifestly—witness Luther's disagreement with Zwingli over the meaning of Holy Communion—the probability that honest people reading the same words will come to significantly different beliefs as a result of different ways of interpretation. Then, how is a difference to be adjudicated? Can it be? Should it be? Finally, from this perspective there is an implicit assumption that people are alone before God (*coram Dei*) with nothing to appeal to but the mercy and grace of God, since no absolute confidence can be placed in an authoritative Church nor even in an authoritative interpretation of Scripture.

CONCLUSION

Were a complete catalogue of beliefs held by some Christians at different times and places to be assembled, volumes would be required just to list the beliefs. This chapter has touched upon only a few of the recurrent beliefs held by certain Christians at various times and places and has drawn connections with the foundational stories for which the beliefs appear as reinterpretations in a new context.

One final comment is required. Christian beliefs are statements of what persons in particular groups or even what individuals who identify themselves as Christians teach and confess to be true. They may, when asked to do so, defend their beliefs by an appeal to the authority of personal insight, or to the cumulative tradition of the church, or to a particular interpretation of Scripture. But regardless of the authority upon which their beliefs are based, Christians all testify to the foundational orientation of the total person. Each speaks of the experience of trust, loyalty, and confidence in the source of whatever authority to which they may appeal. They all retell the foundational stories in their own way.

In the tradition, belief is not simply to be equated with faith, for even the role of faith in the journey of Christian living can become a source of conflict.[20] Some theologians do regard faith, like belief, as the first step of giving intellectual assent to truths taught and confessed by the church. Love is, in such a view (as for instance in the thought of Augustine), the capstone and keystone of Christian

---

[20] The suggestion that "belief" is grounded in the experience of "believing" is carried in the language of the tradition. The New Testament word usually translated by the English verb "to believe" is the Greek verb *pisteuo,* based on the noun *pistis* meaning "faith." The Greek verb is never followed by the preposition "in" as it is most often in translation. It is used with the preposition *eis* meaning "into." So what came to be translated "believe in," in the original text means "faithing into," which carries a very different implication.

The problem arises in translation because Latin, French, and English do not have a verb based on the noun "faith," e.g. Latin has the noun *fides* and verb *credere;* French *foi* and *croire* and English "faith" and "believe," carrying the connotation of believing in something. The problem has not been ignored by the tradition, and attempts have been made to avoid the confusion between faith and belief; Luther preferred *fiducia* to *fides,* for instance, because it means trust and confidence rather than "belief in."

living. Other theologians (such as Luther) regard faith as the total response of the total person and hold that all other characteristics (including belief) of Christian living flow from it. In either such perspective, or any other of the numerous combinations that have appeared in Christian history, an interplay between beliefs, rituals, stories, and symbols emerges. Each differs in its emphasis and each is fraught with the possibility of one-sidedness. But each is in some way an attempt to articulate the experience of the moving force by which the one believing has been empowered and changed. Each is an expression of "faith seeking understanding" that, in some way or another, may enable a living-out of the multiplicity of possibilities that is Christianity.

6

christian worship: the drama of sacrament and memorial

In the previous chapter we looked at the stories Christianity has to tell about itself. We looked at its beliefs, its myths, narratives, creeds, and theological doctrines. The power of a story lies in its being experienced. It is the personal and communal experience of what the story is about that claims the commitment of the believer. But experience is not only intellectual; it also includes the emotional and the physical. For human beings are not only thinking beings; we are also feeling beings; for us, the "heart" is as important to us as the head. And here we find a second form of religious expression, ritual and worship.

THE IMPORTANCE OF FORMS OF WORSHIP

Worship appeals specifically to the bodily and affective dimension of our nature, and occasions the possibility of a whole experience. Christian worship combines moments of deep self-reflection with periods of great celebration. Like other religious traditions, Christian beliefs have been nurtured and maintained within the context of a worshipping community in which the beliefs are dramatized, acted out. Christian worship involves the acting out of the stories of the tradition. Theological reflection and worship have never long been separated in the Christian tradition. Theological doctrines become dry and wooden if they cannot be imaged and celebrated in song and dramatized in ritual. For example, on Palm Sunday, prior to the celebration of Easter, in many churches Christians will walk in procession, waving palm branches, or some symbolic representation of them. As ritual expression, such an activity enables the participant to experience, in some measure, what the crowds felt as they hailed Jesus' entrance into Jerusalem. And the same with Holy Week, which proceeds from Maundy Thursday, Good Friday, Holy Saturday to Easter Sunday. The week symbolically traces the movement from death to resurrection, bearing worshippers through the same series of experiences. On Easter Sunday, most Christians put on their best clothes, adorn their churches with flowers, and sing with full voice, "He is Risen." This is an expression of the affective side of religion. What may seem unprovable philosophically or historically is experienced in worship in the company of the community of faith.

In worship, the Christian is potentially able to experience a union between mind and body, spirit and flesh. At the core of Christianity is the claim that God became known through the particular earthly and physical form of Jesus, the Christ. It is in worship that Christians witness to the mystery that Christ still comes to them. This potential union resides in the power of symbols, symbolic images, and acts. Just as myth and story present images to the mind, so ritual worship centers upon the concrete expression of these images and the ritual actions they invoke in response to the power they manifest. Symbols have special meaning because of the "invisible reality" to which it is understood they point and also in some mysterious way in which they participate. For example, from one perspective, a cross found in the woods may be just two sticks that accidentally fell across each other; a cross on the spire or on the altar of the church means something more. Again, the things that people do in worship—kneeling, crossing themselves, shouting, or singing—do not inherently convey their full meaning and are, in some cases, absurd outside the religious context in which they come to expression. However, acts that are believed to create another, transcendent reality cannot be expected to conform to the purposes and the "reality" of the everyday world. They explicitly show that there is something other. In the Christian sense, the reality of God and the reality of the ongoing saving work of Christ through the Holy Spirit are all expressed in the beautiful orchestration of visual and verbal symbols found in the ritual act of public worship.

Christian worship is "what is done"; it is the *praxis* (Greek for "deed" or "action"). Worship includes all that is done to enact the Christian worldview, all that helps establish the individual's and the believing community's relationship with God within it, and all that draws the community together as a visible social reality. Embracing individual and community, worship includes the main weekly services and much else as well: weddings and funerals, prayers for the sick, private baptisms, pilgrimages and retreats, private prayer and meditation—all meaningful in so far as they are founded upon the Christian religious worldview, as the participants understand it.

Christian worship as we imagined it in an ancient Mediterranean city in Chapter 1 is not carried out in precisely that way anywhere today, but virtually all Christians would find features of that rite familiar. More recent forms of Christian worship fundamentally enact the same reality: a universe of which God is Creator, lover, lawgiver, and judge; a universe in which Christ is God incarnate, crucified and risen Savior, and guide of souls; and a universe in which persons are given new life, both now and hereafter, by sharing in the life of Christ. That life was shared then through experiences of prayer, hearing the Scriptures read and sermons preached, Baptism, Holy Communion, and fellowship. It is so today, though with varying emphases on these features in different Christian traditions. Once more we shall see that the diversity of expression does not obscure, but rather enhances the unity of the Christian vision.

Christian worship may be divided into two classes: those which represent the main worship service at which members of a Christian community gather weekly, usually on Sunday; and those services or practices which are more occasional or individual, such as midweek services, prayers and sacraments for the sick, pilgrimages, and private prayers or meditations. We shall first consider the main service.

For the sake of discussion, these services are also divisible into two types, described as Catholic and Protestant. The Catholic type, observed in Roman Catholic, Eastern Orthodox, and, to a large extent, Anglican churches, is directly derived from the rite of the early church as it had developed by the second or third century, though it has become much more formalized and ceremonial over the subsequent centuries. Known as Holy Communion, Eucharist, Divine Liturgy, or Mass, the service includes Scripture reading and prayers, music and sermon, and centers on the offering and partaking of the bread and wine, blessed and consecrated by a priest to become the Body and Blood of Christ. The Protestant type, as it appears in all of its many forms, centers upon the sermon and Scripture reading, although it may also include Communion, more commonly known as the Lord's Supper in that tradition.

WORSHIP IN THE CATHOLIC TRADITION

A visitor unfamiliar with worship in the Catholic tradition will—whether visiting a Roman Catholic, Eastern Orthodox, or Anglican church—probably first be struck by the elaborate, symbol-laden decor of the church, the richly-colored "robes" or vestments worn by the priests and other officiants, and the ritual character of the sacred acts they are performing. These features will immediately suggest two things: that this activity is special and different from other things that people do, and that it follows traditional patterns carried over from the past.

The tradition aspect suggests that for these worshippers Christianity is a fellowship crisscrossing space and time, in which words and signs and even items of clothing from Christians of times past in places far and near can join with people of the present in enacting the great drama of the Eucharist.

The special atmosphere may strike one as the creation of a space and time

Mass at St. Paul's in New York City. Photo courtesy of Laimute E. Druskis.

that is different, set apart, and full of sacred power. The noted historian of religion Mircea Eliade has commented that, for religious humanity, space and time are not "homogeneous." Every day is not just the same as every other day. Some, such as Christmas and Easter, have a special "feel" of joy and festivity, which, when their spiritual meaning is added to the modern secularized celebration of a holiday, gives them a sacred depth of solemnity that sets them utterly apart. The Catholic tradition makes a great deal of special days—Holy Days, from which comes our word holiday. Not only are there Christmas and Easter, which Protestants also usually keep, but a host of other commemorations, including the Assumption, or taking into heaven at the end of her earthly life of Christ's mother the Blessed Virgin Mary, and the days of many saints great and small, usually on the date of their deaths or "heavenly birthdays."

Some places differ greatly in power to evoke, or channel, divine energy. For this reason places of pilgrimage, like Lourdes or the Shrine of Our Lady of Guadalupe in Mexico, have had a special meaning in the Catholic tradition going back to the veneration early Christians paid to the tombs of martyrs.

But it is not only holy days and special places that are full of spiritual meaning. In a religious worldview, the whole of time and space are sanctified through the setting apart of specific times and places that are felt to be sacred.

Sacred time makes present again the events that founded the world. Christian time begins and ends and begins again with the birth, death, and resurrection of the Incarnate Lord. And all of time, punctuated as it is by significant events, is held to re-present that pattern.

The churches in the Catholic tradition, then, have devised over the centuries a church calendar, focussing on Christmas and Easter, that correlates the major events in the life of Christ and the early church with the seasons of the year—his birth with Christmas and midwinter, his death and resurrection with Good Friday, Easter, and the coming of spring, and so forth. The correlation is largely with the events of the Jesus story which may be called, in the technical sense in which we have used the word, the Christian *mythos*. These are the largely miraculous events, also central to the Apostles' and Nicene Creeds, that Christian faith sees God working in Jesus Christ for the salvation of the world: his virgin birth, his passion, death and resurrection, his ascension, and the pentecostal coming of the Holy Spirit to the Apostles. The traditional calendar also has days devoted to certain other extraordinary events in the life of Christ—such as his baptism by John (Epiphany) and his transfiguration—and numerous days honoring the Apostles and many other saints.

In varying degrees, Protestant churches have adopted parts, though generally not all, of the traditional calendar. We will now summarize the major seasons and festivals of that calendar.

The Christian year begins four weeks before Christmas with the onset of *Advent*. The name comes from the Latin *adventus* meaning "coming." This is understood as a time of preparation for the approaching rule of God and the arrival of the Kingdom which is at hand. It is a time of readying for the event that will not only symbolically take place again upon earth but also within the heart of every believer. The preparation is for the judgment that comes mysteriously in the form of a child.

Christmas comes as the ritual celebration and thanksgiving of the event of the Incarnation, the moment when God took on human form and finitude, lifting all of creation into the divine presence. This festival is also imaged as the coming of light into darkness. It is celebrated near the time of the winter solstice, showing its connection with earlier religious traditions for which the marking of the seasons was of primordial importance.

Following Christmas, *Epiphany* (from the Greek, meaning "to show forth") celebrates the revelation of God in Christ in majesty and glory, to the three visiting Magi.

The season of Epiphany lasts until Ash Wednesday, a day of penance and fast that marks the beginning of *Lent*. Instituted in the fourth century, Lent is the period of forty days that leads up to the celebration of Easter. It is a time of preparation and penitence, and it represents symbolically the forty days of Christ's trial and temptation in the desert. As we saw with the early Christian Church in Chapter I, this was the time during which catechumens rigorously prepared for baptism. Today the time is still observed by many with penance, prayer, study and fasting; a time of cleansing and "emptying out" in readiness for Easter.

Easter comes from *Eostre,* an Anglo Saxon fertility goddess who represented

Spring and the coming of the life-giving light of the new son into the world. Easter also represents the triumph of light and life through darkness and death. This spring festival of the death and resurrection of Christ is, for most branches of Christianity, a climactic event as it was in the early church (see Chapter 1). Preceded by Holy Week, which leads the believer through a representing of the events of the week leading up to the crucifixion on Good Friday, Easter bursts forth into the world of history at midnight on Saturday, although it is generally celebrated on Sunday morning. Christians who gather to celebrate this event also explode from a symbolic grave to rise in glory, reborn once more into the world, yet with new understanding of its and their individual significance.

There follows the *Great Fifty Days,* which is an adoption of the ancient Jewish marking of the fifty days of Passover. This period culminates in *Pentecost* (Greek for "fiftieth"). However, the time is interrupted after forty days by Ascension Day which celebrates Christ's being lifted into the heavens, after having appeared to the disciples on several occasions during the preceding days. His Ascension echoes with the promise to remain always with those who believe, through the power of the helper he will send.

At the end of the fifty days, the Holy Spirit descended like a mighty rushing wind and danced with tongues of fire upon the heads of the disciples as they waited in hiding in Jerusalem for the promised sign. After this visitation, the disciples, now Apostles, went into the streets proclaiming their faith in a strange new tongue that was understood by all who gathered there from different nations to celebrate the end of Passover. And so the festival of Pentecost is also the celebration of the birth of the Christian church as the Apostles set forth to carry the Gospel to all nations. Pentecost is the last great season until Advent comes around again.

Moving from the yearly cycle to the weekly, we return to the Catholic style of worship at the main service we have described, the Mass or Divine Liturgy, that, in marking the end and beginning of the week, creates in an especially powerful way a sense of ritual sacred time.

The church in the Catholic tradition is itself a sacred space of remarkable force. The Eastern Orthodox church, its walls alive with icons and candles and the great iconostasis veiling the deepest mysteries across the front, offers an entry into heaven where the saints are luminously alive and the air is full of grace. Western Roman Catholic and Anglican churches, with their elaborate sanctuaries and altars, and often their candled statues of saints, also kindle a bright visual and spatial sense of walking into a sanctified realm where religious realities are vividly alive.

When, as they do at the main service, sacred space and time come together, the effect is to create "another reality" in which the Kingdom of Heaven draws near and God's grace is freely dispensed. This experience brings us to another "message" of the Catholic style of worship. It asserts the visible presence of God's activity in the world channeled in and through the church. To this Christian tradition, a "church" is not only just a place to worship and learn, it is also, as a concrete institution, a bearer of the power and presence of God in the world. Yet, it is above all an institution made up of its people. God has chosen to entrust himself into the hands of humanity and his presence shines through rites, especially the Eucharist, which they perform, even as his grace may be especially and definitely communicated through their hands as they bless and forgive. Moreover, the church is believed to have assurance of God's guidance in its teaching, so that the dogmas it holds will never be incorrect, a belief rooted deeply in the tradition. In principle, these divine endowments to the church are held collectively by the whole body, but are exercised on its behalf by its empowered leadership: Pope, Patriarchs, Archbishops, Bishops, Priests, and Deacons. For this reason they conduct much of public worship, particularly those sacramental services such as the Eucharist, which they alone are authorized to administer, as successors of the Apostles of Christ, ministers of grace.

Closely linked to the concept of God's power and presence embodied in the church, the Body of Christ, is the sacramental principle. Sacraments are rites in which God's grace is definitely and reliably communicated through a material means administered by human beings. They are, in the words of the Anglican Prayer Book, "an outward and visible sign of an inward and spiritual grace." Traditionally, they are seven in number: Baptism, Holy Communion, Confirmation, Holy Matrimony, Penance (confession of sins and receiving of absolution or forgiveness from a priest), Holy Orders (the ordaining of deacons, priests, and bishops), and Holy Unction (the anointing with oil which is part of the rite administered to the sick and dying). These sacraments will be described more fully later.

In each of these sacraments, there is a material means—water for Baptism, bread and wine for Holy Communion, the forms of the man and woman in their married relation to each other in matrimony, oil in unction, the hands of the priest or bishop in the other three—through which grace is transmitted; and there is a person to administer it, usually a priest, though if need be any Christian can baptize. For those who find sacramentalism fundamental to their image of Christianity, this use of material means and human agents to transmit God's grace in the world reenacts the event of the Incarnation. God entrusts himself to matter and fallible human beings to bring the Kingdom into the depths of the world, and in becoming visible, he shows that matter and humanity can be sanctified. In turn, this divine involvement in the world reveals to the believer that the world of matter is not to be disdained but rather to be accepted as God's creation with humility and love. One is able to receive God's grace through common matter and through the hands and bodies of fellow humans, however unworthy they may seem to be of the power imparted to them from above. In the Catholic traditions, this spirit is at the root of saintliness, and presents a key toward understanding the inner meaning of worship in the Catholic tradition. The church displays a sort of holy materialism, in which matter communicates grace as a kiss communicates love. This materialism is found both in the pomp and splendor of the Church's great festive services, and in the homeliness of the very common elements—water, bread, and wine—in its most basic rites.

The other main Christian tradition of worship, the Protestant, certainly affirms strongly the goodness and importance of God's material creation, and of mutual communication of grace within the church. But it does so in a different way. It is not so much through specific significant rites and persons, though these both have their roles, but more through a changed inner attitude toward all creation and all persons.

PROTESTANT WORSHIP

As we saw in Chapter 5, the basic Protestant principle, articulated by Martin Luther, is that humanity is justified—that is, set right with God—by God's grace working inwardly as it is received through faith. Faith is not simply belief in right doctrines, but an inner attitude of trust and openness toward God and his work in Christ which anyone may have, whether priest or laity, wise or foolish.

This attitude of faith is sparked by hearing the Gospel message, preeminently from the words of Scripture and from preaching proclaiming the message of Scripture. Therefore the emphasis in Protestant worship is on the reading aloud of Scripture and preaching from it. These events set an emphasis on verbal communication as the most important element of worship which is carried over to other characteristic features of it: hymns, prayer, responsive readings. The first two sacraments, or ordinances (things ordered by Christ as they are often called by Protestants), Baptism and Holy Communion, are observed by most Protestant churches. But Holy Communion is usually not celebrated as the main service every Sunday as it is in churches of the Catholic tradition, and it is enacted with considerably less ritual and ceremonial. In most churches in the Protestant tradition, ordinances are not seen as communicating grace in and of themselves but rather as performances that can point toward the Gospel message and stimulate response to it; they are as it were ''acted sermons'' or ''acted Scripture.''

The Protestant churches are called churches of the Reformation, for they derive historically from the religious ideas and experiences unleashed by that sixteenth-century series of events. On a deeper level, though, they may be termed Reforming churches, for a fundamental Protestant idea is that the church should never absolutize any particular structure or practice, but should be continually willing to reform, or reshape, itself as its growing understanding of God's Word compels it to do so.

Protestantism, therefore, characteristically places less emphasis on the classic ancient and medieval liturgical tradition than Catholicism, and its worship will usually be more informal, spontaneous, and unritualistic. (We should, however, note that the Catholic tradition has its own mechanisms for reform of worship, generally through the authority of the Pope and the general councils; and that individual Protestant churches and denominations have developed their own traditions of worship that are often quite strong.) In a lineage emphasizing inward faith and grace, and having a pattern of church life potentially reforming itself continually, the varietal spectrum is wide. Protestantism ranges from often ornate Anglican worship, as much in the Catholic as in Protestant tradition, and stately Lutheran services, to lively Pentecostal churches and backwoods revivals. It includes Methodist worship midway between the extremes of form and informality, Baptist gatherings likely to be a little more informal still, and silent Quaker meetings.

In all this variety, we find that Protestant churches can be said to fall basically into two large groups: those that are or derive from one of the traditional state churches of Europe—the Anglican in England, the Lutheran in Scandinavia and substantial parts of Germany, the Reformed in other states of Germany, Scotland, the Netherlands, and parts of Switzerland—and those of the "Free Church" lineage which embraces those churches that arose independently from the established religions, offering alternatives for those whose spiritual needs were not adequately met by the state church. They include such Protestant "families" as Baptists, Methodists, Quakers, Pentecostals, and churches in the Reformed tradition from England (the Puritans), Ireland, and France. We will now look at the worship traditions of Protestant "families" of churches. We begin with those of the state church lineages, then move to the other less structured life of "free"-church groups.

Anglican worship displays considerable variety. It is formal in the sense that it follows more or less a set liturgy, the standard being *The Book of Common Prayer* in its various national editions. But styles of implementing worship differ, so that in some churches the Anglican Eucharist is virtually indistinguishable from the Roman Catholic Mass, while in others it has a more clearly Protestant character, especially when Morning Prayer, a non-Eucharistic service of psalms, scripture, and prayers, is the main service. These variations represent the fact that both Catholic and Protestant theological currents are strong within Anglicanism. In recent decades, however, there has been a move toward a central position in Anglican worship, so that now the visitor to a typical Anglican church, including Episcopal churches in America, would find the main Sunday morning service to be the Eucharist, celebrated in a relatively simple and modern way but with traditional vestments and structure, not unlike the post-Vatican II Roman Catholic Mass.

The largest of the Protestant "families" of churches, the Lutheran, also has a fairly traditional form of worship. The principle regarding worship of Luther and the Lutheran reformers was simple: the central point worship must communicate is justification through faith; whatever does not conflict with this message may be kept or adapted from the general traditions of the Christian church. Thus Lutheran reformers saw no need to radically alter the patterns of worship centering on the Mass which they inherited. They translated them into the vernacular (which, as noted in Chapter 2, was a major matter) to enable them to transmit better the Gospel message, simplified and modified them here and there to make the primacy of faith more apparent, and gave the sermon more prominence and the sacrament less. The typical Lutheran service consists of the first part of the ancient Eucharistic liturgy, with lessons, liturgical hymns, and prayers, together with sermon. Adding the Holy Communion itself as a part of the regular Sunday service has become increasingly common in the twentieth century, but there are still a great number of churches in which it is observed only monthly or less. On the other hand, the heritage of pietistic movements that swept Lutheranism in the nineteenth century and before, emphasizing feeling-oriented, personal, and subjective modes of prayer and praise, still remains in many places. Lutheranism, always noted for the magnificence of its music, made congregational hymn-singing an important part of Christian worship and has contributed a number of powerful hymns and chorales to the entire Christian world.

The churches in the tradition known as Reformed, influenced by the theology and example of John Calvin, went further than the Lutherans in remodeling Christian worship to inculcate its principles. Rather than simply retaining what did not conflict with the Reformation, they were more conscious of the Reformation as an opportunity to restore the structural as well as theological purity of the New Testament church. Reformed Protestants, therefore, sought to model worship on the usages of the early church, as they understood them. Worship in this tradition centers on the proclaiming of the Word of God through Scripture and sermon, embellished by the singing of psalms and hymns and prayer. It does not follow a rigorously predetermined liturgy, but allows the individual church and its minister considerable freedom to order the service and phrase the words of prayer according to occasion and inspiration. A mood of dignified simplicity is definitely favored, with little use of ornate vestments or ritual gestures. Like Catholic, Anglican, Lutheran, and most other Christian churches in the twentieth century, Reformed churches have experimented with new styles of worship and tended to move from a solemn, didactic mood to a celebrative style.

Worship of Protestant churches not of state-church background has generally adopted the Reformed principle of endeavoring to recover the worship life of the primitive church. These churches have characteristically also put particular emphasis on individual conversion and faith. Their services, then, in a wide variety of ways seek, through simplicity and spontaneity, to give voice to the Holy Spirit speaking directly to the hearts of participants, kindling therein faith and fervor. Following are some of the varieties.

No doubt the most consistent application of this side of the Protestant heritage has been the Quaker meeting. Here, there is no "formal" service at all, but participants sit in meditative silence, open to the guidance of the spirit, until someone, anyone, is moved to arise and speak, pray, or lead a hymn. No minister, therefore, is required.

The worship of "free" churches in the Reformed tradition, such as the Congregationalists (now the United Church of Christ in the United States) is similar to that of other Reformed churches such as Presbyterians, derived directly or by example from the state church of Scotland. However, it often has an even greater atmosphere of simplicity and freedom.

The Baptist tradition is generally quite open to the expression of warmth and feeling in worship. It stresses the importance of the individual and public confession of faith in Christ; preaching and worship will often be oriented toward drawing participants to discover or renew that faith. Frequently the service will culminate in an "altar call" when believers may come forward to make such a public testimony. The emphasis on feeling extends also to the style of hymns and rhetoric common among Baptists as well, and is indirectly shown also in the fact that the outward accoutrements of Baptist worship are usually plain. Churches are simply styled, and vestments shunned.

The Methodist family, derived from the ministry of the Church of England clergyman, John Wesley, preserves reminders of Anglicanism in its worship, especially in the Holy Communion. Because it also emphasizes the centrality of personal inward faith, Methodist worship has a freer, simpler, and perhaps more obviously feeling-oriented tone than the Anglican, and it lays greater emphasis on the sermon.

An important Protestant movement, which originated in the United States in the wake of the great revivals of the nineteenth century, is that simply known as Christian, for its adherents are determined simply to be Christian rather than sectarian in any sense, and to recover the life and worship of the New Testament church. Nothing has to be done that did not have Biblical warrant, and there was to be no creed but the Bible. This movement has now evolved into three major denominations, all of which give the local congregation great autonomy: the Christian Church (Disciples of Christ), the Christian Churches, and the more conservative Churches of Christ. They have preserved several significant worship innovations based on the strict adherence to what is said about worship in the New Testament: instrumental music is not used in the Churches of Christ, and all celebrate the Holy Communion or Lord's Supper at the main Sunday service weekly. Despite this similarity to the Catholic tradition, the service follows the "Free Church" Protestant pattern, and the Supper is observed in a simple Protestant manner, with local elders rather than the ministers praying over the bread and cup.

Another movement of American origin, which has grown so powerfully worldwide that it has come to be called a "Third Force" in Christiandom, is Pentecostalism, sometimes also called the Charismatic Movement. It is not primarily a denomination, though it has spawned several, but a movement that has spread through many denominations, including the Roman Catholic and Anglican as well as many Protestant churches.

Like so many earlier movements, Pentecostalism sees itself as recovering the full power and experience of the early church. New Testament healing and warmth of fellowship are included, but special place is given to the experience of Pentecost, when the Holy Spirit descended on the Apostles and they spoke in new and strange tongues. "Speaking in tongues"—the practice known as *glossolalia* (from the Greek root *glosso,* "tongue," a praying or speaking in words that have no apparent meaning but which can sometimes be interpreted by someone who has that "gift") is the hallmark of Pentecostalism. In the churches of Pentecostal denominations, such as the Assemblies of God, the Church of God, the Pentecostal Holiness Church, the United Pentecostal Church, and others, these manifestations will occur in most services. That may also be the case in those parishes of other denominations in which Pentecostalism is a strong force, within the context of its more traditional worship forms. In other cases, as in many Roman Catholic churches, Pentecostal expression is limited to certain prayer groups, services, or spiritual fellowships that cross parish lines.

Pentecostal worship, whether in a Catholic "Charismatic Mass" or in an old-line Pentecostal church, has a unique and unforgettable quality. Preaching is fiery, prayers by participants warm and heartfelt, and when tongues come they are often a mysterious murmur that rises and falls like the sea. Sometimes motor activity—dancing, jumping, shouting, or falling to the floor upon the laying on of hands for healing or to impart the Holy Spirit—is much in evidence. The service may have a structure punctuated by these events, or—especially in more informal Pentecostal prayer groups—it may develop its own spiritual logic.

We can ask now what messages might be communicated by the Protestant style of worship? First, that it is possible today to be, in the words of the theologian Soren Kierkegaard, "contemporary with Christ," or at least with the infant church of the New Testament, which had the fullness of Christ and the Spirit, and is regarded by those in this tradition to be the eternal model for Christian churches in all times and places. Rather than rejoice with Catholics in the accumulation of ecclesiastical customs and traditions from the intervening two millennia, Protestantism seeks always to collapse twenty centuries into a day, to be again the church of Jerusalem or Corinth or even of the Day of Pentecost. This is evidenced in its acceptance of the Bible as the only authority, its general dislike of post-Biblical usages and ceremonies (though some, like the Lutherans, may not object to these if they are not clearly contrary to Scripture), and above all its belief that the only *essential* work of the church is that of the Apostles in the Book of Acts, to proclaim the Gospel of Jesus Christ.

This points to two more fundamental messages of Protestant worship: the centrality of verbal communication and the appeal to inwardness. Protestantism tells us that the most reliable medium of communication, especially from God and about God, is in words: the sentences of Scripture, preaching based on it, the verses of hymns. Next to the word, non-verbal visual communication—painting, sculpture, ritual gesture, wordless music, the smell of incense—and the inchoate aesthetic or numinous feelings they may invoke are, if not suspect, at least not wholly to be trusted and are found in Protestant churches far less than Catholic. This primacy of the word is clearly seen in Protestantism's tendency to pare down the number, and frequency of celebrations, of the traditional sacraments, though most Protestants do not give up entirely the two main ones, observing the ordinances of Baptism and Holy Communion, since they seem to be mandated by the words of Scripture itself.

It is believed that words, with their presumed precision, can aim directly at inwardness where faith is formed. Faith is not the same as emotion or aesthetic feeling. It is simple openness to God and acceptance of the saving work he has already done for humanity in Jesus Christ, and faith requires no further emotional or ritual "works" but only thankful acceptance with trust and love, according to the classical Protestant teaching. The basic principle of Protestant worship is to create ideal conditions for the participant's inwardly receiving the word of God, which alone can generate true faith for conversion or for the deepening of Christian life.

SUMMARY

The worship and sociological expressions of Christianity center around a weekly act of public worship. By all but a few Christians, this act of public worship is observed on Sunday, the day of Christ's resurrection. We have surveyed how this main weekly service is kept. Most often it has been a form of the Holy Communion, the taking and sharing of small amounts of bread and wine based on Jesus's acts and words at the Last Supper, the evening meal he took with his disciples before his betrayal and arrest later that same evening and his crucifixion the next day. At that meal, he took bread, gave it to them, and said, "Take, eat; this is my body." Taking the cup, he said, "Drink of it, all of you; for this is my blood of the covenant, which is poured out for many for the forgiveness of sins" (Matthew 26: 26–28).

Whether or not Jesus necessarily intended by these words to establish the main weekly worship service of the Christian church, that interpretation was held virtually without question by Christians during the first fifteen hundred years. Then the Protestant Reformation, without generally repudiating the service of bread and wine, urged that the proclamation of the word which engenders faith was really as important. Its services centered on scripture and preaching, with less frequent observance of the communion rite, were the natural results. Later in this Chapter we will explore, in a more detailed way, the various expressions of the weekly ritual.

But, although the Sunday service is absolutely crucial to Christianity in its concrete forms, the faith has many other forms of worship public and private. We shall now look at some of them.

OCCASIONAL SERVICES

As we saw in our discussion of Christian sacred time, the week and also the day are divided up in such a way as to respond to the sacred meaning of their points of transition. We have seen that the central weekly event is the Sunday service that marks the end and beginning of the week, and symbolically marks the end and beginning of time itself, as it reenacts the events of Easter. But there are also other services that are significant. Many churches also have services on Sunday evening and on weekdays. Roman Catholic and some Anglican churches have a daily Mass, often early in the morning; this service is usually a "low mass" without music or formal sermon.

Monastics have not only daily Mass, but also seven or eight "Offices" or services of varying lengths consisting of chanting psalms, brief hymns, Scripture readings and prayers. Priests are expected to read the Offices privately throughout the day. According to the Rule of St. Benedict, they are known as Matins, Lauds, Prime, Tierce, Sext Nones, Vespers, and Compline and extend from the very early hours of the morning until evening. In Anglican Churches, Morning, Noonday, and Evening Prayer are sometimes observed, while Evensong (actually a public worship variation of the old monastic Office of Vespers) is offered quite often, especially in England. In these ways, the significant hours of change in each day are marked and set apart, thus sanctifying the whole day as it repeats the spiraling archetypal pattern laid down in the beginning.

Another sort of occasional service is the festival, the significance of which we have already partially examined. Christmas and Easter are the most widely observed festivals among Christians of all denominations, although the celebration of the birth of Christ did not emerge as a Christian holiday until the fourth century. No other festival which does not fall on a Sunday is widely kept by both Catholics and Protestants, although many Catholic and Protestant churches have services on some civil holidays that have spiritual meaning as, in the United States, Thanksgiving, Memorial Day, and Independence Day.

In the Catholic tradition, Penance or reconciliation, one of the traditional seven sacraments, may be done outside the main service. Individually, persons may confess sins anonymously to a priest, either kneeling in a confessional booth with priest and penitent divided by a grill, as in the Roman Catholic church, or, as is more common in the Eastern Orthodox and—when the rite is used—the Anglican traditions, behind a priest seated or standing near the altar. The priest will give counsel, and absolution (formal forgiveness of the sins in the name of God), and in addition an assigned "penance"—something to do, such as saying certain prayers. In many corporate services a general confession is followed by absolution, and serves as an expression of individual and community penance. Penance, like Baptism, is understood as repentance, washing clean, and beginning anew, restored to a loving relationship with God and with the community.

Less frequent or obligatory, but very much a part of Christian life, are such activities as pilgrimages and retreats. Pilgrimages, the ancient and widespread practice of traveling to places believed to have special spiritual power and significance, have become especially developed in the Catholic tradition. Pilgrimages are made to the scenes of the life of Christ in the Holy Land, to important religious centers such as Rome or the Greek Orthodox monasteries on Mt. Athos, and to sites hallowed by miracles such as appearances of the Blessed Virgin Mary. The shrines dedicated to modern visions of this sort, like Lourdes in France and Fatima in Portugal, are well known. In the Anglican tradition, the medieval shrine of Our Lady of Walsingham in England has, in this century, been revived with success. In Protestantism, pilgrimage does not have the ritual significance it holds for the Catholic tradition, where return to the place is a representation of the event itself, but many Protestants have found meaning in visiting the Holy Land or places of historical importance to their spiritual heritage.

Individual and community retreats have their roots in Catholic practice, and have more deeply impacted Protestantism in modern times than has the practice of pilgrimage. A retreat is a period of time devoted to intense religious study and practice, often at a monastic retreat house where the atmosphere is one of quietness and sanctity that also speaks of deep fellowship. From the Middle Ages onward, many have paid extended or brief visits to cloisters for the sake of nurturing their spiritual lives. Retreats have also been a part of the training of those called to the monastic life and to the ordained ministry. A well-known example of this is the four-week program envisioned by St. Ignatius Loyola for aspirants to his Jesuit order. Today retreats, often rather formal in structure, have gathered a large response from laity and clergy. Something of a similar pattern can be observed in other church activities that involve withdrawal from the usual daily routine, for example, summer youth camps.

There are other occasional services that more clearly follow the pattern we discussed earlier; rituals that mark and sanctify the most significant points in an individual's life. They are the Christian instances of the "rites of passage" that are found in all religious traditions. They give expression to the spiritual meaning of the natural events that occur between birth and the moment of death, and beyond. By recognizing and dramatizing the moments of change from one way of being to another, the whole of the individual's life between these moments is also imbued with meaning. We shall look briefly at the six most well known of those rituals, namely baptism, confirmation, marriage, ordination, unction, and the funeral.

We saw in Chapter 1 that, from the beginning, baptism has been the great rite of initiation, of entry into the Christian experience and the gateway to participation in the wonder of the death and resurrection of Jesus Christ. So, too, it now marks the entry into the fellowship of the church and thus into the mystical body of Christ. As from its earliest understanding, the administration of water symbolically washes away the accretion of sin and death and the believer rises again a new being in Christ. With words echoing the past, the officiate baptizes "In the Name of the Father, and of the Son, and of the Holy Spirit" with the activity of washing being performed by sprinkling, pouring, or total immersion, depending on the tradition involved.

No longer performed only at Easter, baptisms were in the past often celebrated as a semiprivate rite at hours not scheduled as part of the church's daily round. But now there is a growing tendency to bring this ritual into the church's main service when the whole congregation is gathered because, as in early times, it is considered to be a part of the function of the church as a whole. For that reason it is celebrated by the priest or minister as the Church's representative, except in the event of impending death, when anybody may perform the rite.

No longer demanding years of preparation and weeks of discipline, baptism in the Catholic tradition and among the majority of Protestants is administered to infants quite soon after birth. This practice emphasizes its role in sanctifying the first stage of life, becoming the spiritual equivalent of natural birth and giving the infant an identity in the world as a newborn daughter or son of God. This event is marked importantly by the giving of a name, specifically a Christian name; a name signifies both separate personal identity before God and humanity and also a joining and a belonging both to an immediate human and to a larger spiritual family. One of the doctrinal implications of baptism is expressed in the view that original sin is reversed in the baptized person's life (see Chapter 3).

Some Protestants, those in the Baptist and similar traditions, reject infant baptism, interpreting the meaning of the ritual in the early church in a particular way. They believe that the rite should be administered only to believers who make a mature confession of faith on their own. (In the infant baptism traditions, the confession of faith is made by sponsors—commonly called godparents—on the child's behalf.) For Baptists, baptism is an event in which one publicly makes a personal profession of faith and enacts its meaning: sharing in the death and resurrection to new life of Christ. Total immersion, as in the early church, is almost invariably the practice among adherents of "believer's baptism."

The second ritual, confirmation, is also an initiation ritual, this time marking and sanctifying the passage from childhood to adulthood, and it also parallels rituals performed at such a time in many other traditions. It is the time when young adults having undergone special classes for training in Scripture and doctrine, confirm their baptismal vows as adults and are accepted as adult members of the church. In the Catholic tradition, it is believed to convey the gifts of the Holy Spirit, and among Roman Catholics and Anglicans, confirmation is administered by the bishop's laying on of hands and anointing the forehead with chrism, or blessed oil. In the Eastern Orthodox church, confirmation or *chrismation* (anointing with chrism blessed by a bishop) is given at baptism. For Protestants, confirmation is usually a service of joining the church as an adult member, a "rite of passage" even in those denominations not using the word confirmation to name the event. In churches practicing adult baptism, the baptism itself can be said to convey the meaning of confirmation and mark the transition from old to new person.

Marriage, or the celebration of Holy Matrimony, ritually enacts another "passage"—this time the leaving of one's parents' home and the establishing of a new life centered upon the joining together of man and woman in a sanctified union. In its deeper understanding, this rite makes manifest the union between God and Creation, between Christ and the church, which is traditionally called the Bride of Christ. Thus it is a union that reenacts the ongoing divine mission to redeem the earth.

On a more tangible level, most denominations have rules indicating who may be married to whom and, through counsel or regulation, set standards for such matters as divorce, remarriage, and the religious upbringing of children.

Although enforced with varying degrees of strictness, the traditional stand of the Christian churches has been in favor of marriage to one person "till death do us part" with no sexual activity permissible outside of marriage. Closely related are the strong position some churches, notably the Roman Catholic, have taken in opposition to abortion and artificial means of birth control.

The wedding or service for the solemnization of Holy Matrimony is usually conducted in a festive atmosphere, often with procession and joyous music. It is generally performed by a priest or minister, although technically that person is there only to add the blessing and declaration that the marriage has been properly performed; the man and woman actually enact the marriage themselves through the exchange of vows and (customarily) rings. The service usually begins with a word by the officient about the meaning and sanctity of marriage, then proceeds to the exchange of vows and rings, the declaration by the officient that the couple are now "husband and wife," and final prayers and blessing. Scripture passages and music may also be part of the service. In the Catholic tradition, the wedding may be set into the Holy Communion service, which then becomes a "Nuptial Mass," a cluster of symbols that represents Christ's union with the church through the event of his death and resurrection. Innumerable wedding customs, from the entry with bridesmaids and the "giving away" of the bride by the bride's father to the crowns worn by the couple in the Greek Orthodox rite, show the variety of cultural traditions in which Christian marriage is set.

The ritual of ordination marks another transition but not one that is shared by all people. Ordination is a "setting-apart" of those who believe themselves called by God to the ordained ministry of the church. Following the pattern set by Paul and his helpers in the establishment of the early church, those who are called are set apart by the laying on of hands (Acts 13:1–4); in the Catholic tradition bishops ordain deacons and priests with other priests joining in the ordination of priests. A bishop is properly consecrated by three or more other bishops. In the Catholic tradition, there are basically three orders of clergy: bishops, priests, and deacons. Appropriate services of ordination (the term consecration is often used of a bishop) are held for each transition. (Other changes of status, as when a priest becomes a canon or a dean, or a bishop becomes an archbishop, cardinal, or Pope, may involve installation services but do not require new ordination as these are not new clerical ranks with new sacramental powers, but different functions within the grades of priest and bishop respectively.)

Ordination comes at the end of a period of training. Qualifications for the ministry, like the nature of that training, vary widely. Traditionally, the ordained Christian ministry has been exclusively male, but in the twentieth century several major denominations including the Episcopal, United Methodist, United Church of Christ, and Presbyterian have admitted women to it. The issue of women's ordination has been the source of much controversy over the years as some women have sought to give voice to a calling they felt deeply yet were forbidden to exercise. Many theological debates have occurred over this issue and many more will follow as women seek to be ordained in the Roman Catholic and Orthodox traditions.

Sickness is also another event in peoples' lives to which Christianity responds with appropriate ritual. Clergy of all denominations visit the sick in hospitals, nursing homes, and private residences to pray, offer consolation, and, frequently, to give holy communion. Many churches also have healing services, in which there is prayer and sometimes the laying-on-of-hands for healing in body or spirit. In the Catholic tradition, the sacrament known as unction or anointing (sometimes as Holy Unction or Extreme Unction) may be administered by anointing the suffering person with oil. Although often considered a rite for the dying, Unction has been and is used increasingly today as a healing rite for anyone who is in need, in body or spirit.

For the dying, though, the Roman Catholic church retains a set of practices known as Last Rites, which are preparatory to the final journey and include final confession and absolution, final Holy Communion, and Unction. The intention of these rites is to ready the dying person by returning them to the baptismal state of openness to God.

And so we come to the final stage and the final occasional rite in a person's life, that of the funeral and the memorial. Like marriage, this ritual is nowhere in the New Testament explicitly mandated as a function of the church and clergy. But, as is universally the case, death calls forth a deep human response, which Christianity answers in a particular way. Echoing the creation of humanity in the beginning from a clod of earth upon which God blew (Book of Genesis), the Christian community returns its dead to their source: "Earth to earth, ashes to ashes, dust to dust" as God ordained. "You are dust; to dust you shall return." Yet the eyes of faith see Christ risen from the death of the cross and know that at the end of time the glory of the defeat of death will be made known, as Jesus said, "I am the resurrection and the life, he who believes in me, though he die, yet shall he live, and whoever lives and believes in me shall never die" (Gospel of John 11:25–26).

On the basis of this belief, the body of the deceased is committed to the earth or to fire (as cremation becomes increasingly accepted), thus returning it to the elements in the hope of the glorious resurrection, which, paradoxically, is to come and yet like the Kingdom itself is already here, as the spirit of the deceased is given over into the hands of God. The ritual itself consists of these acts of commitment, together with Scripture readings concerning faith in eternal life and prayers for the mourners.

In the Catholic tradition prayers will be offered at the funeral and elsewhere for the soul of the departed, that it may grow in grace and glory. Protestants generally do not do this, feeling the deceased is now wholly in the mercy of God. In the Roman Catholic church, saying the Rosary on behalf of the deceased is a very common devotion. The funeral commonly includes the Holy Communion, known as a "Requiem Mass." Such Masses may be said on behalf of the departed at other times as well, as additional prayers and memorials. In the Catholic tradition, other offerings are made for the soul of the deceased including offerings of flowers and sanctuary candles. In the Eastern Orthodox tradition, food offerings of specific elements are made at regular intervals after the death of a loved one and are enjoyed by all the congregation after the Sunday service. In each instance, the ritual acts combine to represent the events of the Last Supper and Crucifixion. Thus the death of the believer is linked with that of the risen Lord, enabling that soul to participate in the resurrection.

In the next part of this chapter, we will look more closely at the weekly Sunday service in three central manifestations of the Christian faith. We will also examine the diverse ways in which the same founding event, Easter, is remembered and represented on each Sunday of the week.

EXAMPLES OF CHRISTIAN WORSHIP

Eastern Orthodox

Nowhere does the power of liturgical worship to create a separate reality out of ordinary time and space, a reality in which the truths and deepest hopes of faith seem to become tangible, show itself more clearly than in the worship of the Eastern Orthodox church. The interior of the church building itself is truly like the household of God and a foretaste of heaven. It will probably be ornamented in the brightest of colors, gold to suggest the glory of eternity and red to hint at divine splendor. In the dome overhead may be painted Christ as Pantocrator, enthroned as ruler of the universe, surrounded by his saints and angels. To the front may be the infant King in the arms of his mother, a grave and wise woman who has become no less than a personification of divine wisdom.

All around the church are icons, which we mentioned in Chapter 4, those characteristic Orthodox church objects of devotion which so well express its sense that heaven, eternity, is all around us all the time, imminently able to break through into the world of time. Icons are richly luminous paintings of Christ or a saint, done according to rigid conventions to represent the Holy One in his or her glorified, heavenly aspect, and opening the viewer into that transcendent reality. Orthodox people light candles and pray before the icons, and also kiss the holy objects. Usually a church will have a prominent icon at the doorway, for greeting upon entry, and others perhaps adorn the walls. The greatest assemblage, however, will be on the iconostasis, or icon screen, a splendid partition that separates the congregation from the altar. Like a visible face of heaven before earth, or a wall of glory shielding its deepest mysteries, the iconostasis is ablaze with saints in their holy magnificence. The iconostasis also contains the Royal Doors through which robed ministers process in and out during the service, like envoys from another world, to read the Gospel or to present the Eucharistic elements of bread and wine. In the center is an opening, over which a curtain can be drawn at the most sacred moments, and through which the priest is visible standing at the altar. For, in the Eastern Christian tradition, that which is most holy is screened, and allowed to abide in its transcendent mystery.

But if the church is a place of magnificence worthy of its divine proprietor, it is also a household, and there one who belongs can also feel at home. People of the Orthodox tradition treat their churches with a peculiar combination of reverent awe and informality that is not quite matched in Western Christianity. The devotion with which they kiss the icons and pray with the offering of the divine mysteries is unswerving, yet they also move about the church to light candles, or come and go during the long services, with a freedom that suggests being at peace in the halls of an exalted but old and close friend. Evelyn Underhill says of the Orthodox liturgy: "The whole emphasis lies on the sacred wonder of that which is done; and the prevailing temper is that of a humble, contrite, and awe-struck delight. 'He shall take the Holy Body in his hand, and he shall kiss it with tears,' says the Armenian Liturgy at the Communion of the Priest."[1]

The Sunday offering of the divine liturgy will begin in this characteristic atmosphere of reverential informality. Parishioners move quietly about the church, lighting candles and praying before various icons. At one side, a small choir sings a preparatory Matins service and the priest and his party of deacons and servers enter from the side almost inconspicuously. The first act is waving incense before all the icons which is itself an act of worship. After that, the priest proceeds to the altar to chant the opening words: "Blessed be the kingdom of the Father, and of the Son, and of the Holy Ghost, now, and for ever, and from all Ages to all Ages."[2] In the original Greek, "Ages" is "Aeons," and immediately this weekly offering is set in the midst of immense cosmic time where the eternity of the Trinity is manifest here and now.

And it is with the here and now that the next part of the service is concerned. The deacon begins a long series of litany-like prayers, to which the choir responds "Lord, have mercy" at each, on behalf of such homely concerns as the city, the weather, those who travel, as well as divine protection of the faithful, and the commemoration of the saints. The role of the deacon is significant, as leader of the prayers and reader of the Gospel. While the priest represents the divine center of the mystery, the deacon is like an intermediary, catching up the petitions of the people and laying them at the altar, delivering to them the words of the promise of eternal life.

The petitions end in the ancient prayer called the *Trisagion:* "Holy God, Holy and Strong, Holy and Immortal . . . " repeated three times. (The number three echoes over and over again in the liturgy emphasizing the importance of the Trinitarian image.) Then a reader reads a lesson from one of the Epistles. And, after a solemn procession in which the lavishly ornamented book of the Gospels is carried out through the Royal Doors, the deacon intones a passage from the life of the Saviour. The Gospels are much beloved by the Orthodox tradition,

---

[1]Evelyn Underhill, *Worship.* London: Nisbet & Company, 1936, p. 265.

[2]Citations of the Liturgy of St. John Chrysostom, the ordinary form of worship in the Eastern Orthodox church, are from *The Divine Liturgy of St. John Chrysostom.* London: Williams & Norgote, 1914.

and have played a prominent role in Orthodox piety and mysticism, especially in Russia.

After the Gospel comes another prayer climaxed by the celebrated Cherubic Hymn, usually sung to a particularly sweet and moving melody. It begins: "We who mystically represent the Cherubim, sing the Thrice-Holy hymn to the life-giving Trinity." As the liturgy advances and deepens, the assembled church has, as it were, passed into the heavenly places and shares in the adoration of the angels. With this hymn, the Royal Doors swing open once again, and robed servers process out bearing solemnly the bread and wine in rich vessels for the eucharistic offering.

The offering is followed by more prayer and praises as this service like a river winds its way slowly and meanderingly; deep and contemplative, unchanging, drifting almost slower than the eye can detect, yet before its end it accumulates tremendous force. After the prayers, comes the symbolic kiss of peace, and the deacon cries the words, "The doors! The doors!" Though no longer enforced, they recall the days in the early church (see Chapter 1) when from here on the catechumens were excluded and the doors barred; what followed was the "Mass of the Faithful" for fully initiated believers only.

The inner part of the service begins with the Liturgy of St. John Chrysostom, the normal Eastern Orthodox liturgy, with the summation of faith in the Nicene Creed (which we explored in Chapter 5), proceeding to the exchange of verses beginning "Lift up your hearts"—the lines that mark the transition to the great Eucharistic prayer in the Orthodox, Roman Catholic, and Anglican liturgies alike. Then follows another feature common to all three and to the ancient church, the short angelic hymn beginning, "Holy, Holy, Holy, Lord God of Hosts" . . . called the Sanctus.

The Eucharistic prayer in the Orthodox liturgy is typically long. It includes such basic features as the following: Christ's words of institution at the Last Supper are repeated; the Holy Spirit is invoked; the Lord's Prayer is said; and the bread is broken, given out, and the priest and those of the faithful who desire and are prepared receive it in communion.

Communion in the Eastern Orthodox church is given on a spoon, on which both bread and wine are placed. Although there have been movements in the twentieth century to encourage more frequent communion, adults still frequently take communion only once or at most only a few times a year. To communicate properly, one must undergo a fairly serious preparation of prayer, confession, and fasting reminiscent of the preparation prior to baptism in the early church. On the other hand, infants and small children are welcome to the sacrament and, being in a state of innocence and grace through their baptism and chrismation, need not submit themselves to arduous preparation. It is not uncommon to see a line of parents holding babies at communion time in the Orthodox liturgy, while they themselves do not partake.

After communion, thanksgivings are offered as the choir sings a short hymn whose words seem with particular power to sum up the meaning of the liturgy to the faithful as a mystery whose brightness opens into the supernal realities:

> *We have seen the true Light.*
> *We have received the Heavenly Spirit,*
> *We have found the True Faith*
> *Worshipping the Undivided Trinity;*
> *This is our salvation.*

After the formal end of the service, an interesting custom is observed. The priest comes to the front of the congregation and a tray with a large pile of pieces of bread is placed or held beside him. The congregation files forward: each person greets the priest, kisses the cross he wears, and takes a piece of bread. This is not the bread of the Holy Communion as such; rather it reenacts the ancient church's *agape* or "love-feast" held after the Eucharist. But, in view of the infrequency of lay communions in the Orthodox church, it may to some extent take its place, and certainly the practice is in keeping with the intimate, homey atmosphere of informality, which is one important aspect of Eastern Orthodoxy.

Roman Catholic Worship

The interior of a Roman Catholic church generally also glitters and shines. But the general feeling is one of greater openness and directness and less hiddenness and mystery. No iconostasis separates the altar from the people, and today the altar on which the sacrament is celebrated is often free-standing, the priest behind it facing the congregation as the bread and wine is offered. Further, in contrast to the older Gothic or Baroque altars with their cascades of saints and angels (which can still be seen against the forward wall of many Roman Catholic churches), the free-standing altar will have an air of simplicity about it. It is recognizable for what it ultimately is: a plain table upon which a meal is served, as well as locus of a sacrifice eternally offered before God.

Like the table, the Roman Catholic Mass has a public and direct quality about it, well reflecting the Roman temperament in contrast to the Greek. This was really true of the Western Mass when it was said in Latin until the early 1960s and the changes made by Vatican II (see previous chapter), although the straightforward character of the rite had been somewhat veiled by the archaic Latin and by a more ceremonial style of celebration in which the richly-vested priest generally stood with his back to the congregation as he made elaborate ritual gestures.

Now, with the Mass said in English (or whatever the vernacular tongue of the congregation is), and the style of celebration simplified almost to the prosaic, the Mass' concise, unambiguous language and vigorous pace is readily apparent. It moves quickly and has variations for each Sunday (indeed, for each day) of the year, more so than the Eastern rite. The Western church has a dynamic history, which is paralleled in its liturgy. The Eastern church veils that which is most holy; in its Western counterpart the sacramental actions, and the sacred bread itself, are publicly displayed.

As the congregation gathers before the Mass begins, many genuflect (that is, touch one knee to the floor) before entering a pew. This is an act of reverence to the reserved sacrament (consecrated bread) which is perpetually kept in the boxlike tabernacle on or by the altar. The elements therein are used to give communion to the sick in hospitals or homes, and also as a focus of devotion in church. For in that bread Christ is sacramentally present; this presence is indicated by the lamp that continually burns near the altar.

Before Mass, and even during it, a light may also be burning on one of the confessional booths, indicating that a priest is there ready to hear confession and give absolution. A short line may form at this booth as worshippers desire to reconcile themselves to God before receiving Holy Communion.

The Mass itself begins with the entry of the priest, accompanied by one or two servers. On Sundays there will now probably be a hymn led by a layman and sung by the congregation as well as the choir. The priest, standing in front of the altar and facing the congregation, greets the congregation in the name of the Lord, and often talks about the theme and intentions of this Mass.

Mass proceeds with a general confession of sins, and the short liturgical hymns beginning "Lord, have mercy" and "Glory to God in the highest." After that comes the "opening prayer," or collect, a short prayer that is particular to each Sunday.

So begins the Liturgy of the Word. First a lesson from the Old Testament or the Books of Acts or Revelation is presented, usually read by a layman who comes to the front of the church for this purpose. Then, as the congregation stands, a priest or deacon reads a passage from one of the Gospels. Following the Gospel, the homily or sermon is delivered, probably by a priest. It may be by the pastor of the parish, by an assistant, or by a visiting clergyman or missionary. The Roman Catholic sermon often has an informal, unpretentious quality; the real weight of communication between God and humanity is here carried more by the liturgy than the halting efforts of human speech, and the homiletic mood is likely to be one of simply talking about a shared faith rather than one of appeals to conversion or conviction.

After the sermon, the shared faith is expressed in the words of the Nicene Creed. Here begins the Liturgy of the Eucharist, the same inner core of the rite of ancient times and in the East called the Liturgy of the Faithful. It begins with the offering of the bread and wine, now usually brought by lay persons from the back of the church in procession. After the prayers and verses associated with the offertory, the Eucharistic action itself commences with the preface containing the verse "Lift up your hearts" and proceeding to the "Holy, Holy, Holy . . . ," the Sanctus.

Then comes the great prayer of consecration itself which includes several themes: the greatness of God; the sacrifice of Christ; prayer that the Holy Spirit may sanctify the Eucharistic offering of bread and wine; a recitation of the words of Christ at the Last Supper—"This is my Body," "This is my Blood"; a commemoration of the Blessed Virgin Mary and all the saints; a petition for the church, its leadership, the Pope and local bishop, and all its people, and for the faithful departed. The long prayer ends with a solemn acclamation of the divine glory as the chalice and loaf are lifted, like Christ, upon the cross. It is then followed by the Lord's Prayer, the breaking of the bread accompanied by certain short prayers, and communion. Just before the breaking of the bread, the "kiss of peace" is exchanged, when the clergy and congregation greet each other with kisses, handshakes, or whatever gesture they wish, saying to one another, "The peace of the Lord be with you always."

According to Catholic belief, in this rite of blessing and offering bread Christ as it were becomes incarnate once again in the midst of his people and is offered once again for their sins in a spiritual sense. The altar is a perpetual Bethlehem, where Christ is born anew with each offering of the Mass, and a perpetual Calvary, where his one sacrifice is presented at the throne of God continually until the end of the world so that his people may continually participate in its inestimable benefits. Because of traditional Roman Catholic beliefs of this sort about the efficacy of the Mass, the general feeling has been in this church that the more Masses offered, the more God's saving power works in the world. Every priest is ordinarily supposed to say Mass daily, and it is presented daily in all churches with a resident priest. Masses are also offered for special purposes, from Requiem Masses, for the repose of deceased loved ones, to Votive Masses, for special intentions.

Modern theological thinking, however, has counterbalanced this perspective with a renewed sense of the importance of the Mass as the communal act of the church, through which the faithful are bound together in love for one another and for God and become visibly the body of Christ in the world. The new liturgical practices, in which the congregation is symbolically gathered around the altar as a family about the table and in which love is exchanged by gestures such as the ancient and now revived kiss of peace, express this insight. Christ is seen on the altar as incarnate Lord and sacrificial victim, as the loving heart of a community of love.

In the Roman Catholic church, communion is ordinarily given to the laity in the form of the bread only. Parishioners now usually line up and file past a priest at the front of the church to receive it.

After communion, the service comes quickly to an end. There is a prayer of thanksgiving, a blessing, and then, briskly the priest may say, "The Mass is ended, go in peace." (The Latin form of this concluding line, "*Ite missa est,*" gave us the word Mass as the Western church's tag for the Eucharistic rite.) The priest may also say, "Go in peace to love and serve the Lord," and the congregation adds, "Thanks be to God." The service may then close with a procession and hymn as the clergy and faithful depart to do the Lord's work in the world.

The Structure of the Protestant Service

If the dominant theme of Eastern Orthodox worship is participation in the heavenly mysteries, and of Roman Catholic worship is the dynamic renactment of the holy sacrifice, the basic motif of Protestant worship is communication. Protestantism is concerned to clear the way in order to facilitate unobstructed communication between God and humanity in the reading and preaching of God's word, and between humanity and God in simple, direct prayer and praise.

Entering a typical, "mainstream" American Protestant church, we first notice two things. The interior is usually relatively plain, more likely to exhibit the soft colors of natural wood than gilt or gems, and with very few pictures or pieces of sculpture in view. The brightest colors will probably be from stained-glass windows illustrating Biblical scenes. If there is an altar table, candles, cut flowers, and a simple cross or open Bible will be the most that it will display. The pulpit will be impressive and centrally placed as the focal point.

At the same time, we observe the relative informality of the congregation. People take their seats in the pews without bowing or genuflecting toward the altar or with any conspicuous efforts at prayer on entry. They appear "natural" and may even chat quietly with their neighbors until the service starts. These observations combine to suggest that this is a comfortable Christian fellowship for whom the events of the service hold greater significance than the physical structure of the church, which is more like a meeting place than a manifestation of sacred space as in the Catholic tradition.

Before the service starts there will most likely be an organ prelude. The entry of the choir, probably robed, and the minister, usually wearing formal street clothing and often robed in a black academic-type gown, is accompanied by a hymn. The minister warmly greets the congregation in the name of the Lord, which salutation may be followed by a canticle from the choir, or a responsive reading by the minister and the congregation.

The pastoral prayer follows in which the minister prays at some length on behalf of the congregation for their needs and for the needs of the world. Then comes a particularly important and solemn moment as the readings from the Scriptures begin. Scripture is here seen as being, in a very special—even unique—sense, the principal vehicle of communication between God and humanity, and, as we have seen, the whole point of this service is communication. For this reason the whole service is in the common language and, in comparison with the Catholic tradition, is severely shorn of everything, however beautiful, that might impede communication through the spoken word.

That spoken word next comes transmitted in the form of the sermon, which often expounds the message of the Scripture readings. In significant distinction from the more pedagogical or exhortative view of the Catholic tradition, Protestantism sees the sermon as an integral and essential part, indeed the climax of worship itself. The sermon is a vehicle through which the living word of God comes to humanity, who are then called to unite in response to it. The sermon is immensely important: next to the Bible, it is believed to be God's major means of communicating with humanity. Only the Bible can judge the sermon. The service is to make the communication of the spoken word central.

When Holy Communion is celebrated in a mainstream Protestant church, it is most likely to follow the sermon, although occasionally it precedes it. Apart from those few Protestant churches, such as the Church of Christ, which make a point of offering the Lord's Supper weekly, celebration is likely to be quarterly or monthly, although the trend is toward more frequent communion. The format varies in different traditions, from the highly traditional Lutheran and Anglican rite, already discussed, through the very simple but structured liturgies of Methodists and Presbyterians to the more informal and spontaneous usages of Baptists and others. Here communion is often taken from individual glasses distributed to worshippers in the pews, rather than from a chalice. The Protestant communion is fairly brief, consisting typically of a prayer and Scripture reading in which the minister recalls the Last Supper and Christ's mandate to "Do this in remembrance of me," and prays that the congregation may by that act be brought closer to him. Then, led by the minister, the assembly prayerfully eats a small piece of bread and drinks from the tiny cups wine or, more often, grape juice. Solemn thanks follow. As noted, communion is not as central to Protestant as it is to Catholic worship. In Catholic service, Holy Communion is a sacrament rather than a memorial feast and those who partake participate here and now in the founding event of the death and resurrection of Christ; it is, moreover, believed to happen again in and through each communicant and through the community united as the mystical Body of Christ in the world. The simple Protestant communion service, on the other hand, creates a very warm, spiritually rich moment that draws the congregation together and, crossing the centuries, unites them also with its Lord. Following the sermon, the Protestant service draws to a close after an offertory, a musical selection, final prayers, benediction, and a closing hymn.

The service closes with a hymn just as it opened with one. Quite possibly one or two more hymns are scattered throughout the service. During the offertory, the choir or a soloist presents an anthem or other special sacred music. Such music is important and prominent enough in Protestant worship that it is worth pausing for a moment to consider its significance. Many Protestant hymns are quite emotional, emphasizing in their text a warm personal relation to God, Christ, and the Holy Spirit, and in their melody the joy and sweetness of this relation. Others, particularly in the classical Lutheran and Reformed traditions, are stately, stressing God's majesty and might. In any case, they usually channel the emotional side of Protestant religion, drawing the heart as well as the mind to God's splendor and closeness.

For this very reason a few Protestants, mainly Quakers, have harbored suspicion of music in worship, fearing its power to arouse emotion unbridled by reason; yet they also make some use of it.

Nonetheless, music is important to Protestant worship. Because it recovers the New Testament form of worship, of which music was most probably a part, and is based on the model of Jesus and the disciples singing a hymn at the Last Supper and of Paul describing the early churches as raising "hymns and psalms and spiritual songs," music represents something fundamental. The indwelling, saving faith that is at the heart of the Protestant vision is not only an intellectual concept or formula or only an experience made up of words. Its core lies much deeper than reason or emotion; both must be transcended wholly by becoming channels of grace.

CONCLUSION

In this chapter, we have come to see something of the richness and diversity of Christian worship. Uniting body and mind, flesh and spirit, these Christian services allow believers to participate in the mystery of God, who became known in the event of the Incarnation. Each provides drama that opens to the possibility of a religious experience that is complete, not in the sense of exhaustive, but more in the sense of being, in that moment, full to overflowing.

christianity and social settings

The story of Christianity, understood as a particular way of viewing the world and humanity in relation to God, can be told from yet another approach. Earlier chapters have examined Christianity's history, its relation to countercultures; its artistic expressions; and its foundational myths and rituals as manifest in story, belief, and worship. This time the exploration turns to the great variety and complexity of the relationships between Christianity and the social settings in which it has come to expression. Questions concerning the formation, function, influence, and interdependence of one upon the other have become the focus of a modern subdiscipline in the study of religion known as the "sociology of religion." Some of the many insights of this approach and its perspectives are offered in this chapter as another amplification of Christianity in its cultural manifestations.

One of the valuable sets of ideas offered by sociologists of religion to assist in understanding the relationships between Christianity and society has been the comparison and contrast between the "church-type" organization and the "sect-type." Through exploring these concepts, this chapter will present some aspects of the dynamic relationship encompassing Christianity and society.

"CHURCH-TYPE" CHRISTIANITY

Roman Catholicism is perhaps the most enduring instance of the Christian "church-type" organization. This type of organization was clearly characterized by Ernest Troeltsch when he wrote:

> The Church is that type of organization which is overwhelmingly conservative, which to a certain extent accepts the secular order, and dominates the masses; in principle, therefore, it is universal, i.e., it desires to cover the whole life of humanity.[1]

Roman Catholicism so clearly demonstrates these characteristics even in its name: "catholic" *means* universal. The term denotes the aspiration to be the universally extended organization that provides the orthodox understanding of Christianity. Catholicism offers a single standard of faith and morals to all adherents in all times and places. Since the Reformation there has been a situation in which multiple organizations and institutions have named themselves as Christian; the most prominent one to name itself both catholic *and* Christian has been Roman Catholicism. Some Protestant churches also have aspirations to be universal, but none has built up the extensive infrastructure necessary to enable it to claim accomplishment of those aspirations in any way remotely as extensively as has Roman Catholicism.

Troeltsch offers further comments regarding the church-type organization:

> The fully developed Church . . . utilizes the State and the ruling classes, and weaves these elements into her own life; she then becomes an integral part of the existing social order; from this standpoint, then, the Church both stabilizes and determines the social order; in so doing, however, she becomes dependent upon the upper classes, and upon their development.

Troeltsch continues:

> The Church relates the whole of the secular order as a means and a preparation to the supernatural aim of life; and it incorporates genuine asceticism into its structure as one element in this preparation, all under the very definite direction of the Church. . . . The asceticism of the Church is a method of acquiring virtue, and a special high water mark of religious achievement, connected chiefly with the repression of the senses, or expressing itself in special achievements of a peculiar character; otherwise, however, it presupposes the life of the world as the general background, and the contrast of an average morality which is on relatively good terms with the world.[2]

If the struggles of early Christianity in the Roman Empire are recalled,[3] one sees that the issue of what forms of organization would be established for Christians has been a paramount one since the days of the Apostles—such questions as: Are the disciples, who became Apostles to the Jews and the Gentiles, superior to later converts to the Gospel? Was one Apostle, Peter for example, superior to the others? Or, were John, Peter, and Paul to be granted equal authority to each other, but greater than that of the others? Was Christianity to be

---

[1] Ernst Troeltsch, *Social Teachings of the Christian Churches*, Vol. 1 (New York: Harper & Brothers, 1960), p. 331.

[2] Troeltsch, p. 333.

[3] See Chap. 3.

a sect within Judaism, or was it to be an independent religious organization? The fact that these were important questions and that honest Christians plainly disagreed in their beliefs regarding appropriate responses to them was one dimension leading to the conflicts between orthodox and heretical views. This is one indication that Christians early recognized how crucial it was to ask and to resolve the question of the institutional organization of Christianity and, thereby, to settle the manifold issues of how Christianity would relate to the larger Roman society.

In early times, the word "church" was used by many different groups of Christians. Some churches were characterized by their orthodox theological beliefs. At the same time, theological beliefs that orthodoxy called "heretical" characterized others. The word "church" derives from the Greek word *ekklesia,* which means "called out"; in its Christian context, "church" came to mean the people called out by God through their faith in Christ. Thus, it is important to recall in reading this chapter that many groups or communities of Christians called their gatherings churches. The word is not exclusively nor accurately confined to any one group, whether Roman Catholic, Greek Orthodox, Anglican, Lutheran, or any of the other more than three hundred organizations in Christianity.

Even the limited overview of Christian history provided in this book shows quite clearly that the mainstream of Christian practice and thinking has been a church-type formulation. Troeltsch comments: " . . . the Church-type represents the longing for a universal all-embracing ideal, the desire to control great masses of men [sic], and therefore the urge to dominate the world and civilization in general."[4] If any institution aspires to universality, to control great masses of people, and to world domination, it has no choice but to come to terms with the existing social order and its complex of institutions—governments, economic systems, education systems, familial patterns. Exploring how church-type Christianity made such accommodations provides one further perspective on this prominent form of Christian organization in its relation to society.

The first requirement toward institutionalization was to arrive at an understanding of the nature and purposes of the organization of the church itself. The late first century marked the rise to prominence of this question. Over succeeding centuries, with ever-increasing clarity and confidence, the church declared itself to be instituted by God as the repository and possessor of religious power and truth. Then, as now, hierarchical priesthood provides the leadership under the guidance of bishops who stand in the tradition of the Apostles. The Bible, the contents of which were selected on the basis of the claimed apostolic origin of the books, reinforced the theories espoused by the leadership. The Apostles' Creed succinctly summarized the accepted consensus beliefs. The systematic interdependence of these three—priesthood under apostolic bishops, apostolic writings, and apostolically articulated essential beliefs—settled the question of dependable, authoritative leadership. Legitimation processes were near closure.

---

[4] Troeltsch, p. 334.

No alternative vision could remotely compare to the extensive claims of this theory.

Then came the question of how to relate the institutionalized church to the governmental structures of the larger society; initially, of course, that meant to the Roman Empire with its highly structured levels of delegated authority. Appealing to the sacred writings of Christianity, Christian theorists began very early to claim that the Christian Gospel provided a vision of governments, whatever their form, deriving from the creator, sustainer, and savior of the universe. Under the holism of the Gospel, all the orders and structures of society are ordained by God. The logic of the case is complex: the divinely instituted church is the channel for God's having revealed this arrangement of society, but, because all the institutions of society are expressions of God's will, then the church *must* concern and involve itself with them if it is to be faithful to the vision it proclaims. Nothing in society could possibly lie outside the universal vision that the church is charged to preserve and proclaim. When, in the early fourth century, Christianity was made a legal religion by Emperor Constantine and was thereby protected from the persecutions it had experienced during earlier centuries, the act of legalization

Pope John XXIII. Photo courtesy of United Press International.

was viewed by Christians as an ambiguous confirmation of God's plan. When, by the end of the fourth century, Emperor Theodosius decreed that Christianity was the sole legitimate religion within the Empire, that law appeared as the consummation of the vision.

There was a built-in source of tension in the relation between the church and the imperial government, however. If God had decreed that all institutions should conform to the vision revealed in Christianity, and if the Pope is the supreme head of the church—the Vicar of Christ—then how shall the Pope relate to the Emperor, who is the supreme head of the empire, which in Christian theory is also God's instrument? Everything hinged not on the theory but rather on personalities and political power and alliances. Strong popes could effectively prevail against weak emperors, but strong emperors could make pawns of weak popes. The struggle was a manifestation of the eternal tension within the accepted theory. We have seen that in the modern world an altogether different political theory—the separation of church and state—has resulted in the church's becoming only one of the institutions of society among all the others. The traditional Christian vision of a Gospel-oriented organization of society has required radical reinterpretation in the modern world in which other authorities compete with a Christian vision.

Dr. Martin Luther King, Jr. Photo courtesy AP Wirephoto.

MARRIAGE, FAMILIES, AND CELIBACY

All the other institutions of society were, predictably, sooner or later subjected to the theory of the universal vision of the church. The family is one of the earliest and most basic of societal institutions. In the earliest years of Christianity there were instances when families were divided when one member, especially a wife and mother, converted to Christianity and the spouse did not do so. Such a situation reflects the individualistic thrust of the early Christian preaching and the urgency of conviction that could result from awakening faith in the heart of an individual, even if it meant severe disruption or disturbance of preexistent relationships. For church-type Christianity, this became intolerable. In the churches' view, the Gospel provides a universal vision and all institutions of society must conform to it. Christian faith, from this perspective, should cement human relations more deeply, not disrupt them. Little surprise, then, that marriage was one of the earliest Christian concerns, as a study of the New Testament itself indicates, especially the letters of St. Paul.

Another aspect of Christian reflections on marriage focused upon the very powerful issue of sexuality. Sexual desire is without doubt a recurrently problematic area of human experience for church-type Christianity. From St. Paul to the present, the anxiety and uncertainty regarding sexuality on the part of Christian thinkers is evident. "Better to marry than to be aflame with passion" (I Corinthians 7:9), wrote Paul. However, the same Paul also wrote an extended passage that likens marital love to Christ's love for the church and concludes with the comment: "This is a great mystery, . . ." (Ephesians 5:32).

The Catholic church has essentially seen marriage as a channel for sexuality. The chief purpose of sex in marriage is the procreation of children. A significant second purpose is "the avoidance of sin." Confining sexual relations within marriage is one of the ways the church sanctions and controls erotic passion by keeping it within acceptable channels and modes of expression. Strict monogamy is required by the church; through the centuries, divorce has been difficult, at times even impossible. Powerful bonding and transformation occur as a relationship deepens. Then the connection is anything but easy to eliminate from partners' lives. Many studies have demonstrated that the trauma of divorce introduces an enormous degree of stress into peoples' lives.

From the perspective of sociology, the church's comprehensive theory of all social relations underscores yet again how powerful, important, and enduring that theory proves to be. In conserving traditional views of marriage, divorce, and sexuality the church has advocated a controversial theory, but one that has withstood challenges over thousands of years. That staying power marks it as sociologically significant.

The Catholic church eventually elevated matrimony to the status of a sacrament, that is, a means of conferring grace to those who participate in the act. So regarded, the rite of Matrimony carries specific understandings of its meaning in its outward manifestation as part of the liturgical context of the church. Likewise, an inseparable part of the marital relation between woman and man is the creation of the conditions for caring for the children of the family, whose conception and development to term, the modern Catholic church has decreed, must be unhindered by any birth control method other than natural rhythm. The responsibility for caring for the spiritual formation of the children, who are to be received as divine gifts, falls upon the parents. In their desire to fulfill this duty, parents have often banned together with the church to provide schools within which the whole Catholic worldview and sensibility can be instilled and sustained. The system thus formed around the sacrament of marriage is mutually reinforced by each increment in the process.

Closely related to establishing the sacramental view of matrimony, with its corollary familial implications, are the debates in the Catholic church about celibacy (commitment not to marry). Celibacy is another way the Catholic church has dealt with human sexuality. Orthodox Christian churches of the East have maintained a mixed standard: priests and deacons may be ordained, even if married at the time (although they may not marry after ordination), but bishops must be committed celibates (that is, unmarried at the time of their consecration, and for the rest of their lives). The Western Catholic church, however, from as early as the fourth century has demanded celibacy as a condition for ordination. If married previously, the candidate for priesthood is required to live separately and to vow sexual abstinence (chastity). This is viewed as a law of the church, rather than as a law of God. It expresses the view that sexual activity risks a person's being drawn away from exclusively spiritual concerns into temptations of the flesh. The rise of monasteries, which have traditionally required vows of chastity and celibacy for all candidates and full participants, further emphasized the view that sex and sin, if not identical, are so closely bound to each other that it is better to avoid sexual activity.

Many schismatic and "heretical" groups interpreted the Christian message as requiring *all* Christians, not only the leaders, to vow celibacy. Husbands and wives must live apart; unmarried people must not marry. (More of this will be explained below.) All these forces combined to lead the leaders and thinkers of the church-type Catholic church to compromise: lay people can marry and be blessed by the sacrament of matrimony to confirm their procreation of children; priests, when ordained, must choose the way of celibacy and chastity. Priests were further distinguished from lay people even in the dress they were permitted to wear—today obvious in the clerical collar and black clothing that has evolved over the centuries.

EDUCATION: SCHOOLS AND UNIVERSITIES

Education is the last of the social structures to be touched upon here. The notion of the church providing schools for the education and formation of Catholic children was mentioned above in the comments on the family. *Catechesis,* the church's form of instructing initiates in the essentials of the faith by requiring that one learn *the catechism,* inculcates the church's teachings and beliefs. But Catholic-church Christianity has never left the matter there. The monasteries of the Middle Ages often became centers of study and learning during a time that, from the modern perspective that considers the "light of the world" as the advancement of reason and knowledge, has been called "the Dark Ages." Monasteries were often the only repositories of writings from antiquity and from the early Christian centuries. Scholarship was one form of the monastic disciplines. However, as centers of re-treat from the larger society, monasteries could only serve as conservators and preservers of learning. The transmission of knowledge and creative understand-ing was primarily from one generation of monks to the next. Only when someone moved out of the monasteries into the larger church institution did the education going on within their walls spill into an arena of greater influence. Indeed, in cases when certain medieval Popes did make such a move, the church was the bene-ficiary of these uncommon events.

As direct outgrowths of the monastic attention to scholarship and learning, medieval universities arose; their emergence can be traced along with the parallel phenomenon of cathedral schools. In its original Latin form, the term *universitas* designated "community" or "corporation." To indicate the particular educa-tional purposes of a specific institution required additional words like *magistorum et scholarium,* or more commonly simply *studium generale.* A scholarly guild of teach-ers arose on the analogy of the new guilds of artists or tradesmen in the twelfth century. Over several centuries, the name *universitas* became the common word for such educational guilds and centers.

The Catholic church early recognized the importance and potential power of such centers, and Popes and church councils vigorously sought to control their licensing and authorization. The study of medicine and law came to be augmented by philosophical and theological studies. Perhaps no single institution, originally conceived as a part of the system of church-type Catholic Christianity, has been more fateful on a long-term basis. Time after time in the eight centuries since they first appeared in the Western world, universities have been a source of the greatest challenges to the theories and structures of Catholic Christianity. Disciplined study often generates ideas and questions that do not conform to the views of the church's authority in all domains of human life. Speculative philosophy and theology, not to mention theoretical science, careful historical and textual studies, and the new disciplines spawned in the modern world, all have conjoined to raise some of the most far-reaching critiques of the church's teachings it has ever had to endure. The pursuit of particular and universal truths, as the repeated aspiration and ideal that guides the university, requires a freedom and independence that is often not easily reconciled with a religious institution aspiring to universality and social domination. Academic freedom and religious liberty do often become powerful allies; occasionally, however, they violently collide and the claims of one or the other become subordinated. With the rise of independent and state-supported secular universities, higher education has become another force in society that the church has to come to appreciate and incorporate in its self-understanding. For their part, such universities are even less constrained in providing students opportunities to engage in the most rigorously critical and constructive examinations of the claims to universality of church-type Catholicism, and indeed of all religions.

"CHURCH-TYPE" ORGANIZATION: OVERVIEW

The theoretical grounds of one of the most prominent organizational modes that Christianity has conceived has been presented under the name of Roman Catholicism. This church-type organization has demonstrated extraordinary resilience over the centuries in concretely finding ways to incorporate more and more dimensions of society into its theoretical framework and worldview. On the other hand, in the modern world political revolutions and theories of autonomous governments have in turn tempered the Catholic vision.

In the realm of faith and morals, Catholic Christianity speaks what it believes to be the last words because they are believed to be God's words. To live under the umbrella of Roman Catholicism is to have available one of the most carefully conceived and extensive symbol systems and theological views that any religious tradition has ever created. From birth to death, in every recurrent human transition and crisis, this church has resources to offer those whom it embraces and who accept its authority.

However, no external critics have been more critical of it than some within the church over the centuries; few questions that conceivably could be put to it have failed to be vigorously debated within it. Through it all, the Roman Catholic Church has steadfastly adhered to its vision and demonstrated the power of that vision. Still, terrible blights mar the applied work of the church from time to time in its history; its immense power has periodically been misused for personal aggrandizement, often with tragic results. But through it all, the church-type form has often proven its durability and adaptability, and for untold millions of Christians it has been offered and accepted as the medium through which grace has entered and sustained their lives.

Mention of the work of Emile Durkheim serves further to introduce the perspective of sociology as he unfolded his analysis in *The Elementary Forms of Religious Life*. For him, existence was clearly divided between that which is sacred and that which is profane. The sacred, when it is manifest, is experienced as world-creating. There is a human desire to live in proximity to it. The sacred is the recognition of "the eternal truth that outside of us there exists something greater than us with which we are in communion."[5] But it is his locating of the sacred that sets the thinking of Durkheim apart from other scholars of his time. As he says, the human being feels the "existence of a moral power upon which he de-

---

[5] Emile Durkheim, *The Elementary Forms of the Religious Life* (New York: Free Press, 1965), p. 54.

pends and from which he receives all that is best in himself: the power exists, it is society."[6]

For Durkheim, the sacred is expressed in society, which is greater than, and different from, the sum of its apparently constitutive parts. Participants in a society are formed in their internal appropriations of the values, morals, and perspectives that are given to them by that society. Humans are socially formed beings. One may be converted from one social complex by and to another one, but one cannot exist humanly outside some shaping social context. From this perspective, religion is a social phenomenon, a response to specific social needs and a product of collective thought. Religion functions to perpetuate the human behavior that is necessary for the existence of society. Religion is a function of society and, as such, is "something that you do," not only something that is believed. A religion is "a unified whole system of beliefs and practices . . . which unite into one single moral community, called a church, all those who adhere to them."[7] Lest Durkheim's thinking be heard merely as a kind of functionalism, these words echo differently: "men [sic] make their gods . . . at the same time it is from them that they live themselves."[8]

In the work of the contemporary sociologist of religion, Peter Berger, especially as expressed in his *The Social Construction of Reality,* some themes from Durkheim are amplified and extended. For Berger, reality is both socially constructed and at the same time exists independently of human volition. Society has both objective actuality and subjective meaning. As with Durkheim, Berger is concerned with the dialectical relationship between people and society, particularly as it is manifest in institutions. Paradoxically, the institutional world that is experienced as external, objective reality is produced by people; yet it is also experienced as other than a human product. Berger describes this as the dialectical process of "externalization—objectification—internalization."

Institutions, like the church, require (1) legitimization, (2) sanctions, and (3) role-playing to exist. The first provides a "protective canopy," which insists that the "same story must be told to all the children." Secondly, sanctions are established to claim and establish authority over the individual, thereby lessening the chance of deviation from the controlling character of the institution as the representative of the order presented in the story. And, thirdly, role-playing binds individuals to the institution as a cohesive whole, a situation that can be realized only through individuals accepting the institutionally defined and permitted roles.

Berger observes that institutions, such as the church, tend to become "reified." Although demonstrably constructed by human activity, the institution is no longer regarded as a human product but as a fact of nature or divine will. There is a forgetfulness or loss of consciousness that people are producers of reality;

---

[6] Durkheim, p. 60.

[7] Durkheim, p. 62.

[8] Durkheim, p. 333.

rather, they, too, are now seen as products of the world. Society becomes fixated and dehumanized.

Reification is, for Berger, a mode of consciousness that objectifies the humanly created world. A status independent of human activity is accorded to it. For example, marriage can be reified as an imitation of divine acts of creativity, as a universal mandate of natural law, as biologically or psychologically necessary, as an imperative of a social system, or as a combination of all of these. All these concepts tend to obfuscate marriage as an ongoing human creation. In reification, roles are seen as fated, leaving the person without choice while binding the total identity of that person to that role. Reification bestows independent status on a humanly generated role that, from another perspective, is only one part of the self. Berger points out the paradox: human beings continue to produce a reality that continues to reduce, to the point of eliminating, awareness of the human contribution to it.

The work of legitimization orders reality into a ''symbolic universe'' in which everything has its rightful place. It orders society, the individual biography, and history. The primary task of this ordering, as Berger says, is to locate death, to give a recipe that allows the individual to go on living in the knowledge of pending death. Institutional order in the symbolic universe is designed to shield and protect those who live within it from ultimate terror. Berger locates the origin and motive of legitimating in the fundamental constitution of the human who dwells in the anxiety-producing tension between order and chaos.

A symbolic universe is described by Berger as being maintained by ''conceptual machineries,'' such as mythology, psychology, theology, and science, and at the same time, being dynamically changed by new themes that arise in these areas. Berger describes this dialectic as lying between society and the history of ideas, whereas the dialectic of the human condition lies between nature and society. Berger names this realm as the place of transformation of the human. Here people produce reality and thereby produce themselves.

Christianity functions, as has been demonstrated, to provide its adherents with a world view that is sustained and perpetuated by the means Berger lists. The sociological analysis, however, clashes dramatically with one of the chief tenets of church-type Christian belief, namely, revelation. Theologically viewed, all of creation, including society, is an act of God, and revelation enables those who receive it to understand and recognize that to be the case. Sociology and theology, therefore, are not always convergent in their conclusions. But there is a consistent thread in sociological analyses that sharpens some issues, even when theology would urge that those issues be viewed differently.

Berger stresses that all symbolic universes are human products. As such they are based on human lives that have no status apart from them. Symbolic universes are not ontological. For him, society is made by humans, is inhabited by humans, and, in turn, is engaged in making humans in an ongoing and changing historical process.

"SECT-TYPE" CHRISTIANITY

In marked contrast to Catholic "church-type" Christianity stands "sect-type" Christianity. Its most characteristic feature is that it is a voluntary association of individuals who form themselves into communities based upon sufficiently similar kinds of experience to enable them to agree to participate with others in their efforts to live by their understanding of the Gospel. Speaking precisely, nobody can be naturally born into any sect; only those confirmed by personal experience are admitted into membership. Contrast that with the life-long process of socialization in the church-type organization.

Sudden conversions are hallmarks of admission into sects. Troeltsch characterized the church as having aimed at objectifying the institution: the priests, the sacraments, and the cumulative tradition are the objective embodiments of God's purpose, from the church perspective. "The Apostolic Message of the Exalted Christ, and faith in Christ the Redeemer, into which the Gospel has developed; this constitutes its objective treasure. . . . "[9] The sect, however, "starts from the teaching and example of Jesus, from the subjective work of the Apostles and the pattern of their life of poverty, and unites . . . religious individualism . . . with religious fellowship, in which the office of the ministry is not based upon ecclesiastical ordination and tradition, but upon religious service and power, and which therefore can also devolve entirely upon laymen."[10]

Such differences are crucial in understanding the variety of organizational expressions of Christianity both historically and today. Sectarian views are not merely underdeveloped versions of Christian thinking. Rather, they are indigenous interpretations of the same message that in a different way gave rise to church-type Christianity as a highly institutionalized expression. The same Gospel has led to diverse sociological expressions. Church-type Christians, however, have always tended to regard sect-type Christians as radicals, dissenters, or heretics; sect-type Christians, in turn, have always regarded church-type Christians as corrupters and legalists. The student of Christianity in its cultural contexts, however, has the opportunity to see both "types" as equally authentic, although significantly different Christian ways of relating to culture and society.

Earlier in this chapter, some of the central emphases of church-type Christianity were presented. As we turn now to instances of sect-type Christianity, comparisons and contrasts will be obvious. The passage from Troeltsch just cited indicates some of the essential characteristics of the sect-type tendency. Direct, immediate experience of God in a person's life is the message and aspiration of all sect-type forms of Christianity. No priest, no sacrament, no routinized forms of worship, no creed, and, ultimately, no Bible can substitute for direct experience. Straightforward, unambiguous moral purity is the essential criterion for

---

[9] Troeltsch, p. 341f.
[10] Troeltsch, p. 343.

measuring such a person's life. Sect-type Christians have not, characteristically, developed systematic theologies; rather, accepting God's word and abiding by the Law of Nature have been regarded as the obligations of these Christians. Law, God's and Nature's, become the emblem of this view, but understood as expressions of moral responsibilities and duties of service to others. Severity, approaching legalism, is typically a feature of the sect-type sense of Christianity.

It remains to explore some examples to suggest how sect-type Christianity was lived out.[11] Only contemporary United States with its proliferation of "new religions" matches the central European scene of the sixteenth and seventeenth centuries in its explosion of sect-type expressions of Christianity. It was as if the Reformation movements served to rupture a great dam that had more or less effectively been constraining a huge reservoir of spiritual forces. When that dam cracked, and eventually crumbled, forces of extraordinary power, bearing great significance for understanding what sect-type Christianity entails, were unleashed. Thus in addition to the mainstream Protestant reformation—Lutheran, Reformed, and Elizabethan reform movements—and the Catholic or Counter Reformation, there was what has come to be called the Radical Reformation.[12]

By its sect-type nature, the radical reformation produced innumerable small, radical groups significantly different from each other in detail but similar enough in general to allow presentation of some recurrent themes or characteristics of them. The foremost historian of that era, George Williams, has assembled the tendencies under three groupings: the Anabaptists, the Spiritualists, and the Evangelical Rationalists. The small groups within each of the three are assembled on the basis of shared ideas and practices that the historian can now perceive; in their time, however, the groups were most often totally separate and unconnected, as one would expect of sect-type Christians. Reference will be made to specific leaders and groups, but the reader is encouraged to see how each detail contributes to the larger picture of the sect-type rather than to concentrate only on the particulars.

Overriding all other sect-type convictions and dating back to the very beginning of Christianity is the profound and mingled fear and hope that the Kingdom of God—not the church—is about to be ushered in or, as in a few instances, has already come but has gone unnoticed by others. "Kingdom" language is filled with images of newness, promise, and anticipation in contrast to what from the sect-type Christian's view appears as conservative, obsolete, and static in the metaphors of church-type language. The particular expressions of the expectation of the imminent coming of the Kingdom varied considerably, but they are united in the emphasis upon something radically new about to erupt and in their confident knowledge of the nature of that new age.

From the moment any new "sect-type" group appears, there arises the issue of what organizational form the community of believers will adopt. The church-

---

[11] See Chap. 3 on countercultures.

[12] See George Williams, *The Radical Reformation.* Philadelphia: Westminster Press, 1962.

type Catholic view presented one way of response, the various sect-type groups present multiple views. In contrast, none of the sect-type organizations sought the support of established governments, although under later constitutions, and partly under the pressure exerted by the sectarian view of these matters, sect-type churches in some lands enjoy the benefits of a policy of noninterference by government in religious affairs. Originally, it is not too much to say, however, that the sect-type churches were either indifferent to or provocatively hostile toward governments and demanded separation of government from the religious community. Further, they tended to regard the story of church-type Christianity to have been one of corruption from its inception. Thus, sect-type churches most often aspired to a restitution of Christian life to the preCatholic forms it had taken among early Christians. Theirs was more an aspiration to recover "true" Christian community rather than a desire to reform an unredeemable church form that was, in their view, utterly corrupt.

If governmental support and assistance is in principle rejected, and if the ideal of a single voice to articulate and interpret faith and morals is rejected, then the community is thrown back upon itself to maintain its own discipline and control among its members. At the same time, the sect-type churches believed that anarchy, or total individuality in religious matters, missed the social aspect of human existence. Spiritual fellowship was the highest goal, and the most effective and widespread means devised to achieve such social solidarity in the sect-type community was the practice of the "ban." This was a collective decision to exclude an errant person from the common life, until or unless he or she properly repented for the offense. In a situation with all the emotional charge and fervor that characterizes sect-type life, to be prevented from inclusion and participation in the community is a mightily effective means to discipline unwanted or stubborn behavior or thought patterns. Although, from the perspective of the outsider, banning can be seen as a form of coercion, if the larger community has clear identity requirements for participation, few more effective means for maintaining those standards could be devised.

In relation to the larger societies within which they sprang up, the sect-type peculiarities and vocal denunciations of established institutions were often sufficient to unleash persecutions upon them, sometimes of a very violent sort. Burning and drowning of these dissidents was sufficiently frequent to make it clear that the risks of being a sectarian of whatever kind were very real. Martyrdom returned to a prominent place in the story of Christianity, although, in the sixteenth and seventeenth centuries, as it had been since the twelfth century, martyrdom involved some Christians persecuting and killing other Christians. In some ways that is a far cry from Christians being martyred by non-Christians, but, to those defending the boundaries of a sacred universe, any who deviated were the enemy as surely as those of another tradition—and perhaps even more so. In response to the persecutions, the sect-type Christians were, for the most part, consistently pacifistic. The fate of the believer, they felt, in a hostile world had been demonstrated by the death of Jesus on the cross. As the supreme example, Jesus the

Christ had set the model for whatever sincere faith might demand. To resist or renounce one's faith was to reject the example of Jesus. Steadfastly confident of their religious experience of the Spirit in their lives, individually and in their small communities, these sect-type Christians exhibited a calm courage that often shamed their persecutors. However, they did, and this must be emphasized and will be returned to later in the chapter, share one thing with their persecutors: *they were equally convinced that they were right in their views and lives*. In presenting such assured righteousness, the perspectives are identical, despite the polarized contents.

In their strict independence from governmental support and in their efforts to create communities of like-minded believers, the sect-type Christians had to resolve leadership questions. Some of them gave prominence of position to a charismatic leader, who was regarded as "spirit-led." Others adopted a consultative, shared pattern of leadership in a council of elders. Still others rejected all leadership models and gathered the members quietly together to await the visitation of the Spirit among them. On such an occasion, one or several among them would bear witness to the others. This latter model is a form of religious democracy and has been characteristic of the British Quaker movement. In virtually none of the models were distinctions drawn between the members upon the basis of any notion of an ordained, specially educated ministry. They took Luther's principle of the "priesthood of all believers" to its full social embodiment.

In matters of forms of worship, most sect-type groups only retained two rituals—Baptism and a common meal. The highly developed theological doctrines characteristic of Roman Catholicism and mainline Protestant reformers were denounced in favor of what they thought to be simple, straightforward, and consistent understandings. For them, Baptism was a seal or sign of belief, and, as belief was possible only for self-conscious, mature people, it was reserved for adult believers, in contrast to the practice of infant baptism in most forms of church Christianity. The common meal that developed into the Eucharist, Lord's Supper, or Holy Communion in the churches, was regarded by many sect-type Christians as a memorial service in which the fellowship of believers shared the love of Christ by taking a meal together. It was held to be a true and beautifully simple love feast.

Many of the radical reform groups adopted metaphors of the family to express the relations within the community, especially brothers and sisters in Christ. The ties were religious and spiritual rather than primarily blood relations. Some of the Apostle Paul's writings in the New Testament lent special force to such images. The sense of intimacy between members of the sect came to expression in their daily interaction. They aimed to be mutually supportive, loving, and, when necessary, to chastise each other in the spirit of the love of Christ they shared. In traditional theological terms, they emphasized the importance of sanctification, i.e. the importance of a devout and holy life following the example of Jesus. But their self-understanding was far less a matter of carefully articulating a doctrine of sanctification than it was as an admonition to live a sanctified life. For sect-type Christians, to be a Christian was and is to be called out of the larger cultural and societal mores into the family of believers.

THE FAMILY OF LOVE

Among the many explorable instances, one skein of the tapestry of sect-type Christianity may, if followed, help to illustrate the larger collection of groups. This story begins in the Netherlands in the sixteenth century after the Reformation had begun. Holland, the northernmost contiguous part of Europe and far from Italy and the Pope, seemed particularly receptive to religious diversity. The decades from the 1520s to the 1540s was a time during which numerous groups of sect-type Christians, particularly variant Anabaptist groups, arose and flourished in the Netherlands. In 1540 in the Dutch city of Emden, a successful businessman of German origin, named Henry Nicholas (Nichales), appeared as a refugee from Amsterdam, where he had been religiously suspect. Some of the most helpful information regarding this man is found in studies of Christian mysticism, which fact is important not in order to categorize Nicholas, because Christian mysticism has many forms, but to indicate that his spiritualist form of sectarianism has connection with Christian mysticism, albeit an unusual and particular form.

Born in 1502 to devout Catholic parents who daily took him to Mass, Henry at a very early age is reported to have asked his father one day what he thanked God for. His father replied that he thanked God for the forgiveness of sin through Christ and for being led in a life of godliness through the church. Young Henry, perhaps only eight years old, told his father that as far as he could tell the sinfulness of humans had not been changed at all by the coming of Christ. Further, he said, he believed Christ had opened the door to the Kingdom of God but that until a person obliterated sin from his or her life, through an imitation of Christ's suffering, he saw no meaning to faith—especially to the church's understanding and practice of it. Henry's father was confounded and arranged for the boy to be tutored by a Franciscan monk. Henry was no more satisfied by those encounters than he had been by the conversations with his father. Shortly afterward he began to have religious visions. Such experiences led him later in life to call himself, in a wonderfully descriptive phrase, "a begodded man." For the remainder of his childhood and youth, however, Henry developed in conformity with the pattern expected of a conventional church Christian. He eventually became a business merchant and joined a guild of mercers. He was married at age twenty.

At age twenty-seven, Nicholas was arrested in Munster, his home city, on the suspicion of being a follower of Luther, whose work he had read with interest and in some detail. He had significant theological disagreements with Luther, however. After he successfully defended himself against his accusers and was released, he moved to Amsterdam to what he thought would provide a more open religious atmosphere. His business dealings led to further prosperity. He became friends with a spiritualist sectarian named David Joris, from whom some contend

Nicholas appropriated many of his insights and ideas. He was again arrested on suspicion of being an Anabaptist. Again, he was freed and eventually moved to Emden.

Nicholas was a charismatic figure, tall and husky, successful and given to wearing a long beard and colorful clothing—"brave in his apparell" as one scholar put it. Concurrent with his move to Emden, he began his writing career and soon attracted a following that gathered under the name "Family of Love." Eventually this Familist ideal spread internationally throughout the Netherlands into France and even to England where considerably later it was absorbed into Quakerism.

The communities of the Family of Love were often invisible to the larger society in which they grew. But it became clear that their often clandestine prayer meetings were extremely carefully choreographed and organized. Leadership roles were based upon the degree of spiritual experience that had been given to individuals. Thus it was a charismatically based form of hierarchy: Henry Nicholas was the highest elder and under him served a group of elders who were also understood to be "begodded men." Under the elders were three levels of priesthood, the experiential qualifications for which are lost to history. It is known, however, that none of the leaders were permitted to hold personal property as one of the signs of the depth of their religious experience.

Marriage was extolled in the Family of Love, but under the admonition that the end of marriage was the destruction of lust of the flesh and the achievement of enlightened love between members of a family. In the extended religious Family of Love, maintaining discipline belonged, in theory, to the entire community, but one of Nicholas's writings suggests how that was actually to be done by "Fathers":

> . . . every Father of a Family under the Love has doubtless the Liberty in his Family to use services and ceremonies according as he perceives out of the Testimonies of the Holy Spirit of Love that they are most profitable or necessary for his Household to the Life of Peace to keep his Household thereby in Discipline and Peace: . . . [13]

Such a patriarchal, hierarchical organization was qualified by a number of more "democratic" features. Nicholas provided for every inspired family member to be free to speak in any service. But, in recognition of the ever-present risk of conflict and strife, Nicholas admonished the Family to submit to the spiritual leaders:

> Give ear to the Elders of the Holy Understanding: and follow not the will or counsel of your own mind: but, with the Elders, under the service of the Love, follow the mind and counsel of the Wisdom: and always keep yourselves with the Elders in the Family of Love . . . [14]

---

[13] *Introduction to the Holy Understanding of the Glasse of Righteousness,* quoted by Williams, p. 481.

[14] Williams, p. 482.

Such spiritual yielding, paradoxical as it might appear, was the path to freedom from the self and thus to salvation, the end of which is the "freedom of the Children of God."

Religious experience, rather than correctness of belief, ritualistic worship, or even conventionally defined morality, was the cornerstone of the Familist "movement." They required only to be left alone to practice their religion as they believed themselves so led. They, following Henry Nicholas, trusted experiences of the indwelling of the Holy Spirit as sufficient for leading them to live Christianly.

Nicholas may have visited England in 1553–1554—that is uncertain—although he did go there at some time. It is known, however, that groups by the name Family of Love were present in England in the following decades. Queen Elizabeth issued a proclamation in 1580 ordering the "Sectaries of the Family of Love" to be imprisoned and their books to be burned. The proclamation was, however, unsuccessful in eliminating the groups, which continued to be known throughout the seventeenth century in England, after which they were taken up into Quakerism and perhaps other religious bodies, as well. One of the most succinct accounts of the English Familists is preserved by one of their most avid critics, a John Rogers, who in 1579 published an expose and diatribe against them in which the following "confession" before an English magistrate by two members of the Family of Love is preserved:

> They are all unlearned, save some who can read English and are made bishops, elders, and deacons, who call them to one of the disciples' houses; thirty in number assemble to hear scriptures expounded. They have goods in common, new members are received with a kiss, all have meat, drink and lodging found by the owner of the house where they meet. They knock, saying, "Here is a Brother or Sister in Christ." The congregation does not speak until permitted to do so. They go to [the established] church, . . . They did prohibit bearing of weapons, but at length allowed the bearing of staves . . . The marriage is made by brethren, who sometimes bring them together who live over a hundred miles asunder . . . No man is to be baptized before the age of thirty. Until then he is an infant. Heaven and hell are present in this world among us. They are bound to give alms only to their own sect. . . . All men not of their congregation or revolted from them are as dead. They hold there was a world before Adam's time. No man should be put to death for his opinions, . . . They expound scripture according to their own minds, comparing one place with another.[15]

If the views and practices of the group that began in England under the leadership of George Fox in 1668, called "Friends of the Truth" or "Quakers," and since about 1800 known as the "Society of Friends," were examined closely, much of what Henry Nicholas propounded could be seen to have been absorbed by them. Through refinement and amplification, and through some of their own insights, the Quakers developed in their own distinctive ways. But the connection between such names as the Family of Love and the Friends of Truth is itself a

---

[15] Williams, p. 790.

source of insight. When the family circle is extended to a gathering of friends, the social dynamics change. The image of the Father gives way to friendly leader imagery; the indwelling of the spirit as the experiential foundation is replaced by an emphasis upon the "Inner Light." These observations suggest some of the links of continuity between the two groups, as well as indicating some of their differences. Today, the Society of Friends is a small, yet highly influential, sectarian expression of Christianity, most prominent in England and North America, particularly the United States. In both social settings, Quakers have quietly and powerfully emphasized social and educational work and are renowned for their leadership in international relief efforts bringing aid to all forms of human suffering.

Throughout this chapter, the concern has been to offer perspectives on various ways Christianity has interacted with its social contexts. The "church-type" organization has been compared with characteristics of the "sect-type" groups. One other form or organizational pattern must be noted to amplify the picture in the United States and some other countries. There, in addition to several "church-type" and many "sect-type" Christian groups, one finds *denominations*. The word "denomination" does not distinguish between churches and "sect-type" churches. Rather, under constitutional governments, which do not favor one religious group over any other, all such groups are equally free to believe and practice as they choose. So long as they remain within a generally accepted consensus, their beliefs and practices are protected by the constitution. Occasionally, some group's practice crosses that line—for example, early Mormon polygamy—and is subjected to civil intervention. Martin Marty has appropriately observed that:

> The denomination, then, was a tardy Protestant invention for societies where in fact numbers of churches had to coexist and compete. . . . The denomination also allows for free and fair competition. People may join the church of their choice or reject all churches. Meanwhile, within each group the members have the opportunity to work at keeping the integrity of their private and exclusivistic theological positions.[16]

In nations that have taken this view, a political philosophy of toleration has prevented any of the diverse Christian groups from successfully imposing its views upon persons with different religious preferences. Religious liberty has guaranteed the perpetuation of the diversity of Christian churches.

THE DYNAMIC BETWEEN "CHURCH-TYPE" AND "SECT-TYPE"

It is tempting, but inaccurate, simply to equate heresy with the sect-type of Christianity and orthodoxy with the church-type. As was shown in Chapter 3, some

---

[16] Martin Marty, *Protestantism* (New York: Holt, Rinehart and Winston, 1972), p. 138.

of the more important forms of counterculture Christianity arose within the heart of church Christianity. Many heretics eventually did found sect-type organizations, but often only after they were disappointed and rejected by the leaders of church-type Christianity. Thus, although the stories told in Chapters 3 and 5 overlap with this chapter, they are about fundamentally different ways of presenting and assessing the material.

As viewed by Peter Berger, the dynamic between church and sect would appear as the interplay between "institutionalization," "revolution," and "reinstitutionalization," because the sect, like the church, can be seen as yet another societal form of institution, another sacred canopy of meaning. This is so even though the sect members believe they are participating in something entirely different from the church.

Berger describes the dynamic of the process of institutionalization as follows. Problems that arise when society becomes segmented center upon the issue of legitimizing. As "subuniverses of meaning" are created, a variety of perspectives and reflections upon the total society are voiced. Alternative definitions of reality are expressed; the relativity of one's own universe is acutely felt. In the face of this threat to established order, the recognition dawns that "outsiders" must be kept out and "insiders" in. Often restrictions are increased and esoteric teachings heightened to keep each individual in his or her own role. Propaganda, mystification, and intimidation are directed against outsiders. As has been shown, Christianity's history is replete with instances of this dynamic.

The need arises to repress any heretical challenge and at the same time to legitimize that repression, a task that is carried out by what Berger calls "conceptual machineries." Berger observes that a heretical challenge provokes the first move by participants in a symbolic universe to put forward a systematic, theoretical conceptualization of their universe. And, at the same time, these new conceptualizations push the tradition beyond its original form. So a dialectic emerges. As the symbolic universe is legitimized, it is also modified by the "new" story that was constructed to ward off the threat of heresy or the risk of change that it manifests.

There is an inherent tendency of institutionalization toward inertia that increases as it is fed by legitimization, suggests Berger. The more abstract an institution's theories become, the less likely it is to change with contingency. At this point, the institution can continue even when it has lost its practicality; things are done because they are "right," not because they work. Experts say they know better than the practitioners. This results either in rebellion and the emergence of new experts and of new definitions or in conflict that arises between experts who cannot test their theories practically and so use the power at their disposal (that is, police force). They can then say that their theory *works* because it is accepted, taken for granted. The fight is clearly one to win the power to produce reality. Experts are sustained by a unified power structure that deals with opponents either by physically destroying them or by integrating them within the tradition, which in turn enriches and differentiates that tradition. As an example of his description, Berger points to medieval Christendom, which destroyed heresy, incorporated folk beliefs, and segregated Jews and Muslims (which also protected church Christians from contamination). It is the experts, the "conservationalists," who call either for the "fire and sword" or ecumenical negotiations.

When a particular definition of reality is attached to concrete power, ideology results. Ideologies can be affirmed by groups for whom large portions of that ideology are not particularly related to their legitimizing interests, and power holders may support experts in theoretical fights that are irrelevant to their power interests. Berger's example of this is Emperor Constantine's involvement in the Christological controversies of his time. Theologians were determined to define who Christ was, in relation both to God the Father and to Jesus of Nazareth. Constantine wanted to unify the Roman Empire and consolidate his rule. They were interested in Christian "truth," and he in Roman political "power."

In his analysis of modern pluralism, religious and otherwise, Berger describes the dynamic of pluralism as a shared and taken-for-granted core universe with different partial universes coexisting in a state of mutual accommodation, tolerance, and cooperation. This situation presupposes an urban society, a highly developed division of labor, high differentiation in the social structure, and high economic surplus. All of this goes with rapid social change and undermines the tendency toward inertia of traditional definitions, while encouraging skepticism and innovation. On the whole, pluralism is subversive of any taken-for-granted reality structure.

Turning to the subjective reality of society, Berger observes that one is not born a member of society but becomes one through the process of internalization. One is not born a Christian but learns, if one chooses to do so, to become a Christian. One result of this process is the understanding that the members of society not only live in the same world, but participate in each other's being. Socialization is a comprehensive and consistent induction of the individual into the objective world of the society. This, in turn, establishes subjective identity and enforces a view of the reality of the world. In the process of internalization, society, identity, and reality crystallize through language.

The subjective reality is maintained by ongoing routines and reaffirmations through interaction with significant others. This is offered by Berger as a reason why the Catholic church is against interfaith marriage. Conversation is the best mode of maintaining a world view; conversation allocates all things, even doubts, a place in reality. The group has a "common language" of reality which presupposes a much taken-for-granted reality behind the words.

Self-identity is only maintained in confirming the milieu in which one has become the self one is. In a crisis situation, the need is for intense and specific confirmation, for example, in the enacting of ritual in a disaster. There are instances of transformation of a subjective reality, or a move to another world, as in an "alternation" (i.e., in traditional Christian language, "conversion"). But just as socialization is never total, so neither is the transformation. Help is required to complete it. This begins the process of radical resocialization through the dis-internalization of the "old world," and the guidance by significant others into a new reality. The community is indispensable in this process as a "laboratory of transformation." If one becomes a monk, one way of being gives way to a radically different one. Often there is segregation at first until the new reality congeals when there can be a move back into relationships, although this is seen as presenting great dangers and temptations. The process is one of reinterpretation of the old reality with the legitimizing apparatus of the new reality. A result is that there are often aspects added to the telling of the past to bring the story harmoniously into the present. All this is described as a reorganization of the conversational apparatus.

As Berger describes it, change comes about when identity becomes a problem—when there is a radical change in reality (for example, in social structure and psychology). In cultures where there are no options available to one view of reality, that one is often imposed. Change can only occur when individuals congregate around a counter view of reality and thereby enable the rest of society to reflect on their taken-for-granted view. Or in cultures that are more pluralistic, discrepant worlds may be mediated by significant others in the primary society.

And yet, Berger points to still another way of change for the ones for whom socialization is "unsuccessful." For these individuals, those who have undergone disidentification from their "proper place," alternative realities and identities appear as subjective options, and choices can be made. But, at the same time, those options are limited by the context of the individual; the social structure may not permit realization of a chosen identity. In this situation, the chosen identity can become a fantasy identity that, on the level of imagination, is objectified as the "real self." In other words, there is a recognition of, and a turn into, the imagination as the place of reality when society will not permit expression of the self so viewed.

In yet a different move, alternative realities are internalized without identification with them. Each one can be opted for; none is the individual's only reality but a reality that is being used at a particular moment for a specific purpose. Realities are seen in terms of role-playing, the individual "puts them on." So, from this, the turn into imaginative reality suggests at the same time a detachment from identification of the self with any single way of being in the world. Subjective worlds can be multiple.

Berger, in describing the objective social structure in which discrepant worlds are generally available, extends the pluralistic theme. As the recognition of the relativity of all worlds, including one's own, increases, the individual's world is seen as *a* world rather than *the* world. The individual's institutional conduct can be seen as a role that can be "acted out" with manipulative control. Berger summarizes the significance of the changes and differences, both subjective and objective, that accompany the shift in perspective when a person experiences reality not only in terms of institutional identity but also in the imaginative realm that affirms many worlds and many selves:

For example, an aristocrat no longer simply *is* an aristocrat but he *plays at being* an aristocrat, and so forth. The situation, then, has a much more far-reaching consequence than the possibility of individuals playing at being what they are *not* supposed to be. They also play at being what they *are* supposed to be—a quite different matter.[17]

Berger does not extend this network of thought in this work but the suggestions carried by his language can be amplified in at least two ways. From the perspective of ''institution,'' understood as an aspect of both objective and subjective worlds, to live relativity outside the sacred canopy is to be in chaos, to be void of meaning, identity, and reality. It is to be ''out there'' with no shield or protection, face to face with unnamable terror. One is all alone in the midst of the babbling multitude. But, from another perspective, the identification of ''one'' over against ''many'' is not the point, as one is always, already many. Reality is no longer programmed, taken-for-granted, and threatened by change, but it is the place where existence is played out. The one who lives his or her particularity by moving through boundaries is freed to play between the ''oughts'' and ''shalt nots'' of any monopolizing institution or monotheistic religion that has forgotten the many faces of the Unknowable. What from the perspective of ''institution'' is empty of meaning is, from within the interplay of selves and worlds, full to overflowing with possibilities.

Berger's image of the conversation as that which maintains an institution through the ''common language'' of taken-for-granted reality and as that which must be reorganized in the identification with and internalization of a new reality, suggests that language arising within imaginative reality does not record one form over another but plays them all. Language that is ''play-full'' gives rise to conversations that are multilingual, to speaking that is heard in many tongues, an image powerfully carried in the Christian story in the polyvocal utterance out of the fiery tongues and rushing wind of Pentecost when the church as social institution was born. And, like the Apostles, who spoke of the coming of the Spirit in prophecy, vision, and dream, and in heavenly wonders and earthly signs where nature appeared as never before, those who speak of a transformative experience in the realm of *fantasy* (from the Greek, *phantazein*—''to make visible'') are counted as being outside the limits, both socially and psychologically. As with the Apostles in Jerusalem, their speaking confounds and amazes those who represent the established religious tradition; the overflowing of their words makes no sense unless they can be labeled as drunk, their fullness explained as an excess of new wine. But that ''new wine'' and ''drunken speech'' are not merely literal; they are images, metaphors, vessels that carry the hearer over and under. No longer confined by convention, they play in language. And interplay has great depth; those who hear and are carried into the images are ''cut to the heart'' (Acts 2:37).

---

[17] Peter Berger and Thomas Luckman, *The Social Construction of Reality* (Garden City, N.Y.: Doubleday, 1966), p. 158.

The story of Christianity recalls many who speak outside the limits, out of the abyss (from the Greek, *abyssos*—"bottomless") where they fall between church and sect. The story of one of them will serve as a telling example. No society or ideology satisfied him. Neither cultural nor counter cultural, he imagined a different way of being.

Sebastian Franck was born to poor parents in Germany in about 1500. Patrons early recognized his intellectual gifts and enabled him to study for the priesthood to which he was ordained. By the time he was twenty, he had met Luther and was recruited for the Reformation. His allegiance to Protestantism, however, was even briefer than it had been to Catholicism. He was disillusioned as much by the ineffectual Protestant preaching as he had become by the sacramentalism of the Catholic church. A soap maker by profession, he became an important Christian thinker. For his integrity to his own sense of things, he became an outlawed wanderer. No prince nor city in Europe would take him in for long. He was tried for heresy in the city of Ulm. Yet he did manage to escape to Switzerland where he enjoyed a short peaceful time. He died at age forty-three.

The course upon which Franck found himself embarked was dangerous—he was a heretic in the eyes of Catholics and Protestants—church-types and sect-types—and he was lonely in the extreme. The story of Jesus, to Franck must be repeated daily in one's own life if one would be Christian. Franck envisioned a new form of Christianity that " . . . is arising, and it shall sweep aside as needless all outward preaching, ceremony, sacrament, ban, and vocation and move toward an invisible spiritual church in union of spirit and faith assembled among all peoples and governed solely by the eternal invisible word of God without any outward mediations."[18] Against the view that he was a heretic, Franck with steadfast courage expressed his carefully considered view that: "Every man must always suffer, die, go to heaven in the Body of Christ himself, and none can suffer, die, believe, or be a Christian for any other."[19] This was said following his comment regarding the sects of earlier years that had been named as heretical:

> In all times there have been sects and bands; Arian would not admit anyone a Christian unless he were Arian; likewise Ebion, Kerinth, Nector, Pelagius, Manichaeus, etc.—all claimed our Lord for their own. . . . So today the folly persists, each sect seizing and claiming God for itself alone.[20]

Against all such company, including all the forms of church Christianity as well, Franck spoke for this singular form of expressing Christian faith—radical individuals who regard the Gospel as a message of release from feeling human constructs as bondage, whether ideas or institutions by seeing them as they are—

---

[18] Quoted by Walter Nigg, *Heresy* (New York: Knopf, 1962) from Peuckert, *Die Grosse Wende*, p. 338.

[19] Walter Nigg, p. 341.

[20] Walter Nigg, p. 341.

human and thereby relative and thereby changeable if need be found to do so. He wrote:

> Belonging to no party, having no bias I can, God be praised, read all, and am captive of no sect or man on earth. All the devout please my heart, though in many trivial things they may be mistaken, and I am sworn to no man's word, but to Christ, my God and Mediator, to whose obedience I alone acknowledge my reason captive. I cast out no heretic, for that would be to pour out the child with the bath water, and hurl the truth away with the lies. Rather, I separate the gold from the filth. For there is scarce a pagan, philosopher or heretic who did not happen on some good thing, which I would not therefore cast away, but revere as fine gold and find something of my God in heathens and heretics. . . . Therefore a truth to me is a truth and God grant I may love it, whoever says it; . . . And I am accustomed to error and misdoing in all men and hate no man on earth for that, but bewail, know and see myself, my own wretchedness and condition, in them.[21]

Finally, almost as a benediction for this solitary way, Franck wrote:

> As soon as people attempt to frame Christianity within rules and fit it into a prescribed law and order, it stops being Christianity. There is a general failure to understand that Christians are handed over to the Holy Ghost. The New Testament is not a book, doctrine, or law, but the Holy Ghost. Where God's Spirit is, there freedom must be. . . . [22]

CONCLUSION

The very adaptiveness of Christianity has made it available and accessible in some form(s) or other to people under extremely diverse social conditions. The passion with which some Christians have in all times and places taken responsibility for living out and thinking through the implications of their understandings of what being Christian concretely and theoretically means is one measure of the religion's vitality and strength. This purposeful resilience is a major characteristic of Christianity. And yet. . . .

Christianity has also been appealed to as providing a "legitimate" basis for terror and horror perpetrated by some people upon others. In the name of Christianity, at various times, Jews have been persecuted, Muslims have been attacked, and Christians have been tortured and killed by other Christians. Empires and nations have restricted or outlawed other religious practices and beliefs in the name of Christianity. Church-type Christianity has diligently and brutally engaged in persecuting Christian heretics, visionaries, and dissidents.

These are the dark sides of the "Light of Truth" that Christianity has proclaimed with such determination in every nation on every continent under its

---

[21] Walter Nigg, p. 340.
[22] Walter Nigg, p. 338.

evangelical, missionary mandate. Although these activities have been roundly and appropriately excoriated by external critics of Christianity, it is important to recognize that from within its own ranks, Christianity has generated some of its most severe critics: its sectarians, its "heretics," "gnostics," and "mystics," all those who are persecuted, are the ones who have raised from the depths voices questioning what has been forgotten. Moreover, they have sometimes been able to live out the implications of those questions, standing as transformative glasses of reflection for the tradition. Together church, sect, and individual vision circumscribe the boundaries of institution in society and psyche; each iconoclastically shatters the boundaries of some other restrictive, limiting view and each re-forms them newly and sometimes playfully. Together they manifest the spirit that moves the creative imagery, the story that is Christianity.

8

christianity: yesterday, today, and tomorrow

Christianity in many cultural settings has repeatedly demonstrated its resilience and adaptability. The fact that some people in virtually every nation on earth today identify themselves as ''Christian'' is witness to the fact that the resources of Christianity are still powerful and sustaining for some human beings, as they have been for almost 2,000 years. But, no nation today can be properly designated as a Christian nation in anything like the way it is proper to speak, say, of Iran as an Islamic state. Yet, even in nations in which atheism is a part of the politically dominant ideology, Christians are to be found, sometimes even in majority numbers, as in Poland. As the numerically largest religion in the contemporary world, it is also the case that Christianity presents the largest number of separate groups who identify themselves as Christian. From Roman Catholicism, the largest, to the tiniest of the most recent Christian sectarian groups, whose numbers are imprecisely known, Christianity is a religion with many faces and voices. By now this book must simply rest its case: Christianity has, from its beginnings, throughout its history, and into the present, been an umbrella name for significantly different groups and even individuals who have lived and understood the meaning of their faith in diverse ways.

THE UNITY AND DIVERSITY OF CHRISTIANITY

The one thing Christians have in common is the affirmation: ''Jesus Christ is Lord,'' although what they understand that to mean varies significantly. The kaleidoscope offers a suggestive image for reflecting upon this diversity. Within the range of very precisely coordinated mirrors, a symmetrical set of images in an infinite set of patterns is produced by light refraction. The technicalities of the instrument are, however, of less importance than amplifying the metaphor it provides. When Christianity is the focus of attention, the patterns within any one of its formalized expressions, whether church, sect, or denomination, provide a symmetrical set of images. Each of the constitutive elements plays its own role but can be given relatively greater or lesser emphases that result in strikingly different, but no less beautiful or authentic, patterns. In this study, the elements emphasized have been history, countercultures, arts, beliefs, worship, and social organization. Within each element a great diversity has been displayed. If not infinite, the possible combinations are at least very numerous and the elements cohere within each frame of reference to form a particular kind of symmetry.

It is not accidental that for Roman Catholic Christianity with its universalizing aspirations, the sacramentally ordained priest administers the sacrament of the Eucharist and, as guardian of the tradition, the Pope speaks to and for Catholics in matters of faith and morals. For the Eastern Orthodox churches, however, the people of God form a mysterious whole, and especially in the patterns of worship, the liturgy, they give outward evidence of their connectedness and unity. For them beliefs are far less emphasized than in the more creedal Roman Catholic Church. Protestantism in its many different forms is largely a Western Christian phenomenon. Except in some of the leftwing, radical groups, Protestants have largely emphasized the importance of beliefs and morals to identify Christians. The Bible has tended to be the authoritative sources of these churches' convictions. In the radical Protestant groups, religious experience, often phrased as being led by the indwelling of the Holy Spirit, has been the authoritative foundation of common life, although, as voluntary associations, individuals present themselves to the group for membership on the basis of personal, individual experience. Finally, the radically individualistic expressions of Christianity have emphasized the lonely, singular connection between God and each woman or man. The early Christian hermits, who renounced life with other human beings in order to affirm and strengthen life with God, like the homeless, wandering Sebastian Franck in the sixteenth century, cast out by Protestants and Catholics alike, are witnesses to and expressions of still a different vision of what Christianity may be like.

The panorama of Christianity, then, is polyvalent and pluralistic. Further it exhibits cultural and historical adaptability, changing its face by demonstrating newly discovered impulses at its heart at different times and in different places. Such a diversity and plurality of paradigms has led many critics to the view that Christianity has no essential core, no peculiarly identifying characteristic(s).

THE RESOURCEFULNESS OF CHRISTIANITY

This study has taken a different viewpoint. By presenting the diversity of Christianity, we have proposed that Christianity has demonstrated its resourcefulness in coping with diverse human situations and cultural settings. The so-called Third World in the late twentieth century is rapidly replacing the Euro-Anglo-American forms of Christianity as the quantitative center of gravity. In the twenty-first and subsequent centuries, it is a good guess that African and Latin American forms and expressions of Christianity will become increasingly prominent in assessments of Christianity. How significantly different those forms and expressions may develop remains, of course, to be seen. It does appear sure, however, that certain recurrent elements will remain: the Bible, a few traditional doctrinal affirmations, some rituals such as Baptism and Holy Communion, and some way of appropriating foundational and traditional stories through which those Christians-to-come will identify with their predecessors and communicate with contemporary fellow Christians.

Christianity has demonstrated a comprehensiveness, a resiliency, and a persuasiveness to untold millions over its 2000 year history. In announcing a message of promise and fulfillment, it has overcome the distance imposed by differences in languages, in forms of government and economic structures of societies, in assessments of nature and the place of human life in it, and in cultural patterns and worldviews. Christianity has not been proclaimed as a single message in terms of specific content—Marcion's "stranger God" and Meister Eckhart's "God beyond God" are conceptually different from the God of the Nicene Creed of the fourth century or the Augsburg Confession of the sixteenth century Lutherans. It has, however, recurrently and consistently, wherever and whenever it has been proclaimed, pointed to Jesus, the Christ, as its founding and leading figure. The power of that figure to elicit such remarkably varying interpretations of who and what he was in his person and teachings has generated an enormous interest in and curiosity about him over the centuries. "Teacher," "example," "savior," "king," "suffering servant," "Son of God," "Son of Man," "prophet," "priest," "shaman," "moralist," "preacher man," "faithful remnant of Israel," "historical Jesus," "Christ of faith"—all these and many more titles have had currency among Christians. Who was he? Albert Schweitzer's magisterial study of the nineteenth century's attempt to draw a definitive historical portrait of Jesus concludes with these words:

> He comes to us as One unknown, without a name, as of old, by the lake-side, He came to those men who knew Him not. He speaks to us the same word: "Follow thou me!" and sets the tasks which He has to fulfill for our time. He commands. And to those who obey Him, whether they be wise or simple, He will reveal Himself in the toils, the conflicts, the sufferings which they will pass through in His fellowship, and, as an ineffable mystery, they shall learn in their own experience Who He is."[1]

There is ultimately mystery at the heart of every religion. Mystery does not mean unintelligibility as much as infinite intelligibility. Humans speak of their

---

[1] Albert Schweitzer, *The Quest of the Historical Jesus.* (New York: The Macmillan Company, 1957), p. 403.

religious experiences, different as they seem to be, out of encounters with mystery. Little wonder that there are differences. How much more surprising it is, as one compares them, that recurrent themes and patterns appear. For Christians the differences and similarities swirl about the figure of Jesus of Nazareth, whom they persist in calling the Christ. Such is the story that has endured for 2000 years and is today told by people around the world.

No other religion, with the possible exception of Islam, seems to have been so anxiously determined to insist upon the truth and superiority of its faith than have and do some Christian groups. Similarly, few religious traditions offer as many stories of devotees' service to other human beings and to efforts to make life together more livably humane. The impulse to dominate has been paralleled by the impulse to serve humanity. The surge of vitality among the religions in the modern world has begun to modify the eagerness of some Christians to insist upon its unique superiority. Appreciation for the worldviews of others and the recognition that Christianity must coexist with other religions is leading some contemporary Christians to a greater emphasis upon service to others even as they discover that some of the aspects of the faith that were long thought to be unique to it may not be.

Other religious traditions have survived and flourished, sometimes for thousands of years, without making such claims of uniqueness. Perhaps Christianity, in one of the metamorphoses that await it, will number among its spokespeople some who will emphasize what Christianity shares with other traditions, rather than insisting only on its uniqueness. That, too, will be a recovery of insights that some Christians have, over the centuries, contributed to the treasury of resources generated and retained within the tradition in its fullness. The gnostics, the mystics, and some of the revolutionaries within the Christian tradition have repeatedly recognized that Christianity's uniqueness lies in the particularity of its visions of the human connection with the divine. Particularity, however, attaches to every religious vision, that of Mohammed, Moses, the Buddha, Joseph Smith, the Vedic poets of Hinduism, Confucius, Black Elk, and every other specific, concrete figure who inspired followers, no less than to that of Jesus.

THE APPEAL OF CHRISTIANITY

Jesus' vision of the opportunity human life holds for recognizing and being claimed by its connection to ultimate mystery has been sufficiently compelling to evoke affirmative response from many human beings. But there is an even larger number of humanity, who, having heard the God story and Jesus story recounted and proclaimed by Christians, do not feel themselves claimed by the message. For every Christian in the world today, there are three persons who do not so identify themselves. Although some non-Christians may never have heard the Christian stories, many have heard but have not responded affirmatively to it. They have determined to follow the path of the religious traditions of their own people—many of which are as old or older chronologically than Christianity—or to follow no pattern of organized religion at all. It has not been found superior to what was already known to or thought by them.

What does that do to Christian claims to be not only particular and unique, but also superior? It at least suggests that Christianity in its various forms is able to speak only to those to whom it brings hope and fulfillment. Others must be free to find their own ways, just as Christians in many places are free to do themselves, although still others find themselves continually persecuted. Further, it suggests that Christians will benefit greatly when they examine their own lives, beliefs, and institutions and take to heart the words so powerful in their own Bible: "Judge not, that you be not judged" (Matthew 7:1). Such an admonition, when coupled with an appreciation for the view so frequently affirmed by many Christians through the centuries that the ways of God are ultimately and irreducibly mysterious, might lead some Christians now and in the future to a deepened openness to the insights and visions communicated in and by other religious traditions. In a time increasingly characterized as religiously pluralistic in many nations, those Christians who are open to others have great resources to bring to the conversations that such a situation could inaugurate.

THE WORK OF CHRISTIANITY

Wherever people gather in the name of Christianity, whether in the grandeur of the Vatican in Rome or in the open air in African villages, whether in a great cathedral in London or in a house church in Tokyo, they make testimony to the power of the stories, the beliefs, the symbols, and the rituals that combine in one or another fashion to present the Christian mythos. For them the orientation and worldview provided by their faith, as it is expressed in their patterns of worship, their ethical values, and their beliefs, is invaluable. As they faithfully live out their lives, they demonstrate the power of the religious visions at work in Christianity.

Perhaps the Apostle Paul, whose universal vision was so deeply grounded in his own experience of "end times" that it radically changed his perspective, can be petitioned to speak of the variety that belongs together under the name "Christianity." For Paul there is a "more excellent way," a way greater than faith or hope, that never ends and, as he describes so beautifully, "bears all things, believes all things, hopes all things, endures all things" (I Corinthians 13:7). For Paul the mystery of love is the genius of Christianity as it has been for all generations of Christians, although their interpretations have been very diverse. He addresses this through his ruleless rule. He describes the way in which he imagines divine and human works, the psychological and practical work of lifetimes:

Only let everyone lead the life to which the Lord has assigned him, and in which God has called him. This is my rule in all the churches. (I Corinthians 7:17)

Glossary

Absolution. The remission, or forgiving and dispelling, of a confessor's sin by a priest. See *Penance*.

Apostles' Creed. A short statement of Christian beliefs, usually spoken in worship services, that is used widely in both Catholic and Protestant churches. It derives from a baptismal creed of third-century Rome. Compare *Nicene Creed*.

Atonement. In Christian belief, the death of Christ on the cross, which is seen as an act by which the wrath of God against human sin is satisfied, making possible reconciliation with God and the forgiveness of all sin.

Baptism. The sacramental act of sprinkling, washing, or immersion into water which is the general rite of Christian initiation. Practice differs as to whether infants or only adults are baptized. The term can also be used for spiritual initiation, as in "baptism of the Holy Spirit."

Bishop. In churches of the Catholic tradition and in some Protestant churches, a high church official; usually chief pastor of a geographical area who is often viewed theologically as a successor to the Apostles.

Canon. A definite order, as in the "canon of Scripture," the set of books that make up the Bible.

Catechumen. One under instruction to become a member of the church.

Catholic. From the Greek for "universal," the tradition represented by the Roman Catholic, Eastern Orthodox, and certain other churches claiming institutional continuity with the early church, and characteristically emphasizing sacramentalism, rule by bishops, and ceremonial styles of worship; the eucharist is generally the main Sunday service.

Christ. From the Greek for "Anointed One," a literal translation of the Hebrew original of Messiah; a common title of Jesus, emphasizing his role as one sent by God for the salvation of the world, as Christians generally came to believe.

Church. In its most important meaning, the body of Christian believers here on Earth and beyond. For Christians, the church is more than a merely human institution; it is the divinely sanctioned "Body of Christ" called to do his work and represent him. Forms of church order and organization, as well as theological understanding of it beyond that basic concept, have varied greatly in church history.

Confirmation. In many churches, an observance or sacramental act in which young people receive full church membership.

Deacon. An ancient church office established in the Book of Acts. In principle, deacons are primarily "servers" responsible for the care of the needy. In the Catholic tradition, the diaconate (office of deacon) has become a grade of ordained clergy lower than the priesthood; in many Protestant churches, it is a lay office.

Diocese. In the Catholic tradition, a region under a bishop.

Eastern Orthodox. Churches of the Catholic tradition chiefly located in Eastern Europe and the Middle East that do not accept the unique authority of the Pope.

Episcopos. The Greek original of "bishop," literally meaning "overseer."

Eucharist. The Christian service of worship which commemorates and enacts the Last Supper of Jesus with his disciples. It is also known by such names as Mass, Divine Liturgy, Holy Communion, and Lord's Supper. Modes of celebration and theological understanding of the Eucharist vary. Churches of the Catholic tradition are most inclined to employ colorful traditional rites in offering it, to emphasize its centrality to Christian worship and to stress its importance as a means of receiving divine grace. Protestants are more likely to see it simply as a solemn remembrance of Christ's suffering and death. All, however, see this symbolic common (shared) meal as a sign of Christian spiritual unity with Christ and with one another.

Gothic. A medieval style of architecture found in many churches and cathedrals of Western Europe, notable for its soaring spires and pitched roofs.

Heresy. Doctrine considered unorthodox or incorrect by normative Christian standards; hence, divisive and spiritually dangerous doctrine.

Holy Spirit. The third "person" or expression of God in the Christian Trinity, generally thought of as an indwelling, life-giving, divine presence.

Icon. A holy painting of God, Christ, or the saints. Icons have an especially important role in the worship of the Eastern Orthodox churches.

Incarnation. From the Latin for "taking flesh," the important Christian doctrine that God took human form in Jesus Christ.

Liturgy. A formal, stylized Christian rite or order of service.

Messiah. In ancient Jewish belief, one who was to come, sent by God, as a sublime king or righteous leader who would establish the reign of God on Earth; Christians identify the Messiah as Jesus Christ.

Nicene Creed. A brief formula of the tenets of faith, commonly recited in worship. Adopted by the council of bishops at Nicaea in 325 A.D., it emphasizes the oneness of God with Christ.

Penance. Also called **Reconciliation**. In the Catholic tradition, a sacrament in which persons confess their sins either individually, to a priest, or (in a modified form) collectively, in a congregation. Absolution, or a declaration of forgiveness, is then given by a priest.

Pietism. A form of religion which puts great emphasis on heartfelt devotion and, usually, on moral perfectionism.

Presbyter. "Elder" in Greek; an office in the early church that was lower than that of the *episcopos*, or bishop; the title of minister in certain Protestant churches; and the original of "priest."

Priest. In churches in the Catholic tradition, the office of the ordinary parish clergyman. It is believed that by virtue of their ordination, priests are especially empowered to administer the Eucharist and most other sacraments.

Protestantism. The movement originating in the Reformation of the sixteenth century—now represented by many denominations—which stressed, in reaction to many aspects of the Catholic tradition, the authority of Scripture; inward faith as primary to attaining salvation; and simplicity in Christian worship.

Redemption. Release from sin, wrought by the salvational (saving) act of Christ on the cross, which paid the price of human sin.

Resurrection. An arising from death. Christian belief holds that Jesus Christ rose from the dead the third day after his death on the cross; that day was the first Easter.

Romanesque. A style of architecture, popular for churches in the early Middle Ages, characterized by heavy masonry and rounded arches and vaults.

Sacrament. In the Catholic tradition particularly, a rite in which divine grace is believed to be communicated by material means, such as water in baptism and bread and wine in the Eucharist. The seven traditional sacraments are baptism, Holy Communion, confirmation, Holy Matrimony, penance (or reconciliation), ordination (the conferring of holy orders upon deacons, priests, and bishops), and Last Rites (the anointing of the sick and dying).

Salvation. Freedom from sin and, therefore, assurance of eternal life in heaven.

Sect. A small, sometimes pietistic, "withdrawal" religious group that insists on a particularly strict adherence to the teaching and values of the prevailing religion and is, therefore, often in tension with the dominant society. Christian sects would include such groups as Jehovah's Witnesses or the Amish.

Trinity. The Christian threefold divinity; the nature of God as three "persons"—the Father, the Son, and the Holy Spirit—in one Unity.

For Further Reading

An immense amount of writing is available on many of the topics covered in this book. The following lists are far from exhaustive, but may be of help in beginning to locate further resources.

1 AN ANCIENT HERITAGE

GRANT, ROBERT M. *A Historical Introduction to the New Testament.* New York: Harper & Row, 1963.

MCKENZIE, JOHN. *The Roman Catholic Church.* Garden City, N.Y.: Doubleday, 1971.

PAUCK, WILHELM. *The Heritage of the Reformation.* Glencoe, Ill.: Free Press, 1961.

REYNOLDS, STEPHEN. *The Christian Religious Tradition.* Encino, Calif.: Dickenson, 1977.

WAND, J. W. C. *A History of the Early Church.* London: Methuen, 1937.

WARE, TIMOTHY. *The Orthodox Church.* Baltimore: Penguin, 1963.

WELSFORD, A. E. *Life in the Early Church A.D. 33 to 313.* Greenwich, Conn.: Seabury, 1953.

2 CHRISTIANITY IN HISTORY

DILLENBERGER, JOHN, and WELCH, CLAUDE. *Protestant Christianity: Interpreted Through to Development.* New York: Charles Scribner's Sons, 1954.

LATOURETTE, KENNETH SCOTT. *A History of Christianity.* New York: Harper & Brothers, 1953.

MARTY, MARTIN E. *A Short History of Christianity.* New York: Meridian Books, 1959.

SMART, NINIEN. *The Phenomenon of Christianity.* London: Collins, 1979.

VAN LEEUWEN, AREND TH. *Christianity in World History: The Meeting of the Faiths of East and West.* New York: Charles Scribner's Sons, 1964.

WALKER, WILLISTON. *A History of the Christian Church,* Revised Edition. New York: Charles Scribner's Sons, 1984.

WILKEN, ROBERT. *The Myth of Christian Beginnings: History's Impact on Belief.* New York: Doubleday, 1972.

3 COUNTERCULTURES

COHN, NORMAN. *The Pursuit of the Millennium.* New York: Oxford University Press, 1970.

NIGG, WALTER. *The Heretics.* New York: Knopf, 1962.

TROELTSCH, ERNST. *The Social Teachings of the Christian Churches.* New York: Harper & Brothers, 1960.

WILLIAMS, GEORGE. *The Radical Reformation.* Philadelphia: Westminster Press, 1962.

4 CHRISTIANITY AND THE ARTS

BOUYER, LOUIS. *Liturgy and Architecture.* South Bend, Ind.: University of Notre Dame Press, 1967.

DILLISTONE, F. W. *Christianity and Symbolism*. Philadelphia: Westminster, 1955.

HOLL, KARL. *The Cultural Significance of the Reformation*. Cleveland: World, 1959.

HUIZINGA, JOHAN. *The Waning of the Middle Ages*. Garden City, N.Y.: Doubleday, 1954.

LOWRIE, WALTER. *Art in the Early Church*. New York: Harper & Row, 1965.

LYNCH, WILLIAM F. *Christ and Apollo*. New York: New American Library, 1963.

MÂLE, EMILE. *Religious Art from the Twelfth to the Eighteenth Century*. New York: Pantheon, 1949.

RICOEUR, PAUL. *The Symbolism of Evil*. New York: Harper & Row, 1967.

ROSS-BRYANT, LYNN. *Imagination and the Life of the Spirit*. Chico, Calif.: Scholars' Press, 1981.

SCOTT, NATHAN A. *The Wild Prayer of Longing: Poetry and the Sacred*. New Haven: Yale University Press, 1971.

5 BELIEFS

AUGUSTINE, AURELIUS. *City of God*. London: Oxford University Press, 1963.

AUGUSTINE, AURELIUS. *Confessions*. New York: Penguin, 1972.

BERGER, PETER. *The Heretical Imperative: Contemporary Possibilities of Religious Affirmation*. Garden City, N.J.: Anchor Press, 1979.

GERRISH, BRIAN A. *The Faith of Christendom: A Source Book of Creeds and Confessions*. New York: World Publishing Company, 1963.

HARNACK, ADOLPH. *History of Dogma*. New York: Dover Publications, 1961, seven volumes.

LUTHER, MARTIN. *Three Treatises*. Philadelphia: The Muhlenberg Press, 1943.

JENNINGS, THEODORE, JR. *Introduction to Theology: An Invitation to Reflection on the Christian Mythos*. Philadelphia: Fortress Press, 1976.

PELIKAN, JAROSLAV. *The Christian Tradition*. Chicago: University of Chicago Press, 1971 and continuing. Four of five projected volumes have appeared by 1986.

VAN DER LEEUW, GERARDUS. *Religion in Essence and Manifestation*. Gloucester, Mass.: Peter Smith, 1967, two volumes.

WHITEHEAD, ALFRED NORTH. *Religion in the Making*. New York: Macmillan, 1926.

6 CHRISTIAN WORSHIP

BISHOP, EDMUND. *Liturgica Historica*. Oxford: Clarendon Press, 1918.

BOUYER, LOUIS. *Liturgical Piety*. South Bend, Ind.: University of Notre Dame Press, 1955.

CABROL, ABBOT. *The Books of the Latin Liturgy*. St. Louis, Mo.: B. Herder, 1932.

DAVIES, J. G., ed. *A Dictionary of Liturgy and Worship*. Philadelphia: Westminster Press, 1979.

DELLING, GERHARD. *Worship in the New Testament*. Philadelphia: Westminster Press, 1962.

GUARDINI, ROMANO. *The Church and the Catholic and the Spirit of the Liturgy*. New York: Sheed & Ward, 1935.

JAMES, E. O. *Christian Myth and Ritual*. New York: Meridian Books, 1965.

JONES, CHESLYN; WAINWRIGHT, GEOFFREY; and YARNOLD, EDWARD, eds. *The Study of Liturgy*. New York: Oxford University Press, 1978.

SCHROEDER, FREDERICK W. *Worship in the Reformed Tradition*. Boston: United Church Press, 1966.

SHEPHERD, M. H., Jr. *Worship of the Church*. Greenwich, Conn.: Seabury Press, 1952.

SWETE, HENRY B. *Church Services and Service-Books Before the Reformation*. London: Society for the Promotion of Christian Knowledge, 1930.

WHITE, JAMES F. *Introduction to Christian Worship*. Nashville: Abingdon, 1980.

WARE, TIMOTHY. *The Orthodox Church*. New York: Penguin Books, 1978.

7 CHRISTIANITY AND SOCIAL SETTINGS

BELLAH, ROBERT. *Religion and Progress in Modern Asia*. New York: Free Press, 1965.

BELLAH, ROBERT. *Habits of the Heart: Individualism and Commitment in American Life*. Berkeley: University of California Press, 1985.

BERGER, PETER. *A Rumor of Angels: Modern Society and the Rediscovery of the Supernatural*. Garden City, N.Y.: Doubleday, 1969.

BERGER, PETER. *Invitation to Sociology: A Humanistic Perspective*. Garden City, N.Y.: Doubleday, 1963.

BERGER, PETER. *The Sacred Canopy: Elements of a Sociological Theory of Religion*. Garden City, N.Y.: Doubleday, 1967.

BERGER, PETER, and LUCKMANN, THOMAS. *The Social Construction of Reality*. Garden City, N.Y.: Doubleday, 1966.

COX, HARVEY. *The Secular City: Secularization and Urbanization in Theological Perspective*. New York: Macmillan, 1966.

COX, HARVEY. *Religion in the Secular City: Toward a Postmodern Theology*. New York: Simon and Schuster, 1984.

DURKHEIM, EMILE. *The Elementary Forms of Religious Life: A Study in Religious Sociology*. Glencoe, Ill.: Free Press, 1947.

GLOCK, CHARLES. *Religion and Society in Tension*. Chicago: Rand McNally, 1965.

HERBERG, WILL. *Protestant, Catholic, Jew: An Essay in American Religious Sociology*. Garden City, N.Y.: Doubleday, 1955.

LENSKI, GERHARD E. *The Religious Factor: A Sociological Study of Religion's Impact on Politics, Economics, and Family Life*. Garden City, N.Y.: Doubleday, 1961.

LUCKMANN, THOMAS. *The Invisible Religion: The Problem of Religion in Modern Society*. New York: Macmillan, 1967.

WEBER, MAX. *The Protestant Ethic and the Spirit of Capitalism*. New York: Scribners, 1958.

WEBER, MAX. *The Sociology of Religion*. Boston: Beacon Press, 1963.

Index